FISHING IN MANY WATERS

A Fijian fisher-girl with her prawn-net

FISHING
IN MANY WATERS

BY
JAMES HORNELL

CAMBRIDGE
AT THE UNIVERSITY PRESS
1950

CAMBRIDGE
UNIVERSITY PRESS

University Printing House, Cambridge CB2 8BS, United Kingdom

Cambridge University Press is part of the University of Cambridge.

It furthers the University's mission by disseminating knowledge in the pursuit of education, learning and research at the highest international levels of excellence.

www.cambridge.org
Information on this title: www.cambridge.org/9781107475434

© Cambridge University Press 1950

This publication is in copyright. Subject to statutory exception and to the provisions of relevant collective licensing agreements, no reproduction of any part may take place without the written permission of Cambridge University Press.

First published 1950
First paperback edition 2014

A catalogue record for this publication is available from the British Library

ISBN 978-1-107-47543-4 Paperback

Cambridge University Press has no responsibility for the persistence or accuracy of URLs for external or third-party internet websites referred to in this publication, and does not guarantee that any content on such websites is, or will remain, accurate or appropriate.

PUBLISHER'S NOTE

Mr Hornell died in February 1949. He had completed a thorough revision of his manuscript, and had passed proofs of his many illustrations. The book has been seen through the press by Professor J. H. Hutton, and every effort has been made to ensure accuracy of detail. But Mr Hornell wrote from unrivalled personal knowledge of his subject: if there are imperfections in the book, it is because he had no opportunity to make them good in proof.

CONTENTS

List of Plates	*page* ix
List of Text-figures	xiii

Chapter I	Weapons of the Chase borrowed by the Fisherman	1
	I The Spear and the Harpoon	1
	II The Fishing-bow, Cross-bow, Blow-gun and Sickle	12
II	Angling of Sorts	22
III	Animals trained to fish and Fishes that angle for their living	28
IV	Shark-fishing	41
V	The Negro as fisherman	46
	I Sea-fishing off West Africa	46
	II Notable fishing Methods of Negroes on Inland Waters	50
VI	Kite-fishing	62
VII	Fisheries that ring the World: the Bonito, Albacore and Tunny Industries	65
	I Bonito-fishing in the Maldive Islands	65
	II Catching and Curing the Bonito in Japan	70
	III Bonito-fishing in Polynesia	74
	IV Crane- or Tira-fishing for Albacore	78
	V The Tuna fisheries of California	80
	VI The European Tunny and Bonito fisheries	83
VIII	Baiting for Crocodiles and Alligators	87
IX	Catching and Curing the Bombay-duck	94
X	The Grey Mullet takes Evasive Action	99
XI	Netting for Hilsa, the Indian Shad	108

CONTENTS

Chapter XII	Fishing at Port Said	*page* 114
XIII	Catching Flying-fish off the Indian Coast	118
XIV	The fatal attraction of the Shadows	123
XV	Fishing for Octopus, Cuttlefish and Squid	130
XVI	Trapping Devices	136
	I Deltaic and Freshwater Fish-traps	136
	II Marine Fish-traps	147
XVII	The Greatest Eel-farm and Eel-trap in the World	158
	I Mainly about getting there	158
	II Eel-fishing and Eel-farming at Comacchio	162
XVIII	Poison-fishing	168
XIX	Seeking Pearls and Chank shells in Ceylon and Indian Waters	182
XX	The Women Divers of Japan	190
XXI	Fruits of the Sea	199
Bibliography		205
Index		209

LIST OF PLATES

(*The plates are bound together at the end of the book between pages* 208 *and* 209)

       A Fijian fisher-girl with her prawn-net   *Frontispiece*

I   A. How the swordfish is lured within reach, Laccadive Islands; a demonstration
    B. Harpooners watching for swordfish, Strait of Messina. (*Photo by F. G. Crupi, Taormina*)

II   A. Shooting fish with a cross-bow, Malabar
    B. A Chinese illustration of cormorant-fishing. (*From De Thiersant*)

III   A. Adjusting a cormorant's harness. (*By courtesy of Dr E. W. Gudger and the American Museum of Natural History, New York*)
    B. The head cormorant wearing its harness. (*By courtesy of the Field and Stream Magazine, U.S.A.*)

IV   A. Night fishing with cormorants, Gifu, Japan. (*By courtesy of Dr E. W. Gudger*)
    B. An experiment with a remora during a pearl fishery, Ceylon

V   A. Negro woman making a *bimbé*-net, Sierra Leone
    B. Fishing with a *bimbé*-net, Sherbro, Sierra Leone

VI   A. A Kru fisherman landing with a catch of tarpon
    B. A Sierra Leone fisherman using four fishing-lines

VII   A. The Chinese lever dip-net in use in South India, at Beypore, Malabar
    B. Bonito-fishing in Japan; a lookout boat

VIII   A Solomon islander freeing a garfish's beak from the threads of the spider's web lure used in kite-fishing. (*By courtesy of Miss B. Blackwood and the Clarendon Press*)

IX   A. Collecting bait for the bonito fishery, Maldive Islands
    B. The Maldivian bonito fishery; the crew engaged in fishing

X   A. A store-basket for live bait, Minicoy Island
    B. A store-basket for bonito live bait as used by the Japanese

XI   A Samoan bonito-boat showing how two men ply three rods. (*Photo by Tattersall's studio, Apia*)

XII   A. Doing tots on his thigh; a Gujarat fisherman calculates his earnings
    B. Shooting an anchored bag-net off Velan, Kathiawar, India

XIII   A. Stringing 'Bombay-ducks' to dry at Velan, Kathiawar
    B. The fishermen's shrine to Madhvar Devi at Diu, Kathiawar, India

LIST OF PLATES

XIV   A. Drying the threefold portion of a veranda-net, Mauritius
      B. Egyptian mullet-fishers: their veranda-net is rolled up at the stern of each boat

XV   The *changodam* method of catching mullet in Cochin backwaters

XVI   A. Two Italian fishing-boats which trawl in pairs off Port Said
      B. Ancient Egyptians using a primitive trawl. (*By courtesy of the Metropolitan Museum of Art, New York*)

XVII   A. A catamaran used in the flying-fish fishery, Coromandel coast of India
      B. The same catamaran under sail

XVIII   A. A prawn trap, Chilka Lake, Ganjam, India. These traps are set in long rows across the current
      B. Quadrangular fish and prawn traps, Kolair Lake, India

XIX   A. Hand-traps used in Malabar. Left, a sieving device; centre, a plunge-basket; right, a fishing-scoop
      B. Tubular traps of split cane used in Fiji. Below, an eel-trap; above, two wider woven fish-traps

XX   A. Fish-traps (*nasse*) on the quay, Palermo, Sicily
      B. A large fish-trap (*nassa*), Malta

XXI   A. A hooded fisherwoman and her fish-trap. Aramia river, Papua. (*Photo by Capt. Frank Hurley*)
      B. A small type of *nassa* (fish-trap) hung from a buoyed rope, Malta

XXII   A. A stellate five-way fish-trap, Kilakarai, South India
      B. Heart-shaped fish-traps, Madeira

XXIII   A. A two-way fish-trap (*uwea*), Mbau, Fiji (1939)
      B. A one-way fish-trap (*susu*) with entrance on top, Mbau, Fiji (1939)

XXIV   A. Eel-trap of *uwea* type, Fiji (1939)
      B. A shark-fisher of Aua Island, Melanesia. (*Photo by courtesy of G. Lane-Fox Pitt-Rivers*)

XXV   A. Walled enclosures used to trap fishes on the Darling River, Australia. (*Photo by Tost and Rohn, Sydney, Australia*)
      B. A screen-barrier, trapped at the centre in a Cochin backwater, South India

XXVI   A. Outer view of a cordate terminal fish-trap used at Comacchio, Italy
      B. View of the same from within

XXVII   A. A poisoning fish-drive at Ovalau Island, Fiji: hauling in the net. (*By courtesy of Dr Isaac, Suva*)
      B. The end of the drive; hauling the net aboard, Ovalau, Fiji

XXVIII   A fish-drive for shoal of hilsa at the Lower Anicut, Kaveri River, South India

XXIX   A. Divers at work on the pearl banks, Ceylon
      B. Divers from Tuticorin at work on the South Indian pearl banks

LIST OF PLATES

XXX A. Muhammadan divers with their catches of chank shells in net-bags; Rameswaram, South India (1914)
B. A Japanese woman diver on the pearl bank, Bay of Agu, Japan

XXXI A. Three Japanese women divers and their male attendant
B. The same family group at work, Toba, Japan

XXXII A. Life appearance of an edible sea-urchin (*Echinus esculentus*)
B. Shells of *Pteroceras* (five-fingered chank) used as octopus-traps, Palk Strait, India

XXXIII A. The common octopus; attitude when resting
B. A large catch of octopus drying outside a village in Mauritius

XXXIV A. The 'ormer' (*Haliotis tuberculata*) of the Channel Islands. Above, the inner surface of an empty shell; below, the under surface of the animal and (right) the outer surface of the shell. Jersey
B. A number of the Brachiopod *Lingula* dug out of sand, Fiji

XXXV Baskets of the Fijian river-clam, *Batissa violacea*, on sale in Suva market, Fiji (1939)

XXXVI Strings of crabs on sale on the roadside in Fiji (1939)

[*Where no acknowledgement is made in the list above, the photograph is by the author.*]

LIST OF TEXT-FIGURES

1 Indian multidentate fishing-spears; in order from above they are: A, the ordinary form of Bengal *konch*. B, the Nadiya *konch*. C, the *Jutiyā*, a harpoon variety. D, the *Pacha* of Patna and Mymensingh *page* 2

2 An Egyptian nobleman of dynastic times spearing fish with a bident. (*After Maspero*)

3 A fishing canoe of Menado in the Celebes; a trident spear rests in crutches on the outrigger. (*Original*) 3

4 Types of the ornamentation of the wooden 'bonito' lures used in the Laccadive Islands in the swordfish fishery. The two figures at the bottom are side-views of the tails of two of these lures. (*Original*) 7

5 A, the butt of a turtle spear from the north coast of New Guinea, fancifully carved. (*Original*). B, head of another, armed with two barbed spearheads. (*Original*) 9

6 A, propeller-shaped 'retarder' or brake used in the islands off the north coast of New Guinea when fishing for turtle or large fishes. B, longitudinal section through the retarder to show its curvature. (*Original*) 10

7 A, retarder in the form of an ox-ray, Wooi Bay, New Guinea. (*Original*.) B, other forms of retarders used by New Guinea fishermen; pieces of china plates are inserted into the lobes of *b*. 11
 11

8 The simple form of bow and arrow-harpoon used to shoot fishes in Malabar backwaters. (*Original*) 12

9 An Andaman islander shooting a fish with bow and arrow 13

10 A simple form of the Malayali cross-bow from Arathinkal, Travancore; the line receptacle is omitted. (*Original*) 14

11 The ordinary type of the Malayali cross-bow. Note the elongated stock and the stout bow formed of four plates or leaves. The arrow groove and the line pocket are shown but not the arrow; from Valapad, South Malabar. (*Original*) 14

12 Crossbow arrows used in South India. A is a bird bolt; B and E are the forms of fish-arrow in general use; C and D being rarer varieties of the same. (*Original*) 15

13 Varieties of the Malayali blow-gun differing in the form of the mouth-piece. A is a plain reed tube without added mouthpiece. In B, the mouthpiece is a disk of coconut shell; in C, it is turned out of wood, whilst in D and E, it is built up of layers of gummed cloth, painted over. The butt end of E is ornamented with lacquered bands of yellow and red on black. The barrels of all these are made of the stems of the *ita* reed. (*Original*) 16

LIST OF TEXT-FIGURES

14 A is a very massive wooden blow-gun in the Trichur Museum, Cochin. The butt is encased in a turned brass mouthpiece; the barrel is spirally wrapped with strips of fibre, painted black. B is an old blow-gun from Valapad in South Malabar; it is made of wood and spirally wrapped with animal membrane. C shows a retrieving hook on the muzzle of the Trichur blow-gun. (*Original*)   *page* 18

15 Blow-gun darts used when shooting fishes. 1, dart ready for use; 2, details of: (*a*), the shaft; (*b*), the steel-barbed head; (*c*), the mop-like wad, its base not yet pulled down into the cavity at the head of the shaft; 3, a longitudinal section through the head of the shaft, showing the oblique perforation through which the retrieving line is passed. (*Original*)   19

16 Fishing with cormorants in China. (*After J. Doolittle, by courtesy of the American Museum of Natural History, New York*)   30

17 The common sucker-fish, *Echeneis naucrates*. (*Original*)   35

18 A deep-sea angler-fish, *Lophodulus dinema*. A phosphorescent light is emitted from the bulbous tip of its fishing-rod. (*After Regan and Trewavas*)   38

19 The small Indian angler-fish, *Antennarius hispidus*. (*Original*)   39

20 The *Uringalē*, a barrier weir-trap used at Mala in the French Cameroons. (*After Monod.*) A, diagram of the fence in optical section. B, upstream face view   56

21 A lever dip-net (*ndambē*) used in the French Cameroons on the River Faro. (*After Monod*)   58

22 Canoes of the Kotoko people, fitted with the lever dip-net (*zémi*). A, the net raised; B, the net being lowered; C, transverse section of the canoe hull, made of two dugout hulls sewn together longitudinally and with the sides raised by sewn-on wash-strakes. The net is suspended from two long antennae, which take the place of the oval frame used in the *ndambē*. (*After Monod*)   58

23 A fishing kite used in Buka, North-west Solomon Islands. A, apex, where the mid-ribs of the median and outer sections meet; B, the control or flying line; C, the tail line carrying the lure; D, made of reeled filaments from a spider's web; E, E, E, the three strengthening cross-rods; *a, a*, points where the line C is tied to the free end of the median mid-rib. (*From an example in the Pitt-Rivers Museum, Oxford, collected by Miss B. Blackwood who kindly lent this block*)   63

24 A Maldivian bonito fishing-boat. (*Original*)   67

25 Two examples of Polynesian bonito hooks. (*Original*)   76

26 The two-rod fishing gear used on the Californian coast in the bonito and tunny fishery   83

27 Method of hooking an alligator in South America. (*After C. Waterton*)   92

28 A hilsa fisherman floating downstream on the River Kaveri, supported upon a wooden float. (*Original*)   109

29 A fishing dingi drifting down the Ganges with its *shānglā-jāl* lowered into position to catch hilsa. (*Original*)   111

LIST OF TEXT-FIGURES

30 Egg of an Indian flying-fish (*Cypsilurus* sp.) undergoing fertilization. The short, sinuous-tailed bodies are spermatozoa; the long filaments are the means whereby the eggs are attached to floating seaweeds. (*From a drawing by Dr M. Ramaswami Naidu*)   page 122

31 Diagram showing how the *madi valai* is operated. (*Original*)   127

32 Ground baiting of a bush-filled enclosure on the River Benue, Cameroons. (*After Monod*)   128

33 A Samoan example of the 'rat-lure' used to catch octopus in Polynesia. (*Original*)   131

34 A small species of octopus numerous on the *Zostera* beds in Palk Strait, South India, $\times \frac{3}{4}$. (*Original*)   132

35 Shell of the five-fingered chank (*Pteroceras*) used in South India as an octopus-trap, $\times \frac{1}{2}$. (*Original*)   133

36 The common squid, *Loligo*, $\times \frac{1}{2}$. (*Original*)   134

37 A common squid-fishing device in use in the north of Ceylon. On the right is the jigger used to hook the squid. (*Original*)   135

38 A tubular trap used in India to capture murrel (*Ophiocephalus*), $\times \frac{1}{4}$. (*Original*)   145

39 Thorn-lined traps. A, a floating variety used to catch prawns, Fiji; B, another from the Duke of York group, Bismarck Archipelago, with the thorns completely covered. (*Original*)   146

40 The two components of a South Indian three-way basket trap. A, woven basketry shaped to form the top and sides; B, the part to form the floor of the same trap; C, the trap completed. (*Original*)   149

41 Diagrammatic sections through four types of Fijian fish-traps. A, the *susu* type; B, the *uwea* type of Mbau; C, the *uwea* of Rewa; D, an eel-trap of *uwea* type. (*Original*)   150

42 Plans of typical fishing-weirs or pounds, Oceania. A, as used in Vitilevu Bay; B, one seen east of Savu-savu Bay; C, a type with two double pens. (*Original*)   156

43 Plan of a labyrinth for the capture of eels and mullet at Comacchio, Italy.   163

44 Nose-clip used by Arab divers. (*Original*)   186

I

WEAPONS OF THE CHASE BORROWED BY THE FISHERMAN

I. THE SPEAR AND THE HARPOON

STUDY of present-day primitive races still living in the Stone Age, proves without the possibility of doubt that the first men to attempt the capture of fishes other than by means of their bare hands were those in the hunting stage of civilization. The devices employed by the prehistoric men who first turned their attention to this art were the ordinary equipment of the chase, the selfsame weapons as they used in the pursuit of the animals of the forests and the plains. Little by little as experience increased and skill advanced among the various tribes, modifications of the original weapons were devised to increase their efficiency under the specialized conditions encountered when pursuing prey with peculiar advantages for escape, not possessed by animals that run on foot upon the land. The primitive spear, in its simplest form of a pole with sharpened point perhaps hardened by charring in the flames, was the first implement used. But this and its improved successor, the spear with a two-edged cutting blade of flint or of obsidian lashed to the outer end of the shaft, while effective enough against an animal that may be patiently tracked for hours, if wounded, are of little service in the case of a fish. The latter, when hurt even to the death, if once it slips off the spear-point is seldom retrieved; a little strength left will carry it to a safe retreat under rocks and stones, or into deep water or the soft mud at the bottom. Hence the earliest modifications of the primitive hunting spear were designed to overcome this defect. The first of these was to arm the simple spear-head with one or several barbs; these ensured that the fish would be held fast once the barbed point pierced the body. The next improvement was to increase the number of points by forming a number of thin spears into a bundle by tying the shafts together for some distance from the butts, and arranging the prong-like free and pointed ends in such a way as to cause them to diverge from one another and so become a missile instrument extremely well adapted to pin a fish down when struck, or entangle it between the prongs (Text-fig. 1, A). Another variation was to tie a bunch of pointed hardwood spikes in a single or double circle around the end of an ordinary spear-shaft, a very effective contrivance for the capture of the smaller kinds of fish, particularly of those that go in shoals (Text-fig. 1, B).

The next advance was to increase the number of prongs in the barbed fishing-lance to two, three or even more, producing two-, three-, or many-pronged spears—the bident, trident and multident forms. The first is characteristic of fishing scenes depicted in frescoes found in ancient Egypt, where fish-spearing was a favourite sport of the nobles; many charming pictures have come down to us, painted or worked in bas-relief on the walls of tombs. The majority are touching domestic scenes, depicting the great man, accompanied by his wife, and sometimes a favoured child, afloat in a marsh through which they thread their way in a pretty skiff made by tying bundles of the long stems of the papyrus sedge into a

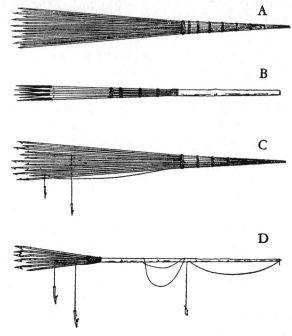

TEXT-FIG. 1. Indian multidentate fishing-spears; in order from above they are: A, the ordinary form of Bengal *konch*. B, the Nadiya *konch*. C, the *jutiyā*, a harpoon variety. D, the *pacha* of Patna and Mymensingh.

floating platform, half raft, half canoe. The husband stands erect and eager, a two-pronged spear in his hand, ready to strike whenever a fish comes within range (Text-fig. 2). Sometimes he is shown with two fishes transfixed upon his spear. In other scenes where the quarry is the hippopotamus,[1] the spears used are fitted with a retrieving line attached near the distal end of the shaft—a transitional stage in the evolution of the true harpoon.

To-day in Egypt the spear has been abandoned for more profitable methods of fishing; a noble class, leisured and passionately addicted to the chase, has disappeared, its place taken by busy officials and a wealthy plutocracy without time or inclination for the country pursuits so keenly enjoyed by the old-time aristocrats.

[1] Tomb of Mereruka at Saqqara, dating from the beginning of the VIth Dynasty.

For some obscure reason the Greeks and Romans of the classic period preferred the trident to the bident; they employed it as we do to-day in the allegorical treatment of scenes representing sea-gods and sea-power. No classic weapon is more familiar to us than the trident of Neptune, now held in the hands of Britannia as stamped upon our bronze coins (Text-fig. 3).

Text-fig. 2. An Egyptian nobleman of dynastic times spearing fish with a bident.

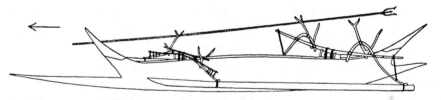

Text-fig. 3. A fishing canoe of Menado in the Celebes; a trident spear rests in crutches on the outrigger.

The ingenuity of early man, having invented various forms of the compound spear, next designed the harpoon, a spear with a detachable head, socketed upon the end of the shaft, and connected to it by means of a strong, thin thong or cord. By this arrangement, when the barbed head penetrates the victim's body, the shaft comes loose; floating on the surface, it serves as a buoy to indicate the position of the wounded fish. It acts also as a check upon its movements, and helps materially to hasten its exhaustion and eventual capture. The utility of this device must have been very early realized, for barbed harpoon-heads, usually made of deer's horn, have been discovered among the refuse of some of the shelters of palaeolithic man in Europe. The final stage of evolution was reached when a mechanical contrivance was devised for propelling short light spears with greater force and accuracy than the average man could attain with mere arm power. This invention we know by the name of 'bow and arrow'; in its turn it was superseded by the cross-bow.

All these methods, in a thousand and one local variations, are still to be met with on the mainland of India, particularly in the lowlands of the Gangetic plain and delta subject to widespread annual inundation. Every little hut there has some of these weapons lying about or stowed away in safety according to the season. Their constant occurrence bespeaks the value set upon them as effective instruments for supplying the daily wants of families too poor to afford the capital necessary to buy the comparatively costly outfit requisite for net-fishing. The hunter's instinct must also be reckoned with. The excitement of the chase is a legacy from our savage ancestors and when this can be combined with profit, need we wonder at the continued popularity of the fish-spear and harpoon?

The simple lance with sharpened unbarbed point is little in evidence in the Gangetic region, but examples are occasionally met with, as in the twenty-four Parganas, having a bamboo shaft tipped with iron. A usual length for the shaft is slightly over 7 feet; that of the point $5\frac{1}{2}$ inches.

The compound spear made up of numerous simple lances firmly bunched together towards the butts but divergent and free for more than half their length are much in evidence throughout the low-country, where it is known generally as *konch* (Text-fig. 1, A and B). It varies in details locally, particularly in regard to the way in which the shaft bundle is secured and in the number of spears bound together. A typical *konch* consists of from ten to sixteen separate split bamboo spears with shafts between $4\frac{1}{2}$ and 6 feet in length. The proximal portions of the shafts are formed into a tapering bundle and secured tightly in position in various ways. In one (at Nadiya) a joint of bamboo, $1\frac{1}{2}$ feet in length, is split through along half its length into four pieces, and slipped over the pointed end of the long conical handle in such wise as to embrace it, and then is tied firmly in this position (Text-fig. 1, B). In some the bundle of butts is bound round with iron rings (twenty-four Parganas) and in others by cord or fibre (Text-fig. 1, A). Each of the numerous shafts is tipped with a short conical iron point, usually not more than $1\frac{1}{2}$ inches long. The *konch* is a heavy weapon requiring considerable strength to hurl. It is generally thrown by a man standing at the prow of a boat, sometimes from the bank of a stream.

The harpoon form of the simple spear is by far the more common of the two. Invariably the harpoon is barbed either single or double. The shaft consists of a bamboo, 9–10 feet long. The barbed point, 9 inches or so in length, is usually fitted to a short wooden handle and this in turn into the hollow end of the bamboo shaft. A cord connects the wooden base of the harpoon point with the shaft.

This form of harpoon (*ek-katyā*) is used principally in the pursuit of tortoises and large fish; the simple unbarbed spears for tortoises only.

The *konch* or compound spear has also its harpoon form, when it is known as *juti* or *jutiyā* (Text-fig. 1, c). It is used in the same way as its prototype but having barbs on the small iron spear-heads, which are attached by thin cords to the long conical 'handle', the prey is more securely held when struck; if the fish is large and puts up a hard fight in its attempt to escape, the great basal cone serves as a buoy easily kept in view by the pursuing boat (Text-fig. 1, c). A variation of this compound harpoon is the *pacha* of Patna and Mymensingh (Text-fig. 1, D). Here the heavy cone-shaped handle of the *jutiyā* is replaced by a single light bamboo shaft, bearing (usually) seven short spears capped by singly barbed iron points, attached harpoon-wise to the main bamboo shaft by thin cords (Text-fig. 1, D).

The fork-shaped spears formed by a number of barbed iron prongs rising from a common base and arranged typically and commonly in one plane, form a distinct class, known in English under the term 'grains'. Usually the forked iron head is secured to the shaft by a cord. The number of barbed prongs varies widely, from two to thirteen; the names have even greater diversity, both according to the number of prongs and to the locality. *Chal* and *pāchkā* are perhaps the most common of these. The bident form of two prongs is not common; it is represented by the *dūkāthi* of Malda. Tridents are much more frequently seen, under the name of *āora* or *ātor* in Bakarganj and Faridpur and *kātā* in Jalpaiguri. The *pāchkā* of Malda has, as its name implies, five prongs, but that of Patna is variable in the number and may have from five to eight. The *sāt-phalā* of Pabna has seven prongs.

In some forms, as in the *tentā* of Nadiya, the iron prongs are bunched together, and in the *pāchā* of Mymensingh the prongs are short straight pieces of split bamboo, inserted in one plane in a divergent manner at the head of a bamboo shaft. Each prong is tipped with a short iron barbed harpoon point, attached by a line to the head of the main shaft (Text-fig. 1, D).

Spearing fish by torchlight is frequently practised. A lighted torch made of dry jute stems or other cheap combustible is placed at the fore-end of a boat, usually a dugout. The paddler at the stern propels it slowly and quietly along while his companion, statuesque and immobile at the prow, rests a long harpoon spear on his left hand, the right holding the butt end ready to launch it at any fish that approaches, attracted by the blaze.

But to see primitive spearing methods employed in a perfected form and on a large scale we must voyage to the Laccadive Islands. The inhabitants of this little archipelago, lying about 200 miles west of the Malabar coast, in race and speech are similar to the people of the adjacent mainland. At an early date they became converted to the Muhammadan faith; the period of Arab sea-power was their golden age.

Their knowledge of the world to-day is limited. Once a year, provided a suitable steamer is available, the Collector of Malabar or his deputy is accustomed to visit the islands, settle disputes, try prisoners for major offences (there seldom are any), see that the islanders continue to maintain the periodical communal rat-hunts, and then return home to prepare a report on his inspection for the edification of the local government. Not infrequently, if the officer be young and enthusiastic, anxious to see 'progress' made and the islanders wakened out of their easygoing philosophic attitude towards life, he prepares an elaborate scheme for the improvement of the material and moral condition of the people; he may wish to see a modern system of agriculture introduced, new fishing methods tried; he may aspire to enlighten the islanders on matters educational and hygienic. This report in due course is commented upon sagely by youthful under-secretaries whose *dicta*, almost invariably adverse, are usually endorsed by government in the orders passed on the report. The primrose path in these circumstances is agreement with opinions that entail no struggle with the treasury authorities. Thereafter the report is printed, and consigned to oblivion in the official archives.

But if the crop of coconuts has been good and the season favourable for fishing, the islanders are quite happy to be forgotten. No tax-gatherer comes to harry them, and the paternal government, to protect them from the rapacity of the mainland traders, buys all the coconut fibre they manufacture at a fair market price. The island sea-going craft make an annual voyage to the mainland with this produce and bring back in exchange rice and curry stuffs, a little kerosene oil and the petty sundries that constitute the islanders' luxuries. Being good Muhammadans, prohibition is their unquestioned custom; so their needs are still further lessened.

In fishing, the harpoon and the many-pronged spear are in everyday employment. By means of the former, the mighty swordfish, voracious enemy of all fishes smaller than himself, is frequently captured. The iron head of the harpoon, usually armed with a single barb, is socketed upon the extremity of a long wooden shaft and attached to it by a length of line so that when the fish is struck and the harpoon-head dislodged, the fisherman may retrieve the fish when its strength is exhausted by the struggle, by hauling upon this line. But first the fish must be lured within striking distance. To effect this, a bait is played on the surface of the water. When possible a real flying-fish is employed, dangled from a short line at the end of a primitive fishing-rod; often such a bait is not available, so the ingenuity of the islanders has evolved a wooden imitation which serves equally well or possibly better. This dummy fish is quite large, usually about 10 inches long. The form is conventional, the body being torpedo-shaped, with two lug-like projections towards the thicker end, to represent the pectoral fins, and a widened tail-like expansion at the narrow end. To increase resemblance to the real flying-fish, the dummy is painted black, with incised patterns picked out in white made with a mixture of lime, resin and oil. In some, a few white bands encircle the body at equidistant intervals; in others the white lines run lengthwise; some have rounded tails, some are bilobed. Individual fancy and a well-developed artistic sense, partial to symmetry and arabesques, find plenty of play in the decoration of these wooden lures (Text-fig. 4).

TEXT-FIG. 4. Types of the ornamentation of the wooden 'bonito' lures used in the Laccadive Islands in the swordfish fishery. The two figures at the bottom are side-views of the tails of two of these lures.

Each family is said to possess its own particular conventional pattern, an advantage in establishing the ownership of these objects if they be lost and then found by others. When fishing, the fisherman stands in the bow of his boat, the long-shafted harpoon poised ready to strike in his right hand, while he plays the 'false fish' (*poĕmin* as it is called in Malayali) on the surface of the sea by means of a short rod and line held in his left hand, making it to skip and dart over the waves in as realistic a fashion as he can manage (Pl. 1, fig. A).

The swordfish comes with a swirling rush and expert must be the harpooner to strike at the precise moment the great fish flashes within reach. An instant's hesitation or unsteady aim and the work of a day may be thrown away; the swordfish though fairly common in these seas, is not to be lured within reach at the beck and call of any impatient fisherman. The game has to be played out with infinite patience on the part of the man, who cannot afford to be discouraged even by several days of failure. The reward is great when it arrives.

The Laccadive islander has still much of our primitive prehistoric ancestor in his make-up; he goes to his fishing with a sense of enjoyment seldom met with in his mainland brethren who too often lead a poverty-stricken and circumscribed life in crowded and insanitary villages. The islander is perhaps equally poor, but his is a freer existence; he owns a few coconut trees and his house stands in its own little compound, well apart from his neighbours. His freedom begets a sporting love of fishing that furnishes him with keen enjoyment when he puts to sea in his graceful little sewn-plank boat in pursuit of the great swordfish or when at night-time he sets forth to spear the elusive flying-fish; on the latter occasion the weapon used is the compound spear, here consisting of two concentrically disposed circlets of pointed sticks at the end of the spear-shaft. To attract the fishes within striking distance great torches made of bundles of coconut leaves are burned, the light bringing the fish round the boat in such numbers that often 100 to 150 may be taken in a single night by one boat.

Nearer home we find the swordfish hunted and harpooned in much the same fashion in the Strait of Messina. As the Strait shrinks to a narrow passage only 2 miles wide at the northern end, the terror of the swirling tidal eddies of Charybdis made this a place of dread to the mariners of the early classic period, navigating in small craft without charts, or pilots or sailing directions. Here, too, a cold current wells up from below and the two influences combine to make these narrows famous for the richness of their fisheries. Among these, the chase of the swordfish ranks high. The most expert fishermen are those of Faro, the little fishing village strung out along the beach near the slender lighthouse or *faro*, from which it takes its name.

These men work in small open boats, manned by a crew of six. Amidships, a high look-out pole provided with a foothold about 3 feet below the top, serves a watcher as a stance when searching for signs of the great fish—the flurry made as it sends a frightened shoal of small fishes racing wildly in flight or the sight of its big dorsal fin cutting the waves. Awaiting his warning cry, another man stands on a short, gunwale-high, fore-decking, harpoon in hand; to right and to left is a vertical board fitted with two half-round hollows cut in the upper edge, rests for harpoon and long-handled gaff when these are not in use (Pl. 1, fig. B).

Another area where spear and harpoon are of notable economic importance in the lives of the people is Melanesia. In 1918 when cruising along the north coast of the Dutch section of New Guinea, I found the dominant fishing methods to be spearing and shooting with bow and arrows. At Wake Island and at Manokwari where I had special opportunities to observe the methods in use, the fishermen are expert in the spearing of fish; the variety in size and in the arming of these weapons is particularly notable.

For large fishes and for turtle two heavy spears, remarkable for their length and for the carved ornamentation of the shafts, are carried in every canoe. The head is quite unusual in form, armed as it is with two barbed spear-prongs, set parallel on opposite sides of the shaft (Text-fig. 5, B). The butt is also richly carved for a length of some $2\frac{1}{2}$ feet. Designs vary greatly; in one instance the end of one of the pair of spears (they are not harpoons) was carved into semblance of a nude female figure, the other being geometrical and fanciful. In many, fishes and human heads are often combined—a fish swallowing a man is a favourite motive (Text-fig. 5, A).

In small canoes these formidable weapons are replaced by smaller ones, still of considerable size and strength. Some have but a single lance-shaped head, made from a stout sliver of bamboo, sharply pointed; mostly there are several of these bamboo prongs, three, four or five in number, with the prongs set slightly divergent.

At Manokwari, the majority of the spears are of similar type; a considerable number are rendered even more formidable by the serration of both edges of the prongs.

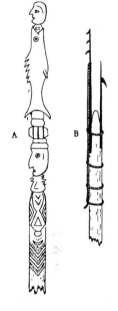

TEXT-FIG. 5. A, the butt of a turtle spear from the north coast of New Guinea, fancifully carved. B, head of another, armed with two barbed spear-heads.

Iron-headed harpoons are in use by the fishermen of every village along Geelvink Bay and in the Schouten Islands, for the purpose of securing turtle, dozing or lazing on the surface of the sea. The shaft is of heavy black wood, slighter at the butt than at the middle or at the head end, in order to give proper balance at the point where it is held at the moment when it is to be thrown. To the butt is tied a piece of tortoiseshell, about $2\frac{1}{2}$ inches long, with a perforated knob at one end, a primitive ring.

The short harpoon-head, single barbed, is of iron, with a conical cupping in the base, enabling it to fit upon the tapered end of the shaft. The retrieving line, attached to the barbed head, passes first to the tortoiseshell ring through which it is rove and then is taken back half-way along the shaft, where it is stopped by means of a slip-knot. This arrangement allows the harpoon-head to remain in place until a turtle or a fish is struck, whereupon the tension set up on the line when the victim makes its first rush releases the slip-knot and brings the line back to the butt.

To shorten the time required to exhaust the turtle or fish after it has been struck, two wooden disks, which we may call stops or retarders, are threaded upon the line; the resistance they offer when drawn at speed through the water affords immense help to the fisherman whilst playing his catch. If the animal be a fighter and strong in its rushes, a second line may be tied to the end of the first; as this is also provided with retarders, the hooked catch finds the brake on its rushes so much increased that it is forced to succumb quickly.

When a line is rove through the central hole of a retarder disk, a strong wooden pin is passed transversely between two of the strands to secure the

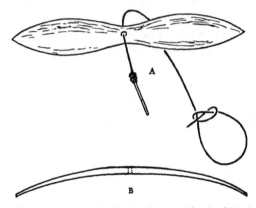

TEXT-FIG. 6. A, propeller-shaped 'retarder' or brake used in the islands off the north coast of New Guinea when fishing for turtle or large fishes. B, longitudinal section through the retarder to show its curvature.

disk in position; alternatively a knot may be made on the line on the proximal side (Text-fig. 6).

The usual form, that of a circular disk, has some geometric pattern cut on one surface; in one example which I obtained, the motive was cruciform, suggestive of a four-leaved clover leaf; another retarder was cut into eight radiating petal-like lobes, with a lozenge-shaped fragment of a china plate inlaid at the centre of each lobe (Text-fig. 7, B(*b*)).

Sometimes the second disk is given a specialized and rather larger form than the first, being carved into the conventionalized form of a predatory bird or of a ray-fish. One of those seen was easily recognizable as intended to represent the horned ox-ray, a fish more feared than the shark by the pearl-divers of the East (Text-fig. 7, A).

In other parts of the world, especially in Africa and America, spearing and harpooning of fish are common practices but nowhere do these methods attain the wonderful diversity and general usage met with in Bengal and

New Guinea. To attempt an enumeration would be wearisome; suffice it, therefore, to mention a few of the most noteworthy and spectacular.

In Africa spearing and harpooning are widely distributed and many of the tribesmen of the Lake region of East and Central Africa are expert in both branches. Prominent among these are the harpooners of the Turkana tribe of Northern Kenya, a nomadic people who roam the country to the west of Lake Rudolf.

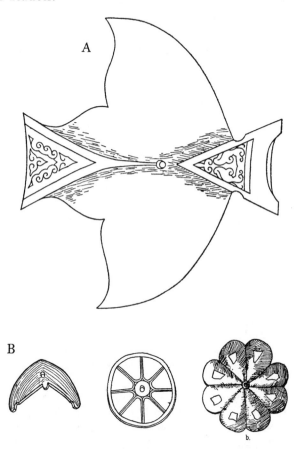

Text-fig. 7. A, retarder in the form of an ox-ray, Wooi Bay, New Guinea. B, other forms of retarders used by New Guinea fishermen; pieces of china plates are inserted into the lobes of *b*.

In Central America the giant sawfishes, often weighing 800 lb. and more, are harpooned as they lie on the sandy bottom of the Bay of Panama, and the spear in several varieties of form is a favourite fishing weapon of the Indians of Brazil.

II. THE FISHING-BOW, CROSS-BOW, BLOW-GUN AND SICKLE

In South India, and in particular in the Malayali country of Malabar, Cochin and Travancore, four peculiar methods of fishing are in use, based upon the employment of implements of an unusual nature. The most notable, as being in general use, are the cross-bow and the blow-gun. The fishing-bow and the sickle are also found in the same locality, but their use is localized and rare.

THE FISHING-BOW. In Malabar the use of the ordinary stringed bow has all but disappeared alike in hunting and in fishing. The fishing-bow (*thettal*) did, however, exist a few years ago, for I have seen specimens, similar to that shown in Text-fig. 8, which came from Malabar. As will

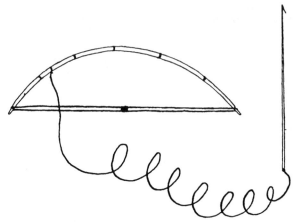

TEXT-FIG. 8. The simple form of bow and arrow-harpoon used to shoot fishes in Malabar backwaters.

be seen from the figure, it is a modification of the pellet-bow; it has twin bow-strings, with a pad at mid-length to take the projectile. This, normally, is a rounded pebble or a dried ball of clay but in the case of the fishing-bow, a barbed harpoon-arrow is substituted. A long and thin cord tied at one end to the bow close to one extremity, is attached at the other end to the butt of the arrow in order to form a retrieving line. The arrow-head is of iron, barbed on one side only (Text-fig. 8).

It is probable that this form of pellet-bow was in general use in Malabar for shooting fish previous to the comparatively recent adaptation for this purpose of the more powerful cross-bow type next to be described. In the Andaman Islands, and on the waterways of Brazil, bows and arrows are likewise used in fishing (Text-fig. 9).

THE CROSS-BOW. In South Malabar, Cochin and Travancore an all-wood cross-bow (*parangi pathi*) is in extensive use. It is employed almost exclusively to shoot fish in the streams and quiet backwaters which occupy extensive areas in the coastal region. Reference to the accompanying photograph and figures made during a tour in 1923 will facilitate description (Pl. II, fig. A).

As will be seen, the bow is compound, made up of several thin wooden leaves, varying in number from two to four, arranged in the same way as the leaves in a carriage spring (Text-figs. 10 and 11). In some instances these are beautifully fashioned and fit together accurately; in others they are coarsely made and rudely put together. At intervals the component leaves are secured in position by encircling bands of coir yarn (sennit).

The stock also varies considerably in detail; in the better made, the butt is obviously a more or less close imitation of that of a musket or rifle. The

TEXT-FIG. 9. An Andaman islander shooting a fish with bow and arrow.

distal portion, some few inches from the end, is perforated by a rectangular hole running from side to side; through this the bow part is passed halfway and then locked in place by means of thin wooden wedges. A shallow groove runs lengthwise along the upper side of the stock, forward of the butt region; in this the arrow lies prior to discharge. The bow-string is a coarse cord of coconut fibre.

The release is notable. As seen in the figures the details are identical with those of the typical medieval cross-bow, as used in the sixteenth century in Europe (see Text-figs. 10 and 11).

The arrows used vary considerably but are generally of harpoon design. The most common is that where a barbed steel head is socketed at the base to fit the pointed end of a light wooden shaft (Text-fig. 12, E). One end of a length of line is tied to the steel head while the other passes through a hole in the wooden shaft and thence to an open-ended cylindrical receptacle made from a bamboo joint, fitted upon one side of the bow close to the stock (Pl. II, fig. A). In this receptacle the slack of the harpoon line is neatly coiled, ready to run out when the arrow is shot. Other forms are shown in Text-fig. 12; these come from North Travancore.

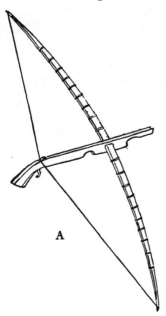

TEXT-FIG. 10. A simple form of the Malayali cross-bow from Arathinkal, Travancore; the line receptacle is omitted.

TEXT-FIG. 11. The ordinary type of the Malayali cross-bow. Note the elongated stock and the stout bow formed of four plates or leaves. The arrow groove and the line pocket are shown but not the arrow; from Valapad, South Malabar.

The dimensions of a typical Malayali cross-bow are as follows:

Length of stock overall	88·0 cm.
Length from distal end to trigger	62·4 cm.
Thickness of stock at mid-length	2·8 cm.
Length of bow when unstrung	143·0 cm.
Length of arrow	76·3 cm.

The Malayali users of the cross-bow are often extremely expert and withal patient. They will wait for hours to get a shot at a fish; they seldom miss, and when they hit, the arrow not infrequently transfixes the body of the fish, so powerful is the force of discharge (Pl. II, fig. A).

There can be no doubt that the Malabar cross-bow is not indigenous. Two considerations suffice to prove this; the first is the deduction to be drawn from the vernacular name and the second is the character of the release. The name is *parangi pathi*; as is well known *parangi* is the Dravidian corruption of *feringhi*, itself a corruption of 'Frank'; in later times it came to connote all *western* Europeans. In South India, the Portuguese being the earliest Europeans with whom in modern times the inhabitants came into intimate contact, the term *parangi* has come to be accepted as the virtual equivalent of 'Portuguese', hence the local term definitely associates the Portuguese with this weapon; the inference is clear that its general form was borrowed from this source.

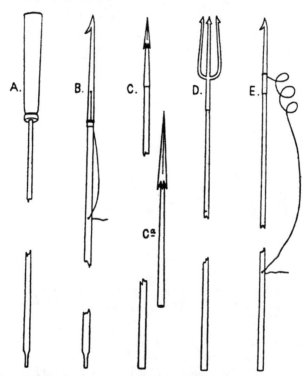

TEXT-FIG. 12. Cross-bow arrows used in South India. A is a bird bolt; B and E are the forms of fish-arrow in general use; C and D are rarer varieties of the same.

The identity of the release with a common European type has already been stated, so we arrive at the definite conclusion that the South Indian cross-bow, in common with that of West Africa, is undoubtedly of European origin; consideration of all the circumstances points definitely to the conclusion that the model imitated was a Portuguese one, such as was in use by Portuguese soldiers during the earlier years of the Portuguese domination of the coastal lands of South India.

In Laguna de Bay, a large lake near Manila in the Philippines, the cross-bow is in use to shoot the *dalag* (*Ophiocephalus striatus*). It is much the same as the Malayali weapon except that the arrow-head is armed with several barbed iron wires, and that it is not always detachable in harpoon fashion; sometimes it is permanently fixed to the shaft (Aldaba, 1931, 7). The weapon as a whole is known as an *Alcabus* or *Arcabuz*, a variation of 'arquebus'; this name is sufficient to prove that it has been adopted by the native fishermen, from, in this case, a Spanish original.

THE BLOW-GUN OR THUMBITHAN. What may be termed the Malayali type of blow-gun, being in use exclusively by the people of Malabar, Travancore and Cochin, is subject to a wide range of variation in the details of its construction, particularly with regard to the material of construction and the form of the mouthpiece. This fact bespeaks usage over a very lengthy period and a high antiquity for its invention or introduction. It is used exclusively for shooting fishes.

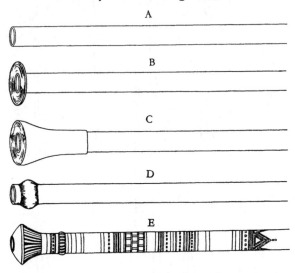

TEXT-FIG. 13. Varieties of the Malayali blow-gun differing in the form of the mouth-piece. A is a plain reed tube without added mouthpiece. In B, the mouthpiece is a disk of coconut shell; in C, it is turned out of wood, whilst in D and E it is built up of layers of gummed cloth, painted over. The butt end of E is ornamented with lacquered bands of yellow and red on black. The barrels of all these are made of the stems of the *ita* reed.

The only other instance of the blow-gun being used for a similar purpose is that quoted by Ling Roth (after Burbridge) of the Muruts of Borneo striking fish 'with unerring certainty with arrows from a sumpitan even at more than a foot below the surface' (1896, II, 184). There is, however, no close connexion between the two instances, for the Murut dart is simple, whilst that of the Malayali is of harpoon form, unique and confined strictly to South India.

In its simplest form (Text-fig. 13, A), as employed by the poorest classes of users, the Malayali blow-gun or *thumbithan* is made from a reed (*Ochlandra* sp.) obtained from the neighbouring forest. If one perfectly straight be found of suitable length, it is taken home and dried thoroughly by filling it with dry river sand. If none quite straight is to be had, the best is selected and straightened by either of two processes. The first is with the aid of fire. In this case the crooked section is soaked with oil and then straightened over a fire by bending. This done, the tube is, as usual, filled with dry sand to extract any moisture remaining and to dry it in proper shape.

If, however, the whole length of reed is slightly curved and not merely bent at one or may be two definite points, then the straightening is done by splitting the reed lengthwise very carefully into two equal longitudinal halves, reversing these end for end and reuniting them by the edges with mucilage obtained from the glue-tree (*Diospyros embryopteris*). When this method is adopted it becomes necessary to wind a spiral bandage soaked in the same kind of gum around the whole length of the tube in order to keep the two gummed edges in contact while drying and to prevent the tube from cracking subsequently.

This bandage is also commonly adopted in certain districts (e.g. Palghat) even when the reed has not been split and reunited. In others the tube is used in its naked condition. Nowadays the bandaging is done usually with narrow strips of mull cloth (muslin) by people called Kuruppans, who are the lacquer-workers of the district.

In Palghat taluk it is the general custom to add a built-up ridge or ring round the tube, composed of numerous layers of gum-soaked cloth strips, a short distance beyond the mouth of the tube, to form a mouthpiece (Text-fig. 13, D). When dry, an initial coat of paint is given over the bandaging and later, a coat of black is applied over the whole length. Finally, about 10 inches of the butt is ornamented with a pattern of fine lines of red and yellow lacquer or paint according to the fancy and skill of the workman. Text-fig. 13, E, represents a typical example.

In the extreme south of Malabar a trumpet-shaped mouthpiece turned out of a block of wood is slipped over the oral end of the tube (Text-fig. 13, c). If the tube be lacquered, the mouthpiece is similarly treated. In certain villages in Calicut taluk (Olavanna and Peruvanna) blow-guns are fitted with a perforated disk of coconut shell as mouthpiece (Text-fig. 13, B).

In many instances the better made tubes have a metal hook (Text-fig. 14, c) tied on by wire or twine to the muzzle end to serve as a retrieving hook wherewith to pick up the harpoon-line from the water when the dart has missed its mark. Or the hook may be soldered to a band of thin metal fitted around the muzzle.

Side by side with guns made from reeds are others shaped out of timber by the local carpenters. This variety is fashioned on the same principle as those reed-guns made by splitting and reuniting two longitudinal halves of a reed stem. Two battens of wood of the requisite length are taken. Each is grooved on one side in semicircular manner, great care being taken to keep the gauge uniform; the other side is suitably rounded. Finally, the two half-tubes are glued together by their edges to form a cylinder. To keep them in juxtaposition the whole length of the tube is bound spirally with a wrapping which may consist of cloth, bark or animal membrane. A mouthpiece of any form may be added at the fancy of the owner. Nearly all are painted black but they may or may not have red and yellow lines of lacquering on the butt (Text-fig. 13, E).

When the wrapping is not of cloth it is usually made of the bast of one of the banyans (*chēla*, Mal.=*Ficus tsila*), dipped in gum made from the juice of *panachinga*, or *panachikka*, the fruit of *Diospyros embryopteris* (*panachi*, Mal.). One specimen obtained at Valapad in the extreme south of Malabar, and said by the owner to be extremely old—an heirloom in the

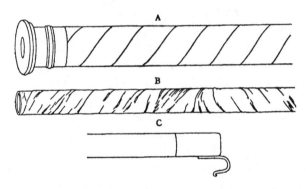

TEXT-FIG. 14. A is a very massive wooden blow-gun in the Trichur Museum, Cochin. The butt is encased in a turned brass mouthpiece; the barrel is spirally wrapped with strips of fibre, painted black. B is an old blow-gun from Valapad in South Malabar; it is made of wood and spirally wrapped with animal membrane. C shows a retrieving hook on the muzzle of the Trichur blow-gun.

family—was wrapped in what appears to be strips of the intestine of some animal, probably a goat (Text-fig. 14, B). It had no mouthpiece but had a retrieving hook soldered to one side of a metal band around the muzzle. Usually these wooden guns are thicker at the oral extremity than at the distal one. A unique example showing this in extreme degree is in the Cochin State Museum; as it was given to the museum by the ex-Rajah, it may be considered as the most elaborate example in existence of the Malayali blow-gun—a weapon made for royalty. The length of the barrel is 5 ft. 6 in., the diameter of the bore, 16 mm. From the butt, which is enclosed in a turned brass cap, the barrel tapers from a diameter of 42 to 24 mm. The form of the brass cap-piece is shown in Text-fig. 14, A. The sole ornamentation consists of plain turned ridges. The muzzle with its retrieving hook is seen in Text-fig. 14, C. The barrel is formed of two half-tubes of hardwood glued together and bound spirally with strips of fibre, painted black. It is much heavier than usual, though by no means so heavy as many of the blow-guns used on the East Coast for shooting birds.

An ordinary example of average length is about 5½ feet but the length may range between 4½ and 6½ feet. Diameter of the bore 16 mm.; of the gun itself from 42 mm. at the butt, tapering to 24 mm. at the muzzle in the case of wooden guns. Reed-guns are about 20 mm. in diameter with a bore of about 10 mm. Most of the wooden barrels are made of a hard, dark-coloured wood, probably rose-wood (*Dalbergia latifolia*); in the Calicut neighbourhood, I was told that there they are made from the wood of the *Areca* palm.

The dart used is of the harpoon variety. It consists of a wooden shaft, 160 to 170 mm. long, a steel or iron single-barbed head about 50 mm. in length, a long carefully twisted cord connecting the two, and a wad of threads, cloth or pith at the butt end of the shaft (Text-fig. 15).

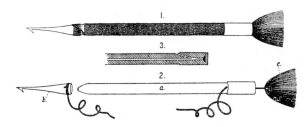

TEXT-FIG. 15. Blow-gun darts used when shooting fishes. 1, dart ready for use; 2, details of: (*a*) the shaft; (*b*) the steel-barbed head; (*c*) the mop-like wad, its base not yet pulled down into the cavity at the head of the shaft; 3, a longitudinal section through the head of the shaft, showing the oblique perforation through which the retrieving line is passed.

The Malayalam terms for its several parts are as follows:

Pongu, *ponthu* and *ulithandu*, the shaft of the dart, which also serves as a float;

Uli, both the dart as a whole and also the barbed steel head;

Kotuppu and *poduppu*, the wad for windage at the butt-end of the *pongu*.

The shaft of the dart is made of different materials in different localities. In Palghat, the side-twigs of the spiny bamboo are used; in parts of Travancore, the wood of the *Areca* palm and in South Malabar, the stem of lemon grass. Whatever be used must be light or else, as in North Travancore, it must have a pith wad added in order to float in water and so indicate either the course of the wounded fish or the position of the barbed head if the dart has missed its mark. The wad on the butt of the shaft in Palghat taluk is formed of a mop of short cotton threads, mixed with some thicker woollen ones. This wad is attached to the shaft in two different ways; either the threads are tied across their mid-length within a shallow groove encircling the end of the shaft and with their lower half reflected upwards to form a mop, or else a conical pit is excavated in the end of the butt, and a hole bored obliquely from the bottom of this pit to a point on the outside of the shaft ¾ inch from the butt-end (Text-fig. 15, 3). The proximal end of the harpoon cord is passed through the centre of a mop of threads, a knot being made on the end to prevent it from pulling through. By pulling on the cord the base of the mop of threads is drawn within the conical basal pit and secured there by a hitch made after passing the cord twice round the shaft. In Ponnani and to the south (Chetway, Valapad, etc.) the wad is often of several disk-shaped layers of cotton cloth nailed through the centre into the head of the shaft.

In certain parts of North Travancore a tapering or conical plug of the pith of *thirupulu* takes the place of a thread or cloth wad. This plug is from 1 to 1½ inches long with the narrow end truncate, into which the sharpened butt of the wooden shaft is driven.

The form of the barbed head never varies. It consists of a slender, cylindrical shaft of iron expanded at the base to permit of a conical hollow being worked in the end, and of a single-winged barb at one side of an attenuate and very sharp point (Text-fig. 15). The forward margin of the barb is ground to razor-blade keenness. The distal end of the shaft is made conical and fits into the hollow at the base of the iron head sufficiently loosely to become detached when anything be struck. The harpoon cord connecting the two is very carefully laid and is tanned periodically to preserve it. When the dart is inserted into the tube this line is wound tightly and evenly around the wooden shaft, leaving no slack (Text-fig. 15, 1).

Sighting is done with the right eye, and then moving the head while keeping the arms steady, the mouth is brought up to the mouthpiece and the dart expelled by a strong, sharp puff. Boys practise aiming at a plantain stem, as this target is soft enough not to damage the point of the dart.

LOCAL RANGE. The use of the Malayali blow-gun has a geographical range coinciding approximately with that of the Malayalam language except that it does not appear at the present time to extend north of the Calicut taluk, while conversely, it extends some distance eastwards into Coimbatore through the Palghat gap—the highway of communication between the Tamil and Malayalam-speaking folk. Trivandrum and Vaikom mark approximately its southern limit, Calicut taluk its northern.

In no locality is this form of blow-gun used except for shooting fish. Its use is not restricted to any caste or section of the population. Generally Muhammadans (Mappillas) take the greater interest in this form of sport than do the Hindus. It is used chiefly along the banks of streams and pools but neither on the coast nor in the seaward parts of the backwaters.

The murrels (Ophiocephalidae) are said to be the commonest of the fishes shot as they have the habit of coming frequently to the surface of the water, where the trouble caused by refraction may be ignored when aiming. Grey mullets (Mugilidae) and the pearl-spot (*Etroplus surantensis*) are other species sometimes shot.

In most localities the use of the blow-gun is much more restricted than formerly, the cross-bow supplanting it as being more effective.

It is significant that the blow-gun, while widely spread among the Malayalis, is not known and seems never to have been used among their neighbours, the Tamils of the east coast, except in the pellet-form introduced from Malaya for bird-shooting, along the seaboard of Tanjore and Ramnad. If this proves nothing else, it demonstrates how isolated from one another were Kerala and the Tamil country prior to the era of British-made roads and railways. It also suggests, when taken in conjunction with other evidence, that the Malayalis are largely of a different stock from the bulk of the Tamil population. But this is a problem foreign to the present subject and cannot be treated here.

THE SICKLE. In a different class to the preceding, which are adapted or developed from weapons of the chase, is a fishing implement derived from an agricultural source—the fish-sickle. This is used in conjunction with torches (*chut*) made of coconut leaves bound into a long bundle. On dark, moonless nights the fisherman attracts large fishes to the surface by the lure of the light of a flaming torch held in his left hand. This he waves constantly to and fro to make it burn fiercely. Any fish drawn by the spell of the light to within striking distance is slashed at and hooked out of the water by means of an ordinary sickle held in the man's right hand.

This is a most unusual method of catching fish and it is noteworthy that it is also practised so far away from India as the Channel Islands and the northern coast of France where sand-eels (*Ammodytes* sp.) are dislodged from sandy stretches at low tide by means of sickles and hooks; no lights are used as the sand-eels lie quiescent, hidden in the sand.

II

ANGLING OF SORTS

Had Izaak Walton been a traveller as well as a garrulous angler and had he penetrated to Bengal, he would have found there the most congenial of company and we should have been the richer by many quaintly told tales of the curious angling devices in daily use on the banks of the Ganges—strange tales, with the stranger merit of being perfectly veracious.

A keen love of angling is strongly developed among Bengalis. More than any other race in India do they love and practise the gentle art. The contemplative repose of angling, joined with the substantial results obtainable, appeal to two of their most marked characteristics. Every man among them, high or low, if true to his racial instincts and not town-bred and emasculated, has an ardent affection for his rod.

The rods used by all except the few who have learned the value of the highly specialized spliced European rod, jointed and furnished with reel and running line, are of the simplest description.

The villager's rod is usually home-made, cut from a carefully chosen length of bamboo. Finer ones, tougher and tapered more evenly, come from the hills and find a place in the local bazaars, for those whose sense of angling refinement is further developed. In all cases where the indigenous style prevails, either the old-fashioned tight line (now abandoned by the European angler in favour of the running line) or an ingenious modification thereof is alone used. In its simplest form the tight line is tied firmly to the tip of the rod. In such cases the rod when used for largish fish is short, strong and little tapered, the line stout and the landing of the fish a matter of a quick strike and a dexterous throw-out upon the bank. If small fish be fished for, the rod is more slender and the tackle lighter.

A modification of the tight line, that renders it possible to play the hooked fish to some small extent, is much more common than the crude original form. This improvement consists in attaching the line not directly to the tip of the rod, but some distance lower down, where it is thicker.

For surface fishing, where a short line will suffice, the attachment to the rod is made at the beginning of the upper fourth of the rod; for mid-water and bottom fishing, the longer line that has to be employed is tied still farther down. When the rod is in use, a considerable part of the line is coiled round and round the rod from the place of its attachment upwards to the tip, where it is secured by two loops being cast round it; these are so loose that the slightest tension sets them free and allows the reserve line, coiled round the rod, to be paid out as necessary.

This improvement, as already stated, enables the expert angler to play his fish to some slight extent. It is infinitely less effective, however, than the running line used in combination with a reel, but it goes some way—as far indeed as its limitations permit—to satisfy the requirements of an angler whose tackle is too slender to permit of his fish being landed by brute force. The superior advantage of the reel is realized readily by Bengali anglers; home-made brass reels and rods with eyes for a running line are nowadays not uncommon. The extra cost involved militates against its general adoption.

Ordinary rods used with tight and semi-tight lines are of all lengths, from 5 or 6 feet up to about 18 feet or even more. The lines are usually of well-twisted cotton or hemp cord, tanned and stiffened by immersion in *gāb* decoction. Stronger and more durable fishing-lines are made from *tasar* and refuse silk chiefly by those curious river gipsies, the low-class Muhammadan Bebajia, a nomad tribe found all over Bengal, living their life out on their boats and combining fishing, thieving, petty trading and sundry other occupations in the approved gipsy fashion. Another gipsy characteristic is their skill in wire-working; from steel wire they fashion most of the larger-sized hooks required by fishermen—the village blacksmith furnishes the remainder. Small sizes are almost entirely of European make, obtainable in the bazaars everywhere. Almost invariably the hooks are barbed. For surface fishing, a single hook is used; for bottom fishing, two or three may be tied on. The indigenous hook is shorter in the shank and with a wider and more angular bend than the typical European pattern.

Great variety characterizes the objects used as floats. One of the chief favourites is a length of the quill end of a peacock's feather. Others are made of short lengths cut from the flowering stems of reeds (*nal*), and certain grasses (*ulu*); a length of jute stem and sections of sola-pith are also frequently employed. Sinkers are nowadays mostly made of lead strips wound round the line till the requisite weight is attained. A more primitive form is that where small iron balls are threaded on; baked clay sinkers are also known.

The ingenuity of the Bengali angler reaches its highest expression in the matter of baits, particularly of ground baits. They comprise everything he can think of to tempt fish to his hook through the senses of sight, smell and taste. For his hooks the favourite animal baits are earthworms, prawns and large silkworms (*chukri*)—the last particularly highly esteemed for almost all kinds of fish. Small live fish, particularly murrel fry and the little *Barbus stigma* are commonly used, together with a variety of beetles and frogs; small mice are also pressed into the angler's service on occasion. Dough made of flour or of baked rice, and fragments of jack-fruit, fish flesh and fish offal are other useful baits. Perhaps the most curious bait is the cockroach used when fishing for the giant cat-fish, *Wallago attu*, so often miscalled the fresh-water shark. This strong-smelling lure is not impaled on the hook but is tied on immediately above it and then lowered a few feet into the water.

The value of ground baiting is so well understood that the manufacture and use of appropriate mixtures have been brought to a high degree of specialization. They are particularly valued in fishing for several of the larger carps. The mixtures employed consist essentially of strong-smelling substances bound up in clay or dough, in order that the diffusion of the odour shall proceed comparatively slowly. The resultant paste, made up into balls, may either be thrown into the water before or during fishing with a view to attract fishes to the spot, or it may be placed in some special contrivance so fashioned that nibbling at the paste ball is betrayed instantly to the angler watching nearby. Three such ingenious devices deserve mention. In the first of these a long bamboo, tapering evenly to an extremely slender tip, is chosen. To this end a white feather is tied by its base, the vane erect and free. A bait made of aromatic substances, previously compounded into a paste, is then tied to the bamboo a few feet from the thick butt end. This done, the bamboo is planted upright in the tank or pool where fishing is to take place, the butt being driven down into the mud to such a distance as permits the feathered end to stand clear of the water, and the mass of ground bait paste to be at what is considered an appropriate distance above the muddy bottom. Fishes are attracted by the strong odour of the bait, and nibbling at it causes the feather to vibrate. The angler then casts his line close to the bait stick. The length of the stick varies with the depth of the tank; a usual length is between 9 and 10 feet.

A variation employed in Lower Bengal is to insert a ball of bait paste into the middle of an internode of bamboo in which a number of long slits have been made; by pressure these may be made to gape and so permit of the introduction within of a mass of paste. At each end, a length of the adjoining internode is left, forming a short tubular cavity. To put this baited cylinder into operation the butt of a fine bamboo wand, several feet in length, is set loosely in the hollow in the upper end, while the lower end is set loosely upon the thinned summit of a stick set upright in the bed of the tank. The slits in the centre of the baited cylinder gape sufficiently to permit fish to nibble at the bait. The whole device is so extremely sensitive that this is sufficient to set the wand vibrating wildly, the indication waited for by the fisherman before making his cast.

Another ingenious contrivance sometimes used in Lower Bengal when fishing for the voracious fresh-water shark (*Wallago attu*) is the *jota*. It is arranged thus: A length of split bamboo sufficiently long for the upper end to project well above water is planted firmly in the tank bottom. A small brass bell is affixed to the projecting end and then some distance below the surface of the water a nest of baited straw, oval in form, is tied to the bamboo pole. Concealed in the straw is a strongly barbed hook attached to the end of a strong line belonging to a powerful fishing-rod held by the fisherman. The arrangement has to be most carefully contrived, for the point of the hook must be directed upwards and so loosely fixed in the straw that nothing will come in its way when the time to strike arrives. The line is then carried over the projecting end of the bamboo stake. The fisherman having finished his preparations, stands attentive, waiting the time when the tinkling of the bell shall announce that a fish is nibbling. Instantly he strikes with a rapid upward jerk. So skilful is the *jota* fisherman, that it is seldom he fails to hook his fish in the chin. Aromatic ground bait is employed in charging the straw nest.

The composition of the more popular of the ground baits employed in Bihar and Bengal is often most complex. A typical example consists of cinnamon bark, fenugreek seed, cotton seed, sesamum, mustard cake and rice, all parched over a fire, then pounded together and mixed with stiff clay into a highly pungent and aromatic paste.

The bait used on the hook employed when fishing with the aid of ground bait is usually made of some such paste mixture as flour and ghee or decayed cheese made up with clay, or bread and cheese kneaded together.

It is notable that neither gaff nor landing-net is found among indigenous angling appliances.

Like fellow-disciples of Izaak Walton in other countries, the Bengali angler gives thought to the provision of a supply of simple comforts for himself when he sets out on an angling excursion. These he carries in the little box where he stores his supply of bait, his floats and hooks, all in separate compartments. Together with his food, stored in the largest compartment of the box, he usually carries (unless he has fallen a victim to Western habits of smoking) tobacco made into a paste with molasses, his earthen pipe-bowl (*kulika*), charcoal cakes used for kindling the moist tobacco and a box of matches. The never-failing hookah is carried in the hand.

Where the villager or cultivator fishes purely for profit while engaged in other work, he employs a number of stout rods, each furnished with a short tight line carrying a baited hook, set at intervals along the bank of a stream, the butt ends planted firmly in the soil. These the owner visits from time to time, to remove any fish that may be hooked or to renew the baits.

An automatic rod-fishing device which properly speaking should perhaps be grouped under the head of snares, is employed occasionally in Lower Bengal. It consists of a medium-sized bamboo rod, provided with a short stout line, $7\frac{1}{2}$ feet long, tied to a rod $2\frac{1}{2}$ feet from its tapered extremity round which it is coiled, and loosely secured at the tip by a loop knot. A large native-made hook is bound to the end of the line, while about 8 inches above the hook a splint of bamboo, a few inches long, with a notch at the lower end, is tied on to the line. The butt of the rod is driven securely into the bank and then its tip is pulled down by the line so that the notched bamboo splint attached to the line will catch into a notch at the top of a bamboo post, 3 feet high, fixed in the bed of the stream or tank and submerged to within 6 inches or so of the summit, the baited hook hanging down into the water for a few inches. When a fish takes the hook, the tension set up, even though slight, frees the little bamboo splint from its hold on the post, permitting the rod to spring upwards and backwards with great force, carrying the hooked fish with it, if the hook has caught.

The hand-line (*tuggi*) is also in common use and has several distinctive features. In nearly all cases, the line is wound round a perforated cylindrical roller, which revolves upon a short bamboo stake driven into the bank of the tank or stream. The roller in its simplest form is made from an internode of a medium-sized bamboo ornamented frequently with fire marks. A gourd is also sometimes employed for the same purpose. More elaborate rollers are turned from teak, and often have the ends ornamented with lacquered patterns. The lines are usually of silk, sometimes of cotton, and always soaked in *gāb* or other tanning mixture to prevent rotting. The length is much greater than any line used in conjunction with a rod. A heavy lead sinker is fastened upon the line, helpful and indeed necessary when casting the line from the bank.

A *tuggi* and its roller are not complete without the addition of a little contrivance to notify the fisherman when a fish is hooked. It consists of a splint of bamboo having a long notch at one end. After the line has been paid out, this piece of bamboo is fixed into the earth in front of the roller, and a loop of the line thrown loosely through the notch. The slightest traction pulls out the loop and attracts the attention of the fisherman. Either one or two hooks are tied to the end of such hand-lines.

Frequently these lines are used for moonlight fishing. On dark nights a fire-fly is occasionally fastened on a float attached to the line; the dancing of the illuminated float warns the angler when a fish is nibbling.

Upon the sea-coast, surf-fishing or casting is a favourite sport; usually two snoods with baited hooks are used, together with a heavy lead sinker. In casting the weighted end, the fisherman whirls it twice or even thrice round his head, when, on release, it shoots out over the surf to a distance of 30 or 40 feet from the shore. The line is played slowly for a few minutes and then pulled ashore if no bite comes, to be cast again and again in the same way.

The most popular bait in the neighbourhood of Madras is a species of Eunicid worm, that takes the place of *Nereis* and *Arenicola* on the British coast. The method of capture is so ingenious as to be worthy of record. The home of this particular species of worm is in the sands below half-tide level, so, to collect a supply, the fisherman goes to the shore towards low tide, preferably when springs are on. He goes armed with a little receptacle slung from a cord attached on opposite sides of its mouth, so that it can be carried suspended from between his teeth, leaving him both hands free. It is usually a tiny earthenware chatty, or two-thirds of a coconut shell. Crushed within the palm of one hand is a smashed-up crab, usually an Ocypod, soaked freely in water, with the end of a disjointed limb held between the thumb and the index finger. When the retreating wave momentarily exposes a stretch of suitable or likely sand, the man runs down to it, flicking drops of dilute juice from the hand holding the crushed crab over the sandy surface. The worms sense this instantly and then, when one pops its head out of its burrow, the fisherman if he sees it, bends down and tempts the worm to protrude still farther by holding the broken crab limb protruding from between his fingers close to it; with the other hand he makes ready to seize hold of the worm's head as soon as it stretches out sufficiently to afford a grip. Instantly finger and thumb close upon its head and with an expert but cautious pull, he hauls the worm from its burrow, usually intact.

Since the Rainbow Trout was successfully introduced into the streams issuing from the Nilgiri Hills in South India, some of these turbulent little rivers, the Bhawani in particular, have become favourite resorts of enthusiastic European fly-fishers who make use of the local form of coracle in order to move from pool to pool and to thread the rock-strewn stream whenever miniature rapids are encountered.

Good fly-fishing is also to be had in the hill streams among the foothills of the Himalayas whenever trout have been properly protected after introduction.

III

ANIMALS TRAINED TO FISH AND FISHES THAT ANGLE FOR THEIR LIVING

MANY animals catch fish to satisfy their daily needs by methods as simple as they are effective. Some of these may have proved suggestive to ancestral man living in the Stone Age, when hungry and eager to enrich his depleted larder with some of the toothsome fishes playing about, sometimes in shoals, in quiet reaches of a stream, or darting hither and thither in shallow coastal waters or imprisoned in some of the rock-pools on the seashore. Some he may have caught by hand, a method not unprofitable when practised in shallow streams.

Early men when settled in a warm deltaic region would often see a converging semicircle of solemn-looking pelicans paddling in stately fashion towards a shallow patch of water near the bank, sometimes the cul-de-sac of a tidal creek. Frequently have I come upon such a scene when on fishery duty in that labyrinth of deltaic creeks and channels through which the waters of the Indus thread their way to empty into the sea.

The actions of these great ungainly birds are purposeful. There is no flurry, no haste in their movements. It is soon manifest that they pursue a familiar and well-tried plan, rich in ultimate reward. Beating their way through the shallowing water with their great webbed feet, their heads all turn towards the same focal point. As they move methodically forward they keep station perfectly. No company of soldiers could keep their curving and converging line better ordered. Moving steadily towards their objective, the slowly paddling semicircle of birds gradually lessens the space enclosed until at last a place is reached where the water is less than a foot in depth. By this time the lessening of the semicircle has brought the birds very close together.

The moment now arrives when, in some queer way, the birds sense that the time has come to gather in the spoils of their collective labours. A flurry of white wings strikes the water, the ungainly pouched bills flash downwards; as quickly, is each back again, now pointing skywards as, with a deft twist, the fish just caught is slithered down, head foremost, into the capacious pouch below the mandible.

Contrasting strangely with the slow and dignified converging movement of the birds during the preliminary drive, the feathered fishers now become greatly excited; they strike furiously and often, and they continue to gulp their prey hurriedly until their pouches are distended to their extreme extent with a spasmodically struggling mass of dying fish, sufficient to assuage their hunger and render the birds ready to spend the heat of the day in the luxury of a plethoric doze.

Whether the daily sight of such a co-operative fish-drive influenced early man we cannot say, but the fact remains that fish-drives by Indian villagers, carried on in much the same way, are of common occurrence as the monsoon floods slowly subside. Often the whole village will turn out; men, women and children troop down to the appointed place on the bank of a shrinking pool or waterspread; there they arrange themselves in a tumultuous cordon across the pool or in the broad sweep of a semicircle if the waterspread be wide and shallow. With joyous shouts and the maximum of splashing they move slowly forwards, any fishes in their path scurrying forwards before them, eventually to be hemmed in by the living chain of laughing and shrieking village folk. Many of the people are armed with plunge baskets, sub-conical funnels, open at both ends; these are thrust down upon the bottom as often as their owners can plant them in the mud, wider end downwards, on the chance of imprisoning any fish hiding on the bottom. If one be caught, it is pulled out through the small opening at the upper or narrow end of the funnel. But many have no plunge basket and are compelled to play a game of grab, the fun waxing fast and increasingly furious as the end of the drive draws near, with the fishes gradually collecting in a wildly convulsed mob at the apex of the area of the drive; in their terrified frenzy many fishes leap ashore where they lie gasping and floundering till some of the village children pounce upon them with shrieks of delight.

The next step in the evolution of the fish-drive is seen when the fish are driven towards a net held by two or more men across the line of retreat. Usually other men, starting from a distance in front of the net, stampede the fishes with shouts and splashing into flight towards the net; dogs and horses have also been used as 'beaters', the dogs sometimes trained to seize and retrieve the larger of the fishes in flight.

Sea-birds are the keenest of all feathered fishers, for fishes to them represent the staff of life; foremost of all are the gannet and the cormorant. The gannet's dive from the sky, driving down with bullet speed, wings folded tightly against the body, to cleave the water above the fish that has been espied from on high, and then to emerge a few seconds later with the prey held firmly in the beak, is a sight never to be forgotten.

Here, too, men of the warm seas pursue a similar technique. In the clear water within the encircling coral reef, I have seen the lithe and tawny Tahitian leap overboard from his canoe and cleave the water just as cleanly as does the gannet. Armed with a sharp-pointed lance he pursues the fish he has spotted and he seldom fails to transfix it on the point. More clever than the gannet, he is not content with a single capture; several times have I seen the diver emerge with three fishes impaled upon his lance-point.

Then there is the cormorant, a ruthless and insatiable enemy of the smaller shoaling fish, so much so that at times its depredations cause it to be recognized officially as 'Bird enemy No. 1'.

In Europe to-day no people utilize its ability as a clever fisher to supplement ordinary methods of fishing for market needs. In the Far East it is otherwise. From a very early period the nimble-witted and versatile Chinese fishermen have been training cormorants as fishery helpers. At the present day this curious fishing method is practised on a commercial scale on many of the lakes, marshes and quiet, slow-moving rivers throughout the length and breadth of the great plain of China. As is to be expected when operations extend over such a wide area, the methods employed vary considerably. In most places fishing is conducted in a very simple manner; the craft employed is commonly a small raft-platform of bamboos, manned by a single fisherman in charge of some half-dozen trained cormorants. The birds usually never know a free life; cormorant eggs are set to hatch under a hen and the chicks thus hatched partake of the family life of their owner from the very first. Even so, when they grow old enough to be put with fully trained old birds, their wings are clipped and a ring of rattan placed around the lower end of their neck, below the gullet pouch. The presence of this ring does not wholly prevent them from feeding; they are still able to pass small fishes beyond the ring but not when they are of large size.

Text-fig. 16. Fishing with cormorants in China.

When trained, they fish from their owner's raft, returning aboard with their catch if they find it too large to swallow past the gullet ring. Whenever a bird gives up its catch, care is taken to reward it with a morsel of fish. When fishes are plentiful the fisherman may lift the captured fish aboard with a dip-net and then encourage the cormorant to try again (Text-fig. 16).

On the small rivers, creeks and pools connected with the Yangtze in the vicinity of Ichang, a peculiar form of small double-canoe takes the place of the bamboo raft. This consists of two tiny canoe hulls, each about 5 feet long and 8 inches wide, joined together by a board at a distance of 18 or 24 inches apart. On this frail platform the fisherman stands, one foot on each hull (Donnelly, 1936, 419). Poling his way along, the cormorants, perched along the gunwales, dive overboard at the word of command, searching the water in quest of fish; any caught are brought aboard and delivered, the bird being up-ended in order to make disgorgement easier. Fishing by this method takes place by day (Pl. II, fig. B).

The imitative Japanese appear to have borrowed cormorant fishing from the Chinese at a very early period, certainly not less than 1000 years ago, probably much earlier. Keen and clever fishermen as they are, it was not long before they elaborated the Chinese technique. To-day the Japanese exploit this method of fishing on an extensive scale and even tag on a secondary industry; they make capital out of it as a show piece! Gifu, on the River Nagara, is the chief centre to-day of cormorant-fishing in Japan, both in its primary aspect as sport and in its secondary one as a tourist attraction.

During a visit to Japan in those peaceful days when friendly relations existed between Britain and Japan, I had an opportunity to watch operations being carried on. At Gifu, fishing takes place only during the dark of the moon, during the warm weather between mid-May and the early part of October; windy nights are avoided—broken, wind-swept water makes it difficult for the birds to sight their quarry.

Word had come from the fishery officer who had been appointed to be my guide by Professor Kishinouye, the then Director of the Fisheries Bureau, that weather conditions being favourable, cormorant-fishing would begin as soon as darkness fell. Meeting the officer at the appointed rendezvous, I found seven or eight fishing-boats about to set off. Several tourist barges were in attendance, crowded with a happy throng of Japanese visitors, mostly noisy young men bandying jokes, with a bevy of gaily dressed geishas scattered among them.

As soon as the light began to fade, the crews of the pleasure barges lit the pretty paper lanterns festooned along the sides—Gifu is famed for the variety and tasteful ornamentation of its lantern products. This was the signal for departure. The fishing-boats led off, dark shadows just discernible in the decreasing light. A few minutes later the gloom lifted as the fishermen lit the flares that are needed to lure the fishes to gather within the lighted area and thereby render the task of the cormorants the easier. As if by magic the scene was transformed; the long canoe-shaped hulls of the boats became distinct; all details were revealed.

With few exceptions the boats, about 40 feet long with a beam of 3 feet, were manned by a crew of four men. The master-fisherman stood at the prow, a picturesque figure wearing a peaked head-dress and a ceremonial kilt of dried grass, everything being seen clearly in the light given out by the wood chips burning in a brazier hung from the end of a long crane-arm that can be switched from dead ahead to either side as desired. It is this man's duty to regulate the course and to tend the lines or traces, twelve in number, which control the work of the same number of cormorants; amidships is his assistant, who tends the lines of four birds. Near him is a boatman armed with a punting-pole, and at the stern is another who steers as directed by the master-fisherman (Pl. iv, fig. A).

Before fishing begins each bird has its harness put on, a matter of much delicacy, for the cormorant has to be coaxed into submission (Pl. iii, figs. A and B). But the master-fisherman knows his business well; with caressing strokes he placates the bird, the while he adjusts a ring of metal or rattan or cord around the lower part of the neck just big enough to enable the bird to swallow small, undersized fishes, yet too narrow to permit the passage of those of marketable size (Pl. iii, fig. A). At the back, between the wings, one end of either a strip of whalebone or one of pliant bamboo, about a foot long, is fastened to the gullet ring; this strip serves as a convenient handle when lifting the bird from the water (Pl. iii, fig. B). To the other end of this 'handle' is attached a light cord leash from 12 to 15 feet in length, made from cypress bark for this is less liable to tangle than hemp or cotton twine. As the master-fisherman has to look after the fishing of twelve birds, it requires unwearied and skilful attention and the extreme dexterity of super-nimble fingers while holding these twelve lines in the left hand, to use his right in the constant effort to prevent them from becoming hopelessly entangled (Pl. iv, fig. A).

The cormorants are a temperamental company. They are exceedingly jealous of their rank and of the privileges belonging to seniority; they scold like fishwives if there be any infringement of what they consider their rightful status. The oldest and most skilful bird is called *Itchi-ban* or 'Number one'. His position is on the overhanging prow. Woe to the bird that would intrude on this privileged 'seat of the mighty'. So with the others; according to their experience and proficiency, so must be their respective stations on the gunwale, the cleverest being allotted the station nearest to proud *Itchi-ban*.

As the fishing progresses the 'master' keeps a keen watch upon his team, spread out fanwise in their search for fish. When one is caught, the bird's head emerges from the water with the fish held crosswise in its beak, then, deftly, it is swallowed head first. If small, it passes the ring and becomes the perquisite of the bird; if too large to pass, it remains in the gullet pouch; if others are already there, the keen-eyed 'master' hauls in the particular leash, lifts the bird from the water by its bamboo or whalebone handle and, with a deft motion, up-ends the bird and with adroit pressure forces it to disgorge the contents of the pouch, three, four, six or even seven at a time if fish be plentiful. This done, the bird is returned to the water, where, annoyed by the loss of its previous catch, it redoubles its efforts, for experience has taught it that good reward is assured if it works to the satisfaction of the 'master'.

When fishing ceases, the catch of small fish swallowed by each bird as food is estimated by 'hefting'; those that feel below weight are given an extra ration of small fishes, for hungry birds are apt to be resentful or sulky and this leads to squabbles with their companions.

Whenever fishing is to take place, the birds are taken down to the boat in covered baskets woven from strips of bamboo, with a partition down the centre; in each chamber one bird is placed, care being taken that only birds friendly disposed to one another are put together.

During the winter season and when the weather is stormy, the birds become a heavy charge upon their owner. They are greedy feeders, blessed like all birds with a very rapid digestion and therefore always hungry.

The taming and training of cormorants is a tedious task. In Japan they are caught by spreading bird-lime over rocks in their known haunts; as soon as one is caught, it is used as a decoy for others, its eyelids being sewn up temporarily. Its cries attract its comrades, which are caught in turn. Only the younger are kept; the older are too set in their ways to be tamed effectively. Those kept have their wings clipped and undergo several months training before they are fit to be admitted as qualified to take their place among birds working in the regular fishery.

OTTER-FISHING. Another animal forced into the fishing service of man is the otter. In some ways it is more amenable to training than the cormorant; in consequence its employment in fishing is more widely distributed. It often develops a dog-like affection for its trainer and gives him personal and willing service rather than assuming the impersonal attitude of the cormorant which works for man because he is forced to do so in order to be given food.

In Europe, accounts of the use of trained fishing otters are current in the literature of many countries—from England, Scotland, Scandinavia and France, through Switzerland and Germany; thence into Poland. Records of its use in North America also exist (Gudger, 1927, 219).

In Asia, tame otters are employed by fishermen in several provinces of China, especially in the Yangtze valley; in India, accounts of its use in fishing come from Bengal (the Sunderbans in particular) and from the Indus and the Cochin backwaters.

In Europe, although otters were once fairly often used in fishing trout streams, its occurrence was sporadic and restricted to small-scale operations carried on by occasional individuals for sport rather than for gain. It had no general vogue. In China and in some Indian localities its employment is a current practice. Writing of what he saw in 1883 in the neighbourhood of Ichang, on the Yangtse Kiang, Archibald Little (1898, 39) says:

After tiffin I cross the river...to inspect the otter fisheries peculiar to this place. The opposite shore rises in pyramidal cliffs.... Attached to the rocky shore, in a small bay, sheltered somewhat from the violence of the current, the fishermen have their otter station. From the bank, and overhanging the water, depend small bamboos, like fishing-rods, to the extremity of each of which is attached an otter by an iron chain fixed to leather thongs crossed round the animal's chest and immediately behind the shoulders. Some of the animals were playing in the water, swimming as far as the length of their tether would allow them; others had hung themselves across their bamboos, resting, doubled up, and looking for all the world like otter skins hung up to dry in the sun. When required for use, the fisherman, after casting his net, which is heavily loaded all round the foot, draws up its long neck to the water level, and inserts the otter through the central aperture; the otter then routs out the fish from the muddy bottom and rocky crevices, in which they hide. Fish, otter, and net are then all hauled on board together, the otter released and rewarded, and a fresh cast is made.

A variation in this method of using the otter in conjunction with the cast-net is described by Gordon Moir (1909) who states that the otter is put overboard immediately after the net has been thrown; while it descends slowly through the water, the otter swims round the periphery of the net chasing any fish it sees into the area above the net, herding them there just as a sheep dog will shepherd a flock of sheep into a small pen. He adds that if there be no fish about, the otter will rise to the surface and give the fisherman warning that a different place should be tried.

Nearly the same technique is in use with the *tar-jāl* of Bengal, a variant of the Chinese lever-arm dip-net worked from the prow of a boat on the streams meandering through the delta of the Ganges. Two or three trained otters are let loose at the beginning of operations; these precede the boat and hunt out any large fishes which may be lurking at the bottom. Very cleverly do they chivvy them towards the net. When the fisherman sees them directly over the immersed net, he deftly raises it, thereby throwing the captured fishes into the bottom of the boat (Hornell, 1924, 234).

A number of other writers, including Hosie (1897), confirm Moir's account, and Percival (1889, 128–9) adds that an otter, wearing a muzzle, is put into the water when one of the huge lever-armed dip-nets in use near Ichang is let down into the river; the otter, swimming around, drives all the fish he can find towards the net, herding them carefully together, rounding up stragglers whenever the wayward ones attempt to stray. When the otter is seen to have collected a good bunch of fishes immediately above where the net rests, the fisherman ashore sets his mechanism working; as the net is raised noiselessly and without disturbance, the fishes are caught in its shallow bag before they have time to take fright and scatter.

In Europe the taming of a young otter appears to have been due to some predilection on the part of individuals fond of animals and intelligent enough to appreciate its possible usefulness. The story that someone had trained an otter to fish and to carry its catch to its master would soon be told as a marvel throughout the neighbouring countryside; here and there an imitator would try his hand. But it always remained as an individual experiment, even in Scotland whence come most of the instances on record for Britain (Gudger, 1927).

FISHES USED IN CATCHING TURTLE. Strangest of all methods of fishing with the aid of animals is the employment of the sucker-fish or remora (*Echeneis* spp). when the hunt is on for turtle—either the edible green turtle or the hawksbill turtle which yields the valuable tortoiseshell of commerce. Stranger still is the fact that this method is of world-wide distribution; Columbus noted it as one of the marvels of the New World which he gave to Leon and Castile; the blacks of Australia are adepts in its use; the Chinese are said to employ it, while off the east coast of Africa, the fishermen of Zanzibar and the Mozambique Channel employ this fish in exactly the same way as the aboriginal fisherfolk of Australia and as the Caribbean Indians continued to do until their tribes dissolved under the cruel yoke of the Spaniards.

TEXT-FIG. 17. The common sucker-fish, *Echeneis naucrates*.

The remora, of which there are a number of closely allied species, is easily recognized by the curious oblong sucker borne upon the top of the head and from which the group derives its common name of 'sucker-fishes'. This specialized organ, formed by modification of the first dorsal fin, is compound, being made up of two parallel series of transverse plates, set in a long oval frame (Text-fig. 17). By its help these fishes are enabled to affix themselves securely to the bottoms of ships, the piles of jetties and to the bodies of whales, sharks, turtle and other large inhabitants of the sea and thereby to get carried about without effort on their own part (Pl. IV, fig. B).

The power of adhesion of a large sucker-fish is marvellous; experimenting with a medium-sized sucker-fish measuring about 2 feet in length, I found that it is able to sustain the pull or weight of a pail of water weighing over 20 lb., if it be allowed to obtain a firm grip by its sucker upon the inside of the pail and then be lifted by the tail.

During the pearl-fishing season off Ceylon, whenever the old barque which formed my headquarters was anchored on the pearl banks, several of these fishes were often to be seen swimming lazily around the stern on days when we had a spell of fine weather. They never moved far from the vessel; they hung around the stern, ever on the watch for any scraps of food thrown overboard; we reckoned them good scavengers. At other times they attached themselves to the hull, generally towards the stern, for there they could still watch for any morsels of food that might drift past. Sometimes we caught one and made experiments on its power of adhesion. We found it difficult to dislodge one by a direct pull backwards or at right angles to the body, but if the head region were slid forward detachment was easy.

When kept in captivity the sucker-fish, like many fishes that live on the bottom or among rocks, shows marked ability to adapt its colour to harmonize with that of its surroundings, the dark stripes on the body fading when on a light ground, whereas the white stripes along the sides disappear or darken when moving amid dark surroundings or when adhering to a dark surface.

Among the ancient Greeks the remora's habit of clinging tenaciously to a ship's bottom was well known; so extravagant was the common belief in its power of adhesion that this was considered adequate to impede or even to halt the progress of a ship. From this sprang the belief, long current, that the battle of Actium went to Augustus because a remora, 'ship-holder' as the Greeks called it, had affixed itself to Antony's galley and had thereby been the cause of that delay which led to the defeat of the fleet collected by Cleopatra. The same reason was adduced to account for the slow progress of Caligula's galley when he was voyaging from Astura to Antium; the populace of that age preferred to believe in the magical power of the fish rather than to credit the prosaic explanation which suggested that slackness on the part of the galley's crew, induced by a bout of heavy drinking, was the real cause.

Coming to later times, Columbus is the first of the early moderns to record the use of the remora in fishing. Among other stories which he sent to Ferdinand and Isabella about the strange things to be seen in the newly discovered lands, he included a description of how a sucker-fish was used by fishermen of Hispaniola for the capture of turtle and large fishes. With a cord attached to its tail, he related how it was liberated by the fishermen near to any turtle which they may sight; to this it swam and attached, for no other reason than that it was a large solid mass fit to serve as a resting-place whence short excursions could be made in search of food.

When a remora becomes attached, the grip of the sucker is sufficient to permit the turtle to be played till it tires, when it is hauled within reach and seized if small, or harpooned if so large and strong as to require to be played for some time longer.

At the present day this ingenious method of fishing is no longer practised by West Indian fishermen. To find it in use we have to go to Zanzibar or to the islands dotted about within the Great Barrier Reef of Australia, provided there be a few aborigines living there. E. J. Banfield (1908, 240–5) gives a graphic description of the capture and use of the remora by Australian blacks. When a remora is wanted, as soon as the haunt of one is located, the blacks ground bait the place for several days before using a baited hook. Once captured, a line is fastened around its tail, just tight enough to prevent it from slipping off. By this it is tethered to a canoe in shallow water until it is wanted.

When the day to hunt turtle comes round the canoe, with the remora adhering to the bottom, is paddled seawards till a turtle is spotted, oftentimes sleeping on the surface. Paddling noiselessly onwards till within a suitable distance, the remora is pulled off the bottom without ceremony and its sucker vigorously scrubbed with dry sand or the palm of the hand to remove any slime present, for this might prevent it from functioning perfectly as a suctorial organ. Wearied of being tethered, as soon as liberated, it dashes off towards the turtle resting all unsuspicious of the approaching danger. Once the remora gets a grip on the underside of the turtle's shell, skilful and patient handling of the light line attached to the tail of the fish is as necessary as when an angler fishing with a fly hooks a mighty salmon intent on getting free from the thin line that is all that bars the way to freedom. Alarmed when the fisherman begins to reel in the line, the turtle dives, exerting all his power to escape; more line is paid out hurriedly. Thereafter the struggle is one where man's skill and patience are pitted against the wild rushes of the captive. Usually man is the winner but in the struggle the tail of the poor remora suffers; should it be cut very deeply, the owner has no compunction in passing the line through a hole bored transversely through the flesh of the tail; it may serve for one more hunt and then—well, there are plenty more remoras in the sea!

Zanzibari fishermen use a technique almost identical (Holmwood, 1883, 382). According to this account, the remora, here called *chazo*, is caught when young and it undergoes a certain amount of training before being used in fishing. After an iron ring or loop is let into the tail, the fish is kept in a canoe filled with sea-water till the wound heals, embedding the ring firmly in the flesh. The water is changed from time to time and the fish is fed sparingly with pieces of meat and fish. If it survives, it soon becomes used to the man who feeds it and tolerant of being handled. When it reaches a weight of between 2 and 3 lb., it is considered strong enough for use and is taken out for trial.

A line is fastened to the iron loop around the tail; on sighting a turtle, the *chazo* is put overboard. It has to be prevented from affixing itself to the canoe, and then it soon makes for the nearest floating object, to which it instantly adheres, and generally allows itself to be drawn with its quarry towards the boat. Should it prove too timid to stand this treatment it is discarded as worthless, but if it will hold on, it soon gets bold enough to retain its hold until taken into the boat, when it is at once detached from the prize by being drawn off sideways, and being returned to its tank is at once fed. They are said soon to learn what is required of them, and it is reported that they have been trained to catch sharks. When in Madagascar some years ago, I was told that the *tarundu*, which the fish is called there, had been trained to catch crocodiles, numbers of which infested the rivers and, as I observed, came down to the neighbourhood of the fishing villages on the coast, without being affected by the salt water.

In the sea where few species of fishes are vegetarian in diet, the life of the vast majority resolves itself into a ceaseless hunt for food, in which they prey for the most part upon those smaller or weaker than themselves, with reliance either upon superior speed or upon clever subterfuge to enable them to seize their victims. In particular, one family, the *Pediculati*, termed most appropriately in common parlance the 'sea-anglers', has evolved a method

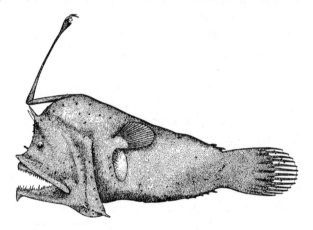

TEXT-FIG. 18. A deep-sea angler-fish, *Lophodulus dinema*. A phosphorescent light is emitted from the bulbous tip of its fishing-rod.

of capturing prey which may, of a verity, be called angling; designedly and of set purpose they lay themselves out to lure other fishes within striking distance by the display of a tempting bait, fixed at the upper end of a fishing-rod, which frequently is jointed. The family is widely distributed, its members living in every imaginable environment. Some, such as our common British angler-fish (*Lophius piscatorius*), live on the bottom, partly buried in sand or in mud; others spend their lives concealed in clumps of marine vegetation—some even amongst the brownish fronds of the wandering Sargasso weed, while a number of fishes belonging to a closely related family, the *Ceratioidea*, living in the abysmal depths of the ocean, gain their infrequent meals by luring fishes, plagued with fatal curiosity, within range of their capacious jaws, armed with inwardly projecting fangs, by the exhibition of a brilliant beacon light set at the tip of a jointed fishing-rod set well forward on their back, immediately behind the head (Text-fig. 18).

In all instances, the fishing-rod is a modification of one of the foremost spines of the dorsal fin.

When in India I have often watched the curious procedure of one of the local angler-fishes when engaged in fishing for his living in a tank in the Madras Aquarium. The particular species was the yellow angler (*Antennarius hispidus*), a dumpy little creature about the size and shape of a lemon (Text-fig. 19). Here we find the fishing-rod quite short, but, as usual, jointed at the base which is just above the forward angle of the mouth between and on the same level as the round expressionless eyes. The outer end of the little fishing-rod ends in a rounded yellow tassel of short filaments, representing the bait. The habits of this Indian angler or 'toad-fish' as some prefer to call it, differ markedly from those of its big British relative; instead of lying spread-eagled on the bottom of the sea, more or less hidden in the mud, the yellow angler loves to conceal his grotesque

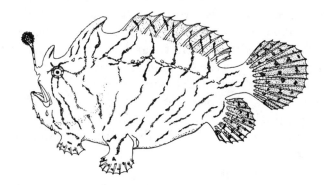

TEXT-FIG. 19. The small Indian angler-fish, *Antennarius hispidus*.

and corpulent yellow body, streaked with brown, in the centre of a gently swaying bunch of brownish seaweed. There he remains motionless, camouflaged exactly in the same way as is a tiger in a thicket of reeds or bamboos. All that ever moves is the rod and the bait. The rod being hinged at the base can be flicked up and down so as to make the tassel-bait gyrate oddly and thereby attract the inquiring eyes of some little fish or prawn. Woe to those who give way to their curiosity!

The little angler may be inert as a stone while awaiting his prey but on the near approach of an inquisitive fish, his jaws and throat are galvanized into surprising activity—the victim is instantaneously sucked into the gaping cavern of a monstrous mouth, the jaws shutting with a snap. If danger threaten the 'bait'—it would be a misfortune to have it bitten off—the rod folds down and the tassel-end snuggles down into a little pit between the two stout fin-spines immediately behind the fishing-rod.

In those angler-fishes which live on the bottom or among the branches of sea-weeds, the breast or pectoral fins and in rather less degree the ventral ones also, are modified into hand-like feet, most useful to enable these fishes to creep quietly over sand and gravel or among the branches of their leafy hiding place.

The members of no other family of fishes may rightly be said to obtain their living by fishing, properly so called. A vast number capture their prey by the employment of various curious and ingenious methods but these devious ways come under the head of hunting and not of fishing. In any case they are so diverse and so numerous that they require far more space in which to describe them than can be afforded here. Suffice it if allusion be made to some of the most outstanding instances.

There are, for example, the hypnotic stare of the John Dory, the aimed drops of water shot from the elongated mouths of the blow-pipe fishes (*Chelmo* and *Forcipiger*) that topples the luckless fly from off its pitch on a leaf overhanging the water, and the similar habit of the so-called archer-fish (*Toxotes jaculator*), the ruses of camouflage and mimicry which enable many fishes to deceive their prospective prey into the neglect of ordinary precautions, the development of electrical and poisonous devices that numb or kill unwary victims and the lightning clutch of the prehensile, sucker-beset arms of the octopus, cuttlefish and squid.

These are but a few examples selected from the list of the snares set by the wilier of fishes skilled in the craft of the hunter, dodges that have become elaborated and fixed through the course of untold generations of their predecessors.

IV

SHARK-FISHING

THE voyage from Samoa to Tonga had been disappointingly slow. Ten days had passed since we had said good-bye to Apia and nothing had happened to relieve the monotony of idle days. True, I had signed on in the capacity of purser (on a nominal wage of 50 cents a month) but as I had to pay the captain a substantial sum for the privilege, the job was a sinecure.

The ship, laden with a cargo of lumber, and rigged as a four-masted schooner, was a sluggish sailer. The twin auxiliary Diesel motors, provided against emergencies, were equally sluggish; the crew declared there was an understanding between the two 'coffee mills', as the sailors called them, that there should be no competition; if one was in action, it was tacitly agreed that the other should be given a rest. But there were, unfortunately, occasions, usually critical, when both desired to rest at one and the same time!

When at last we rounded the north end of Vavau, northernmost of the Tongan group, and met a strong head-wind, lassitude and depression took a firmer grip upon the ship's company until one of the sailors called out that four big sharks were following the ship. The prospect of a spell of shark-fishing cheered up everybody. A decaying piece of salt pork was conjured forth by the cook, skewered on a hook and thrown over the rail at the end of a stout line. The sharks proved a greedy crowd. No sooner did the odour of the dainty morsel begin to diffuse than our lithe attendants sprinted forward and the bait vanished.

A few minutes later the winner of the race was dragged aboard, lashing out furiously with its tail. Hardly did it touch the deck when the carpenter, axe in hand, leaped forward and severed the tail from the body.

Here our Chinese cook intervened; swooping on the tail, like hawk on cowering bird, he carried off his prize, intending later to convert it into savoury soup. The first mate would have liked to affix it to the end of the jib-boom, to ensure good luck and good weather for the rest of the trip, but the cook gained the day; the bait had been provided by him, and this gave him prior claim.

After the tailless carcass had been thrown overboard, a number of Tongans who were carried as deck passengers began to bewail this as woeful waste, declaring that shark flesh is first-class *kai-kai*. To console them another baited hook was put out and a second shark was hooked; we failed to land it for it bit clean through the wire trace. A third try was made and this time the floundering monster was safely landed and duly handed over to the Tongans to their great delight, on the understanding that the cook should have his perquisite—the fins. And that night there was high revelry around the fo'c'sle galley.

Experience gained after our arrival at Neiafu, the port of Vavau, confirmed all that our passengers had said about shark flesh as a local dainty, and about the methods employed to capture these fishes. At one particular season, round about the latter part of April and throughout May, fishermen set out in little outrigger canoes to fish for sharks off the north-west coast where sharks then congregate. When the fishing-ground is reached and sharks are sighted, one of the crew stands in the bows with a piece of meat, none too fresh, dangling from a short line at the end of a pole. Holding this in one hand, his other is busy vigorously shaking a rattan hoop on which coconut half-shells are strung in pairs, with the convex sides turned towards one another. The large size of the threading holes permits of considerable movement and a loud clattering noise is made when the shells are jangled half in and half out of the sea. The men believe that this noise has an attraction for sharks, so when the bowman is shaking his rattle, the while he apostrophizes a shark to come and pay his good friends a visit, a second man gets ready to noose the fish; he stands with a stout lasso in his hands, ready to drop the running loop over the shark's head as it rushes alongside, eager to seize the bait. The lasso is made by plaiting together narrow strands of split rattan cane.

When a shark decides to make a rush, the bowman and the steersman must co-operate closely, the one to play the bait in the right way, drawing it slowly and temptingly along one side of the canoe, from the stern towards the bow, the while he utters soft persuasive words to the shark, and the other to manœuvre the canoe in such a way that when the rush comes, the shark shall be swimming towards the bait from astern and not from any other direction.

If these moves be properly co-ordinated the man who holds the lasso will be given a good opportunity to drop the running noose over the shark's head, a split-second before the bait be reached.

This is the critical moment; if the noose be placed adroitly and in the right place and then drawn tight the shark's head should be brought into such a position as will permit the steersman to drop his paddle, seize a club and deal the shark a stunning blow between the eyes. If the shark be large and powerful and likely to prove riotous, a second noose is passed around its tail if possible.

Clever fishermen count on landing several big sharks as the day's work of one canoe.

When inviting a shark to pay a visit to his friends, he is addressed in the most respectful terms and called by some polite name such as 'Hina'. Should a small shark come alongside in response to the call and the clatter of the shell-rattle, the fisherman requests it to oblige them by going in search of a big relative and by telling it that some kind people have prepared a feast to which it is invited. The men who relate this, declare that it is usual for the little fellow to return after a short time, escorting a big shark well worthy of their attention.

A variation upon this method, common also in Samoa, is found almost everywhere in the fishing villages of the Bismarck Archipelago, lying off the north-east coast of New Guinea. The differences are partly in method but more particularly in the gear used, for the lasso is here provided with a large propeller-shaped brake or drag upon its free end (Text-figs. 6 and 7).

In these islands, of which New Britain and New Ireland are the largest, when the shark-fishers reach the fishing-ground, the bow paddler picks up his rod, a long and supple bamboo, baits the line with a fish and plays this bait just under the surface of the water. He lets it drift aft and dances it about merrily by delicate twitches of the rod. A second man stands next to the rod fisherman shaking a coconut-shell rattle vigorously in the water.

When a shark, attracted by the bait or by the clattering of the rattle, comes nosing along, the first man draws the bait slowly towards the bow where he stands. If this succeeds in inducing the shark to make a rush, the bait is whipped smartly out of the water just before it is reached; his companion, who has meanwhile exchanged the rattle for a plaited lasso, slips its running loop into the water exactly in the place where the bait had been a second before.

If all goes well, the shark's head passes through the loop thus cunningly substituted; a jerk on the rope tightens it and away the shark goes, carrying off the lasso complete with its propeller-shaped drag, which is thrown overboard as soon as the loop is tightened. The fish tears along at great speed in the vain endeavour to shake loose from the incubus of the wooden 'retarder'. Every attempt to gain relief by swimming away or by grounding is hampered and slowed down by the drag attached to the end of the lasso. The direction of this slow flight is also indicated by the splashing made by the retarder. This the fishers follow up, and when they judge the fish to be sufficiently exhausted, they pull the canoe alongside.

It is now the turn of the young men in the canoe. Eager to show their prowess they seize their clubs and rain a shower of blows on the shark's head, until it ceases to struggle.

When the canoe, with its prize safely aboard, returns to its village, its success is heralded by blasts upon a conch-trumpet made from the shell of a large triton.

On the Malabar coast of India, shark-fishing was formerly a thriving industry; to-day it finds employment for few men. The smallest of dugout canoes are used, manned by a crew of two. In search of a catch they go farther seaward than any of the men who fish for the regular run of food fishes.

They fish with hand-lines made fast near the fore end of the canoe. When a fish is hooked, they play it in such fashion as to convert the canoe itself into an even more efficient brake on the wild rush of their victim than the propeller-retarder used in the Bismarck Archipelago. When the fish is tired out they paddle alongside and despatch it. Now the men seem to face an exceedingly difficult problem: How to get the big carcass into a canoe not much bigger than itself?

To these men it presents no hardship; they jump into the sea, rock the canoe till it fills with water up to the gunwale. Canting it over on to its beam-ends, they slither the shark's carcass into the canoe and then begin to bale out the water aboard. When this has been partially accomplished, they scramble aboard, finish the clearance of the water and head for home, content with their day's work.

The three methods above described appear to form a developmental series. Most primitive is the Malabar method. Next comes that employed in the Bismarck Archipelago where an artificial 'retarder' replaces the canoe as the drag upon the fish which entails its eventual exhaustion. Finally, in the Tongan method we find that the great skill of the fishermen enables them to dispense with any form of braking device.

Two forms of the rattle are in use. In Tonga and Samoa the pairs of coconut half-shells are strung upon a single hoop of rattan cane; in the Bismarck Archipelago the fishers use the loop doubled and of a smaller diameter.

When a propeller-shaped retarder is employed, the length varies from 4 to $4\frac{1}{2}$ feet (Text-fig. 6).

The noise made by the rattle is said to be mistaken for the excited cries of a flock of sea-birds feeding on and hovering over a shoal of fishes, by any sharks that may be in the vicinity; hearing the sound they hasten towards it, eager to participate in the feast. Another reason given is that the noise resembles the sound made by a travelling school of horse-mackerel —fish of which sharks are fond.

Finsch says (1888, 207) that this coconut-rattle is also used in shark-fishing in the Trobriand Islands; from the context he appears to indicate that the shark is caught with a line armed with a wooden hook, $1\frac{1}{2}$ feet in length.

In the Gilberts the shark is sometimes hunted in its own element by a diver armed with a long knife (Burnett, 1911, 19); the same writer describes how Rarotongan fishers at Aitutaki are accustomed to watch for a shark enjoying a siesta at midday with its head and most of its body withdrawn within one of the cavernous hollows common on the ragged and undercut margin of a coral reef. When the fisher sees a tail protruding from one of these, he slips overboard from his canoe; swimming quietly down he slips a noose round the tail and signals the fact to his friends above, who haul the shark to the surface and spear or club it to death.

The same story comes from other parts of the Polynesian island-world; I found it current in Fiji, and Hadfield records this way of fishing sharks as practised in the Loyalty Islands, lying off New Caledonia (1920); the same writer adds that a precaution sometimes taken by divers in the South Sea is to bind something dark coloured over the white soles of their feet.[1]

Sharks with flesh of good edible quality being plentiful in the waters off the southern coast of Arabia, a long-established trade in sun-dried shark flesh, cut into long baton-shaped pieces, continues to be of great local importance in the commercial relations of this locality with the east coast of Africa. The fishermen engaged in this industry inhabit the Kuria Muria Islands and the numerous villages scattered here and there in the coastlands of the mainland opposite, between Ras Sharbut and Ras Nūs. These people, who belong to the Bautahara and Beni Janaba tribes, are fearless and indefatigable hunters of the shark, for this is the mainstay of their livelihood. Wood being scarce and expensive, these poverty-stricken folk are driven to continue the primitive procedure of their forefathers without change or improvement; hence we find them employing their inflated water-skins, made from the pelts of sheep or goats as a makeshift device to go afloat in pursuit of their quarry. With the aid of such buoyant floats these Arab fishermen put to sea without fear and seldom return without a satisfactory catch; happily the temperature of the sea along this coast is high and there is little hardship if they have to remain afloat and swimming for several hours should success elude them for some considerable time.

The use of inflated skins on this coast is of high antiquity; the *Periplus of the Erythraean Sea* (first century A.D.) records that frankincense was transported on 'rafts held up by inflated skins after the manner of the country and in boats...to Cana', probably the modern Bir Ali, a harbour about 240 miles east of Aden. And if inflated-skin rafts were used, we may be certain that skin swimming-floats existed concurrently.

---

[1] From my own observations in India and Ceylon, I am satisfied that sharks seldom attack dark-skinned divers; instances of attacks by sharks on the native divers employed in the pearl and chank fisheries of India and Ceylon are extremely rare; of these, several of the alleged instances which engaged my personal attention, were discovered to have been caused, not by sharks as reported, but by the savage Barracuda; the sharp teeth of those of large size can inflict very severe wounds. Conversely, in waters where native divers work with almost complete immunity, white men are exposed to much danger when they swim in the same waters; witness the fatalities which occurred in Colombo harbour when soldiers bathed from troopships moored there during the War of 1914–18.

V

THE NEGRO AS FISHERMAN

I. SEA-FISHING OFF WEST AFRICA

To meet the real negro, go to West Africa. Elsewhere you usually get him so modified by contact and admixture with other peoples as to form thereby fresh sub-races, generally, as in the case of the Bantu, an improvement in certain directions upon the original pure negro stock. But the true article is a good fellow in essentials if not spoiled by the absorption of some of the bad features of so-called European civilization; when he has opportunity and satisfactory inducement, he can make a fair show at most things. He makes a most remarkably efficient soldier; he can work wonders in brass and iron and leather with the crudest of tools; he is a good farmer and is indeed the foremost cocoa-planter in the world of to-day; before the coming of the white man he had no acquaintance with the sea—nowadays he goes down to the sea in many ships and although he seldom moves aft, there have been good negro skippers of sailing ships, and the launches on the big rivers are usually run entirely by natives. And who has greater skill and renown as surf boatmen than they! In inshore fishing they excel and in a few instances they have even launched out into deep-sea fishing, remaining at sea for days at a time, taking their chances in small open boats.

On the coast of Sierra Leone, the fisherfolk are worthy people, whether they be English-speaking Creoles, descendants of freed slaves from the United States and Jamaica, or the wild and superstitious aboriginals of the land. The latter live in small hamlets clustered along the shores of the great estuaries and sandy beaches where fish are found in most abundance. Sherbro Island is a typical fisherman's country and it is to this place and its people that most of the following notes refer.

Were a Sherbro hamlet more neatly kept, it would form an excellent example of how to plan a garden village. The houses are scattered in picturesque irregularity around several wide and open spaces; if a Chief's village, a big hall or *barri* is conspicuous, where rough-and-ready justice is meted out. Away from the Creole towns, British law and order function through the local notables. Prison is used as little as possible; fines and a sojourn in the stocks are the chief punishments inflicted. Fraudulent and recalcitrant debtors are soon brought to reason by the latter method, and, if we may judge by the large number of leg-holes in a typical set of stocks, epidemics of unwillingness to pay up the tribal rates and taxes must occasionally occur. The gaping jaws of the stocks are commonly carved into a rude representation of a crocodile's head—grim jest, chiming in with negro humour!

The village houses are commonly circular in ground-plan, built up of a basketwork framework, excellently finished, made of the pliant aerial roots of the mangrove. The interstices of the walls are afterwards filled in with clay and neatly plastered smooth, the roof being thatched with grass or with palm leaves. A fetish amulet such as a tuft of fern leaves or a mass of orchids, often adorns the roof apex in newly built dwellings—a pretty finial. There is more comfort shown in the design of these houses than might be expected. The single entrance leads into a small veranda, often with half-walls on the outer side. Behind is what answers to a dining-room and from this doors open into two sleeping-rooms at the rear; the partitions are of latticework to allow for the adequate ventilation so essential in hot and steamy climates.

On the landward side of fishing villages the bush closes in, unkempt and gloomy, difficult to penetrate save by narrow footpaths which lead to small fields of cassava, the chief cultivation of the inhabitants. The hamlets are usually of very long occupation, and in these, noble mango trees, with an occasional breadfruit and massive forest tree, give shade to the houses. Gigantic termite nests towering 8 to 10 feet in height, are not uncommon on the outskirts, left standing either from superstitious fear or as boundary marks. Flocks of ever-twittering little weaver-birds, gregarious and with a curious love for the vicinity of mankind, often hang their nests from the leafy crowns of tall oil-palms growing close to the houses.

Life runs smoothly in these fishing villages. The men are more industrious than in the agricultural districts inland and the womenfolk have a better time, with more spirit and intelligence in consequence. The men are out fishing most of the day or are busy making or repairing their nets and thus a partial equality of effort between the sexes is fostered to an extent seldom seen elsewhere in Africa.

These people have many curious methods of fishing; they use fish-spears for barracuda and ray-fishes; they angle with hand-lines and they employ numerous kinds of nets and weirs; in inland streams basket-traps of many ingenious forms are employed extensively. Even the women engage actively in fishing when fry are about. The women's net, *bimbē* as it is called, is wholly different in form and mesh from any of those used in the sea. It is made by the women themselves, upon or with a framework of split bamboo cut into narrow ribbon-form of as great length as possible. The cord used, made from palm fibre, is laced around a spirally twisted bamboo strip in such a way that a deep basket, about 2 or $2\frac{1}{2}$ feet wide, is formed; the sides and bottom are formed of tightly packed bamboo coils, concentrically arranged and worked over with twine in a most ingenious manner (Pl. v, fig. A). When judged to be sufficiently large the bamboo framework is removed by breaking it at intervals and the pulling out of the broken pieces. This done, what was a small, deep basket changes as if by magic into a great bag-net, several feet in diameter. Could anything be more cleverly conceived and executed? A light oval framework of thin branches keeps the mouth open. With this net (Pl. v, fig. B) two women sweep up immense quantities of anchovy fry which, when sun-dried, are sold in Freetown under the name of 'whitebait'. Thousands of sacksful are collected in this manner during the season.

The fishermen are splendidly built fellows without a superfluous ounce of fat on their bodies. They work exceedingly hard and their methods are most ingenious in several instances; for shoaling fish, which have to be caught by the hundred and thousand, they use nets of various forms, varying with the locality. In some places where there are many channels and deep sandy bays, they use long barrier-nets held upright in position by stakes driven into the sandy bottom. Elsewhere, in deep water, they employ gill-nets buoyed by hundreds of cylinders of light wood strung on the head-rope. The shore seine is also much in evidence in the vicinity of Freetown, but in Sherbro Island it is proscribed under the severest penalties —to be inflicted by the local all-powerful 'devil'; the fear of this unseen power, fostered by the annual, awe-inspiring ceremonies of a semi-secret society founded to placate this demon and to carry on the cult, is sufficient to prevent the introduction there of the seine-net; this prohibition is probably founded on the belief, possibly correct, that the unrestricted use of this net might be detrimental to the general prosperity of the local fisheries. Secret societies are still all-powerful in this part of Africa and the most noteworthy and powerful—the Porro and the Bundu —are actually of great disciplinary and educational value to a rude people without a religion that inculcates the cardinal duties of man to his fellows.

The most valuable fish under present methods of fishing is the *bonga*, a kind of shad. It occurs in enormous shoals in the estuaries and is dried in immense quantities to supply Freetown and the inland markets. It has the appearance of a very deep herring. Every fishing-hamlet has a number of specially built sheds for the cooking and drying of this fish. The method adopted is ingenious and the only effective one that people with restricted resources can employ under the peculiarly humid conditions of the local climate. The *bonga* when brought ashore are laid out on low platforms made of closely set thin poles supported 2 feet above the ground. Fires of mangrove wood are lit beneath; the fish are really grilled in the first instance and in this cooked condition decomposition is held at bay just long enough to permit of the fish being reduced to a bone-dry condition; the process takes 3 days to complete for the final sun-drying of the product. This treatment is obviously inadequate to give satisfactory results; the actual condition of this imperfectly preserved fish is well expressed by the name commonly applied to it by Europeans, i.e. 'stink-fish'.

When the drying operation is considered to be complete, the fish are packed into large baskets and sent to market. Boatloads are despatched daily from the fishing villages opposite Freetown during the season. Thousands of people—seemingly the major part of the female population of Freetown and a goodly proportion of the menfolk—crowd the shore at King Jimmy market to await their arrival and to buy the daily supply of *bonga*. The seething multitude is a fitting subject for the artist and the colour photographer, for the Creole women love to clothe themselves in gowns of wondrous hues and marvellous patterns; and there is plenty of material, for they love them of generous and even voluminous proportions—they have no use for abbreviated skirts and it is well that it is so! But the women do not monopolize all the colour; up-country men in handsomely striped flowing robes made of native cloth are numerous, anxious also to make their purchases for the day's requirements.

To return to our fishing villagers; apart from the men who devote themselves to netting, many hundreds concentrate on fishing with hand-lines worked from dugout canoes. The finest of these small canoes are found on the coast of the Sierra Leone peninsula; they go by the name of Kru canoes. In fine weather scores of them are in sight almost anywhere along the coast. Anchored to a stone or a small killick, they lie there for hours; each contains a single fisherman who angles with either two or four lines (Pl. VI, fig. B). When four are employed, two are held on slip nooses on the big toes, two upon the legs or in the hands. The fisherman reclines comfortably at his ease near the stern, with his feet resting on the gunwales of the canoe. He may seem asleep but a tweak to his toe or leg brings him instantly to life.

It is of interest to find that America has no monopoly in the sport of angling for that famous fighting-fish, the giant tarpon; a Sierra Leone Kru fisherman thinks nothing special of hooking a 5-foot tarpon, though he is never sure that the fight will end in his favour. He takes the adventure in the day's work, and can afford to laugh at the white man's efforts in the same direction, for the European in West Africa has seldom landed a tarpon, fishing from a boat. But the native fisherman sometimes lands a couple in a day and the Kru canoe seen in Pl. VI, fig. A, had actually two fine tarpon aboard when the photograph was taken.

These beautiful craft are prized highly by their owners, who bestow great care upon them. When not in use they are turned bottom up and raised several feet off the ground upon a light trestle platform. They are never painted and when the Freetown harbour-master recently issued metal disks to be attached to the hulls for identification purposes, it nearly broke the hearts of some men to find the metal causing rust stains upon the adjacent wood.

The paddle used has one of the most elegantly modelled forms anywhere to be seen in the world, a triumph of artistry among a people who have few of the advantages common among Europeans.

II. NOTABLE FISHING METHODS OF NEGROES ON INLAND WATERS

Considered broadly, many of the fishing methods and appliances found in use on the inland waters of Africa in those parts which may be considered as constituting Negroland, are either identical with or closely related to those commonly used on Asiatic inland waters, particularly in regard to those of India.

It is evident that related conditions of life and environment, physical, economic and, to some extent faunistic, have led the African to the adoption or loan of many of the devices evolved by the fishermen who work the rivers, tanks, marshes and waterspreads of India and China; in some instances the negro may have invented some methods and some fishing implements independently—certainly they have greatly modified and even improved upon some Asiatic models. That parallel development of the basic ideas underlying certain primitive methods of fishing has occurred both in Africa and Asia is seen to be extremely probable when we compare the fishing practices in common use among the peoples of the great Gangetic plain in India with those of the fisherfolk of the great lake and river basins of Central and Eastern Africa. These Asiatic resemblances are most strongly marked among those forms of fishing appliances abundant within the basin of Lake Chad and on the waterways of the Central and Western Sudan—a fact suggestive of long-standing culture contact between East Africa and India.

To give a few instances of these parallel methods and devices: in the Lakes Region of Africa we find, as in the valley of the Ganges, that the plunge-basket is the fishing implement in most general use wherever marshes, pools and shallow waterspreads are common, especially shortly after the close of the rainy season. So, too, with individual, non-return wickerwork basket-traps, as well as with fish-fences and earthen embankments (bunds), furnished at intervals with wide-mouthed, funnel-shaped basket-traps of design related to those employed individually; there are also numerous varieties of fishing weirs, built sometimes of stout palisading, sometimes slenderly constructed of reed matting supported on rough jungle poles. These fences may be arranged in a variety of designs, all with the common object of inducing the fishes to deflect their course in such a direction as will lead them eventually to enter certain basket-traps set by the fishermen or, alternatively, to pass through the trapped entrance of a terminal pound or enclosure, usually heart-shaped, less often circular. Other parallel methods are the use of the hand dip-net, multiprong spears, the primitive bow and arrow, and the pernicious poisoning of the waters of quiet pools and tanks with decoctions made from various plants—*Tephrosia* and *Euphorbia* among others; common parallels are also to be found among the ways that hand-lines, long-lines, gill-nets and seines are employed; to these has to be added that most complex and highly developed fishing engine of all—the great lever dip-net, frequently operated from a stage on the bank of a stream or lake (Pl. VII, fig. A), and just as often from a fulcrum fitted aboard a plank-built boat; nor must we omit the quaint tandem-float ridden astride by the fisherman when plying his fishing operations without the use of a boat, in water beyond his depth. Of these particular two, the lever dip-net whether worked from the shore or aboard a boat is in use both in China and India; the tandem-float is recorded from South India (Hornell, 1924, 233 and 1946, 18).

Other parallels exist but those enumerated are the most important.

When considering the respective value and significance of these various parallel or closely related devices, the conclusion is inevitable that in the fishing domain, the negro has shown himself capable in many instances of improving in various ways upon the basic ideas which have led to the invention of particular methods and of adapting these to conform to specific and special requirements rendered necessary by local or unusual conditions; he has also shown initiative in devising improvements in fishing technique by the combination of two methods of fishing whereby the resulting catch is greater than the total obtained when the two methods are employed separately. Most conspicuous among these improvements and adaptations are (*a*) the novel forms of the plunge-basket found in Africa, (*b*) the use of basket-traps as a component part of a specialized seining outfit, (*c*) the elaborate adaptation of the lever dip-net for use aboard a boat, and (*d*) to a less extent, the designs of some non-return basket-traps. These are of sufficient importance to require separate notice.

PLUNGE-BASKETS. In the design of these the African shows considerable ingenuity; in two instances at least, he is more versatile than his Indian brethren. For example, the fishermen of the Kuanza River in Angola, instead of adhering with conservative ardour to the truncated cone form, open at both ends, have fitted their plunge-basket with a long handle at the apex, rendering it easier to carry but causing the elimination of the usual apical opening. To compensate for the loss of the latter, a small aperture is cut out of the basketwork on one side, fairly high up, and furnished with a light door, in order to permit of the removal of any fish which may happen to find itself imprisoned when the wide and open base of the basket is thrust suddenly into the muddy bottom in places where fishes are believed to be lurking (Leith & Lindblom, 1933, 9). When a fish caught in this manner is too large to be drawn out through the side-opening or is suspected of being armed with dangerous or poisonous spines, a spear is passed through the opening and the fish pinned to the bottom to be removed when rendered harmless.

A novel and ingenious variety of the same implement is the *tereben*, used on the lower reaches of the El Beïd, a river flowing into Lake Chad. Here the sub-conical basket framework is reduced to four rods which diverge from the apex of the trap, splaying out below to make attachment at equal intervals to a ring of cane, 30 to 40 inches in circumference. Within this skeleton frame is a net-bag, its mouth laced to the cane ring joining the lower ends of the four rods. When in use, the fisherman grasps a knot marking the tail end of the bag and holds this pressed against the apical meeting-place of the four rods, afterwards manipulating the implement in ordinary plunge-basket fashion. Every time the implement is thrust down upon the bottom, the tail knot is cast loose, thereby allowing the net to fall loosely downwards. Should a fish be present within the area covered by the frame, its struggles to escape entangle it the more fully in the folds of the fallen net (Monod, 1928, 306).

An equivalent of this unusual form of the plunge-basket is found in India on the waterways of Bengal (see p. 139).

As in India, the plunge-basket is the chief fishing implement of the women of the community. At certain seasons it is a common sight to see a happy crowd of women advancing slowly in line abreast in shallow water, or converging in circle form upon a central point; as they advance, their baskets rhythmically rise and fall in their attempts to capture any fishes which may be hiding in the mud in front of their feet. It seems an unlikely way to catch fishes but wherever mud-living species are present, the catches made are often fully satisfactory.

In some instances the fisherwomen's plan is to converge upon the inner side of the apex of a V-shaped fish-fence where several of their menfolk are stationed, some armed with plunge-baskets and some with fish-spears, all eager to capture or transfix any large fishes fleeing from the disturbance caused by the fisherwomen's splashing as they methodically work over the bottom with their plunge-baskets. Another method in use in conjunction with the V-shaped fence is seen on the Semliki River, flowing out of Lake Edward in Uganda. Here the fishermen wade out into the water with lights at night-time and drive the fish into a huddle on the inner side of the apex of the V, where they catch them with plunge-baskets (Worthington, 1932, 35).

NON-RETURN WICKERWORK TRAPS. These vary greatly; many are the changes rung upon the bell-shape and upon the arrangement and number of the trapping devices. Some are more or less cylindrical; others are pear-shaped; one variety is bottle-shaped, another has a small chamber atop of a larger one, after the style of the cottage loaf. Some are suspended from a buoyed line, with or without bait, but the great majority are set in shallows and in marshes amid a tangle of water-weeds and papyrus. One of the largest is the 'cottage-loaf' trap, measuring about 6 feet in height; this is the kind used in the Victoria Nyanza to capture the Lung-fish, *Protopterus*. Water-lily leaves are the bait used, but as *Protopterus* feeds almost entirely upon water-snails, it would seem that the snails which attract this fish to the trap are those commonly found living upon water-lily leaves (Graham, 1929, 95).

FISH-FENCES AND WEIRS. A common and extremely effective form of the palisaded fishing weir is found in the Victoria Nyanza. This, known locally as *kek*, consists of a stout walling of jungle sticks stretched across a creek or subsidiary stream; narrow gaps are left in it at intervals and in each is placed a large wicker fish-trap. The fencing is so closely set and interlaced that only the smallest fish may pass; the larger ones are compelled to pass through the gaps, only to find themselves imprisoned in the wicker traps which sieve out of the running water any objects that travel with it.

An ingenious device forming an alternative way of trapping running fish in the same lake, is the *obalala*; in this the fence is made of closely fitting bamboos and is folded at intervals in such manner as to form a series of rounded chambers when the design is seen in plan; the entrance to each is narrow and apart from this the only exits lead into basket-traps placed invitingly in the hinder wall of the chamber. Several variations occur, dependent upon the fancy of the fishermen and the physical conditions present at any particular site (Graham, 1929, 87).

SCARE-LINES. These are made of leaves tied upon a long rope and are valued in Africa, as in India, as an effective way of driving fishes into a line of basket-traps or into short lengths of nets held by a pair of fishermen. From this idea, native ingenuity among the fisherfolk of Victoria Nyanza has developed the great *ngogo* device. This is a long stretch of matting made of the buoyant stems of papyrus bound together with plaited papyrus cord, used as a scare-line with the object of driving any fish present into the mouths of a line of traps set close to the shore. Some are of great length and Graham (1929, 91) records seeing one at Kibos, about 250 yards in length. A fisherman poling a bundle-raft of papyrus stems, tows one end of the *ngogo* out into the lake, leaving one warp ashore, afterwards carrying the second warp to the beach after making a half-circle in seining manner. The two warps are seized by two groups of men who set to work to draw the *ngogo* ashore. Midway between the two gangs a row of basket-traps has already been placed in position; the object of the men is to drive all fishes fleeing before the *ngogo* into the open mouths of the traps set in line abreast in shallow water in front of the shore.

From this, the transition is not great to a form of compound seine in which the basket-traps, instead of being separate and fixed in a stable position, are incorporated in the scare-line itself which now is converted into a functional seine, a transformation that reflects much credit upon the native intellect.

The complete apparatus, called *usambo* by the Wabudu of the western shore of Victoria Nyanza is complex, and difficult to describe satisfactorily in a few words. Its essential features are (*a*) a row of about a dozen large-mouthed basket-traps lashed securely together side by side; (*b*) a screen backing of light bamboo matting, the upper edge extending well above the baskets, (*c*) a strong foot-rope of plaited papyrus attached along the bottoms of the basket-traps and the matting screen; this functions as an efficient scare-line for it is decorated with many closely set banana leaves designed to frighten away any fishes which see it. Each of the two warps is attached to one of the outer ends of the row of basket-traps already mentioned.

The Budu fishermen, using rude rafts 'made of the midribs of a palm' (Graham, 1929, 97) tow the contrivance as far out into the lake as the warps will permit, going even to the distance of a quarter of a mile. The work completed, the men return to shore towing the whole outfit after them. Landing on the beach they find the shore hands, about fifteen in number, ready to begin the haul. When at last the 'bag' of the seine (which here consists of a row of basket-traps) is brought close inshore, the driven fish, massed in a surging, splashing huddle, swim in front, frantically seeking for some way of escape. Behind and on both sides, escape is barred by the swaying banana leaves of the scare-line; only when close to the beach does a way of escape seem to be open, for now the fishes perceive numerous openings through which escape may be possible; unfortunately these are the mouths of large basket-traps and all fishes that pass in find themselves prisoned in a small chamber whence there is no escape. Dr E. B. Worthington measured the dimensions of a typical *usambo*; the basket-traps, which numbered eleven, were each 4 feet in diameter and were weighted with stones; the matting of horizontally placed reeds, laced together after the fashion of an Indian *tatti* screen, measured 14 yards in length. The foot-rope under the traps and the matting screen was weighted with stones, tied on at intervals; each warp was 250 yards long. The whole operation of setting and hauling took $1\frac{1}{2}$ hours and the men stated that they make five or six hauls in a day (Graham, 1929, 97).

In the Lake Chad basin and in that of the Niger the fishing devices used by the natives differ greatly from those of the lakes of East Africa. Some show less ingenuity than is found among corresponding methods in East Africa as, for example, in the class of basket-traps; in other classes the advantage is with the people of the Western and Central Sudan, notably those semi-permanent fishing engines built on the fish-weir principle. In the northern area we find also that lining and net-fishing methods are more diverse in operation and in more general use; the same remark is applicable to that class of fishing apparatus classed under the heading of barriers, intended to capture fishes on their way either up or down stream. Only a few of the most ingenious can be described here.

In the Central Sudan these fishing barriers, usually herding fish into pockets, prison chambers and other forms of trap, assume extreme importance in the economics of the riverine and lacustrine tribes, particularly in the rivers which feed Lake Chad and in the marshes and waterspreads of the adjoining parts of Nigeria and the Cameroons. In these waters fish-weirs attain an elaboration and diversity of constructional detail probably greater than can be matched anywhere else in Africa and Asia; within the space available attention can be given only to those of exceptional interest.

One of the simplest is the guiding barrage which the Kanuri use on the River El Beïd in Bornu. This consists of a V-shaped barrier fence supported on stout posts, with the apex directed upstream. Each arm just fails to reach the river's bank, thus leaving a narrow passage open between the barrier and the shore on either side; as fish descend the river their course is deflected by the diverging arms towards the side-passages. Each of these is, however, guarded by a fisherman armed with a dip-net of triangular form; with this he deftly whips up any large fish which attempts to pass (Monod, 1928, 309).

Another type, a derivative from the simpler form just described, is also a fence of V-shape in plan but it is commonly turned with the apex pointing downstream or in whatever direction the fish are known or expected to run. When the stream is of moderate width the arms may extend from bank to bank, a variation which converts the V-arms into 'leaders', guiding the fish towards the interior of the apex, where a trapped chamber, round, or, more frequently, heart-shaped has been constructed to receive and detain the incomers. By reason of an infolding of the walls at the entrance, egress is barred.

In broader streams or in lakes, the plan of this weir is liable to great variation to suit it to peculiarities of local conditions which may be caused by some unusual physical characteristic or some abnormal feature in the run of the fish at this particular place. Types of these weirs are worldwide in distribution, derived as they are from the primitive stone-walled tidal weirs such as I have seen in Australia, Fiji and the island of Coiba, off the Pacific coast of Panama; in Africa, Graham (1929, 87) records them from Uganda and states that Guise Williams saw one on Ruwondo Island.

From these relatively simple forms of fish-weirs we are led through several connecting developmental variations to that most elaborate type seen at Mala on the River Shari where it is called *uringalē* (Monod, 1928, 339). Used only during the dry season, it stretches as a stout, two-row set of matting-covered stakes across the river (Text-fig. 20). The upstream row, stout and set vertical, have a matting backing, the lower edge ending just

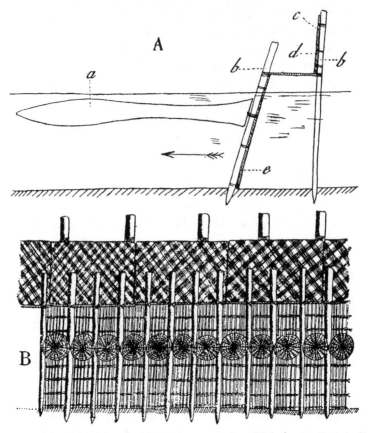

TEXT-FIG. 20. The *Uringalē*, a barrier weir-trap used at Mala in the French Cameroons. A, diagram of the fence in optical section. B, upstream face view.

above water-level. The hinder or downstream row, less stout, are fixed obliquely in the bottom, their upper ends inclined towards the front row and somewhat shorter in length; their upstream face is filled in to a point a little above the water with a permeable walling of closely set reeds. In this reed walling a row of openings is left immediately in front of lightly constructed wicker-traps, long and narrow, shaped like very slim soda-water bottles; the mouth of each is wide and everted and leads into a roomy chamber behind, unprovided with any means of exit at the end. These long, sleeve-like traps are set in pairs, both hung from the same stake, each by an attachment at a point to one side of the mouth. When the downstream current enters the small openings in the fence which lead to these traps, its strength drives any fishes which pass with it, into the open mouths of the traps swinging sideways in such a position as makes it easy for the fish to enter and pass into the swollen bag at the hinder end. The narrow neck, markedly constricted, precludes any attempt on the part of the captive fish to turn round and escape. To empty a trap it has to be up-ended and the captured fishes shaken out.

Between the two rows of stakes at a height a few inches above the stream, a long and narrow strip of matting is stretched horizontally, its downstream margin tied to the stakes of the hinder fence, while the other margin is similarly tied to the taller and vertical upstream fence posts along the lower margin of their matting backing. By this arrangement any fishes which endeavour to avoid the barrier by leaping over it, fall upon the horizontal platform thus created and are gathered up by the watching fisherman.

Another most highly specialized type of fishing apparatus is the great *ndambē* net characteristic of the methods in use on the rivers Benue and Faro by the Batta tribesmen of Southern Bornu. In essence this fishing engine is a variation of the Chinese balanced lever dip-net so common a sight on most Chinese rivers and estuaries and well known to visitors to Cochin on the west coast of India, where its presence and its local name of *Cheena vala* bear witness to the active trade which existed between China and India in medieval times, when Chinese junks were a familiar feature in the harbours of Cochin and Malabar (Pl. VII, fig. A).

Although the principles on which the construction and operation of the *ndambē* are based are similar to those pertaining to the Chinese net, notable divergences are noticeable in the African examples. To give them in detail here is impossible; suffice it to say that (1) instead of the net being suspended from the four ends of two stout bars crossing at mid-length, the African form fits the net into an oval frame springing from a short cylindrical roller working in a deeply grooved socket, and (2) that the lowering of the net into the water and its raising are controlled by a long lever fitted at one end into the roller at right angles to the sides of the net. To assure the rigidity of the sides of the net-frame, two rods diverge from the free end of the lever arm, to be attached to the sides of the frame somewhat proximal to its mid-length (Text-fig. 21). Control is further assured by several accessory ropes made fast to the distal margin of the net-frame.

When raised, the frame is held in this position by a rope attached at one end to the free end of the lever arm and at the other to a stake driven firmly into the river bank. When the net has to be lowered into the water, this rope is cast off the stake and the net allowed to descend into the river by its own weight. To raise it, as has to be done frequently during fishing

Text-fig. 21. A lever dip-net (*ndambē*) used in the French Cameroons on the River Faro.

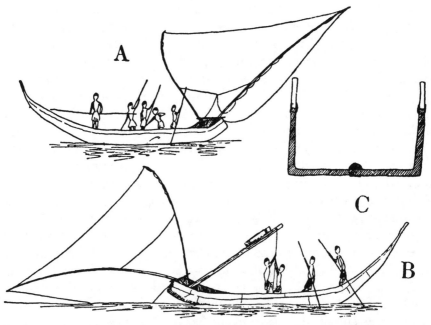

Text-fig. 22. Canoes of the Kotoko people, fitted with the lever dip-net (*zémi*). A, the net raised; B, the net being lowered; C, transverse section of the canoe hull, made of two dugout hulls sewn together longitudinally and with the sides raised by sewn-on wash-strakes. The net is suspended from two long antennae, which take the place of the oval frame used in the *ndambē*.

operations, the fisherman and his assistant tail on to the rope attached to the free end of the lever arm and, hauling upon it, raise the net as quickly as possible; if fish have been caught, they slide down into a pouch arranged at the lower end, worked in braided straw. To counteract the force of the current striking against the net, a guy-rope runs from a stake ashore on the upstream side to a point on the upstream side of the net-frame.

In rivers this net is operated from a rough staging erected on the bank, whereas on board the Kotoko fishing-boats on the river Chari in the country south of Lake Chad, this great net, now made triangular in shape and termed a *zēmi*, is suspended from two long and powerful branches or antennae instead of from an oval frame. The lever arm is loaded with some heavy weight as a partial counterpoise in order to lessen the effort necessary to pull it down when the net, spread between its two antennae, has to be raised out of the water (Text-fig. 22).

Though different in details, this engine parallels the Chinese lever dip-net in essentials and is operated in identical manner (Pl. VII, fig. A). In Africa its use is confined to the rivers coursing through the country of the Kotoko people living to the immediate south of Lake Chad.

The *zēmi* is sometimes operated from a stationary boat, tied up against a bank after the fashion of the *ndambē*; more generally it is operated from a number of boats working as a co-operative group, attended by a fleet of small dugouts, each with a crew of one man and a boy, the man to paddle or pole, the boy to enjoy himself by beating an ear-splitting tattoo on the canoe's side with the aid of two hardwood sticks. The usual procedure is to ascend the river to a considerable distance from the fishing-village and then to let the current take charge and carry the boats slowly downstream. As far as possible the boats keep line abreast, with their huge nets submerged. As soon as this happens, the dugouts begin to play their part; they dart ahead of the nets, the canoemen poling the light skiffs at top speed, the while the boy beats a frantic tattoo, in a monotonous rhythm 'ko-to-ko' which Monod queries as possibly the onomatopoeic origin of the name of the tribe, the Kotoko, the people whose special fishing engine is this *zēmi* (Monod, 1928, 331); their orders are to describe a semicircle in front of the net-equipped boats on the downstream side, an operation designed to drive any fish present before them and into the nets. Ever and anon the nets are raised and emptied, only to be lowered again and the operation repeated time and again, to the cacophony of the boys' harsh tattoo and the cries of the jungle animals awakened or alarmed by the noise.

In striking contrast to this highly complex fishing engine is the simplicity of a method which some of the Mundang fishermen find to be very effective in the Lake of Lere, in the north of the Cameroons. This is their use of dried gourds as floats for baited hooks, each hung by a short line from the hook-like remnant of stalk left on at the time of drying, for this specific purpose. The fisherman takes a number of these gourds in his canoe, baits the hooks with grasshoppers or earth-worms and casts them overboard when the water is calm and unruffled by wind. Any fish that takes a hook is betrayed immediately by the violent oscillations of the gourd caused by its struggles to escape—the signal awaited by the watching fisherman (Monod, 1928, 253 and fig. 57).

Strangely enough, in view of the close relationship of many African fishing methods with those of Asia, as already stressed, there is one striking exception—the cast-net. This net, widely distributed in Southern Asia, as yet has found little favour with the inland fishermen of Africa. Graham (1929, 97) was surprised to find that it is not native to the Victoria Nyanza, where the only users of it in 1927–8 were Goanese from India. Monod (1928, 254) also remarks that cast-nets are unknown to the inland indigenes of the Cameroons although they are a familiar sight on the coast, introduced there through European influence. Two of the explanations given by him for their absence—the lack of boats suitable for its satisfactory employment and the statement that it can be used effectively only under exceptional circumstances—are shown to be invalid by the fact that the cast-net is in general use by the Dravidian fishermen of the Malabar coast of India; the African's disability is in truth due to his lack of skill. It should be noted that the Indian finds no difficulty in throwing this net, even from craft of low freeboard such as an unstable dugout where his stance is little if anything higher than water-level. The statement sometimes made that some greater elevation is necessary for the manipulation of the cast-net is incorrect.

Regarding the proximal sources of the fishing devices in use to-day on the inland waters of Africa, it would be an impossible task to attempt to particularize the source outside of Africa for each type. Indeed, what may be true of the origin of one in a particular area, may be quite erroneous in another. The cultural borders of Africa have so many gateways facing towards Europe and Asia that the route of entry of any one method can seldom be indicated with any degree of certainty. Especially true is this of the tribal lands of the Sudan and of the Lake district of East Africa. For many centuries B.C., Egyptian technical methods and ways of life seeped insidiously into Negroland along the valley of the Nile. Of later date, through centuries of exploration and trade, the influence of settlers from the Phoenician cities of Syria, radiating from Carthage, crept slowly southwards among the tribes of the Sahara and the Sudan; Indian influences and industrial techniques from an equally remote date were active on the east coast with Malinde and Zanzibar as the focal points—influences that continue with increasing strength at the present day. Persian and Arabian cultural influences entered by the same gateway, with Moslem-Arab culture forcing entry into the Sudan both from the Mediterranean and by way of the Nile and the river routes and caravan tracks into the interior from ports on the east coast. After them, European influences entered in an ever-increasing stream which was initiated by that far-seeing organizer of African exploration, the great Prince Henry of Portugal, rightly surnamed 'the Navigator'. Under the stimulus of his enthusiasm, Portugal introduced European culture into Africa from many settlements along the western coast, and then, turning northwards at the Cape, she carried the banner of Europe into the great seaports of the eastern coast and thence across the sea to India and Ceylon; to-day the language of Portugal prevails as the official language of several important seaports in India and may even be heard sometimes in the bazaar at Colombo where artisans continue to follow in the steps of their forefathers who married native women and settled in their new home where they continued to work at the trades learned in Portugal. No wonder that many artisans of Colombo and fisherfolk of Southern India bear names reminiscent of the great sailors and soldiers who emulated the exploits of the Spanish *conquistadores* in Mexico and Peru, albeit without exhibiting the cruelty and treacherous conduct of the Spaniards. In passing, it is worth recording that wherever the Portuguese have gone, they have left a record of improvements made in the fishing methods of the coast people who came under their influence from time to time. From China they introduced into India the great mechanical dip-net worked by leverage which is the characteristic fishing engine in use in Cochin and which still has Portuguese terms for its several parts.

In Africa, Portuguese technical influence upon fishing has been followed in more recent years by the French and the Italians chiefly in the north and east and by the Dutch and the British in the south. The east is now being influenced in increasing measure by the flood of immigrants from India, bringing with them new habits of life, and in fishing some new methods and new appliances. Unfortunately some of these are undesirable as being unduly destructive, especially of fry and of immature fish. As in Fiji, these hordes of incomers, too often sprung from a stratum having a low standard of living, will effect radical changes in the whole range of African culture; wherever their mounting numbers approach equality with those of the native people of the land, there will be imminent danger that the latter will be driven to the wall, unless they bestir themselves quickly. Native African culture is often marred by serious defects but if to these be added those common to the immigrants from India, the outlook will become dark; it may even be similar to that which follows upon the introduction into one country of an animal which at home is harmless and maybe even useful but when placed in a new environment becomes a nuisance and perhaps a plague and a danger to some element of the indigenous fauna, just as the introduction of the mongoose has proved in the West Indies and that of the grey squirrel in England.

VI

KITE-FISHING

No account of strange forms of angling would be complete without reference to kite-fishing. This most curious method of luring fishes to bite, although now practised in two discontinuous areas, each distinguished by its own characteristic technique, would appear to have originated at a single centre; if so, this was probably somewhere in Eastern Indonesia.

The two areas lie respectively westward and eastward from New Guinea whence no record of kite-flying is known. The western area extends at the present day from Singapore and Java in the west to the Moluccas and the Banda Islands in the east, but excluding Borneo, the Celebes and a number of the islands towards Australia. These exceptions, however, may be due either to our lack of adequate knowledge of the local fishing methods, or to disuse of this contrivance.

In both regions the basal technique consists of the use of a small kite to fly a fishing-line with its bait or its lure in such a way that the bait or lure will dance and bob about over the surface of the sea, skipping lightly from wave to wave in imitation of the jumping movements of certain small fishes and prawns upon which larger fishes are accustomed to feed.

In the western region the fishing-line is usually baited with a prawn or a small fish, threaded on a running noose made from a single strong fibre of *Arenga saccharifera* or of fine copper wire when this is procurable. The only kind of fish sought to be caught by this device is the garfish (*Belone* spp.), for this is the only fish which responds to this peculiar form of allure; no sight is more common in eastern waters than that of garfishes leaping from the water in the attempt to seize a prawn or small fish seeking to escape by a frantic jump from the enemy that pursues it; sometimes the garfish takes even greater leaps when it, in turn, is pursued.

The contrivance generally used in Indonesia consists of a slender bamboo rod with a fishing-line passing through a ring at the tip; to the farther end of the line a small kite is attached, made of the stout pinnate leaf of the epiphytic fern, *Polypodium quercifolium*, often seen growing on the stems of palms or in the forks of forest trees in the tropics. What is usually the tail of the kite is here replaced by a line armed at the free end with a running loop of fine fibre or metal wire, whereon is threaded the bait. Equipped with this device the fisherman paddles out from shore until he sees that unmistakable sign of the presence of garfish, the flutter of their occasional leaps from the water; he gets out his rod, adjusts his line, fixes bait upon the running noose, and casts his little kite into the wind, manœuvring the kite-cord until it attains sufficient elevation and stability, a matter of comparative ease in a latitude where the seasonal wind blows steadily from one quarter. Neither is it difficult to keep the bait dancing close to the waves; with luck and skill the fisherman soon begins to land fish. Garfishes alone are caught, for no others have the leaping habit combined with the curious form of the jaws seen in these fishes; their jaws are prolonged unduly into an extremely long lance-shaped beak, armed with a multitude of teeth, sharp as needles.

To take the bait on the noose, the lower jaw usually goes through the loop, the upper closing upon the bait from above, or the performance may be reversed; whichever it be, the violence of the thrust tautens the noose and the fish is caught.

Sometimes as at Karakelang Island, to the north of the Celebes, a rod is absent, the line being wound on a wooden reel held in the hand; neither bait nor noose is used, being replaced by a brightly shining hook (Weber, 1902, 60–1).

Passing eastward to the Melanesian region, we find in the Solomons and adjacent groups a most extraordinary lure in use. Instead of a baited noose, a tassel of tangled spider's web, 3 or 4 inches long by ½ inch thick, is tied to the free end of the fishing-line. This proves an equally effective killing device. The garfish takes it for something worth seizing, and when it does, its many sharp teeth become so tangled in the mass of fine threads that it is unable to free itself and is hauled ignominiously alongside the canoe, to be dipped out with a small landing net.

The kite in these islands is more substantial than that used in the Malay Archipelago (Text-fig. 23); it is made of strips of dried palm leaf, pinned or sewn together and strengthened by slivers of palm-leaf midrib; one is placed across at the top and another at the base, with a third usually attached midway between these two (Balfour, 1913).

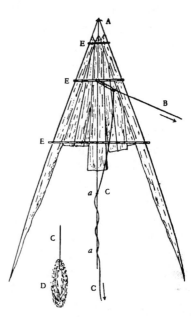

TEXT-FIG. 23. A fishing kite used in Buka, North-west Solomon Islands. A, apex, where the mid-ribs of the median and outer sections meet; B, the control or flying line; C, the tail line carrying the lure; D, made of reeled filaments from a spider's web; E, E, E, the three strengthening cross-rods; a, a, points where the line C is tied to the free end of the median mid-rib.

The lines used are often of extraordinary length. MacGregor (1897–9, 46) states that the kite-line used at Dobu Island, off the south-east tip of New Guinea, is not less than a quarter or even a third of a mile in length. He adds that in making the tassel of spider's web used as a lure, 'spiders are tossed on a long cleft reed or bamboo until a close double tissue of web is obtained about three or four inches broad and four or six feet long. These are laid past to furnish material for the fishing tassel as may be required.' Or a looped tassel may be obtained by winding the thread on a long stiff leaf, from which it may be pushed off eventually and worked into a long thin cord, which is wound round and round the fingers until it forms a loop about 2 inches long (Edge-Partington, 1912, 9).

Early in the present century, two instances of the adaptation of this kite-flying fishing technique appeared independently in England and in California.

In 1901, the *Daily Mail* of 21 September recorded how an enthusiastic angler had hit upon the ingenious idea of utilizing box-kites flown from a long wire, to carry a number of baited fishing-lines out to sea with the help of an off-shore breeze, so that sea-fishing from the shore became practicable.

The American adaptation is somewhat later in date for it was not till 1909 that a Santa Catalina angler developed the idea of using a kite to 'jump' a flying-fish bait when fishing for tunnies and swordfishes.

As in the English 'invention', the kite is used as a means of carrying the angler's baited line to a distance—in this instance from a boat.

The method of operating the device is as follows: The boatman puts the kite in the air, and pays out about 200 feet of line or more as circumstances require. Another cord, 10 or 20 feet long, is then attached to the kite-line and its free end connected with the angler's baited line by a short and thin cord, breaking at about 12 lb. strain. The boatman and the angler thereafter pay out kite-line and fishing-line together. In this way the bait may be carried to any distance from the boat. With experience the bait is made to skip and jump and to act as if it were making frantic efforts to escape. On hooking a fish the weak cord connecting the kite-line and the fishing-line breaks, leaving the angler free to play the fish and the boatman to reel in the kite (French, 1916, II, 15–16).

The American invention did not die out as did the English one, for Whitehead in 1931 (pp. 75–9) reports that kite-fishing was then in use by sportsmen fishing for the marlin and the broadbill swordfish and for both the yellow-fin and the blue-fin tunnies.

How far the two instances quoted above represent independent invention, we cannot determine on the information we have. It may be that they do, or it may be that one or both are to be considered as the result of 'diffusion'; the inventors may have had some knowledge of the Malayan and the Melanesian kite-flying fishing device and have adapted it to the capture of larger fish.

VII

FISHERIES THAT RING THE WORLD: THE BONITO, ALBACORE AND TUNNY INDUSTRIES

In many of the warmer seas of the world the pursuit of those aristocrats of the mackerel family, the bonito, the albacore and the tunny, is the subject of diversified fisheries of vital importance to the prosperity of the off-shore fishing communities of the adjacent coasts.

As the habits of these fishes became gradually known, appropriate methods of capture were evolved; in every instance these are ingenious and often are complex in operation. Generally there is some basic relationship between them due to the fact that the pelagic habits of these fishes are fundamentally similar in every sea. However, man's ingenuity may devise various alternative solutions to any particular problem; hence the diversity that characterizes the apparatus and the methods employed in the prosecution of these fisheries in different parts of the world.

Restricting the present survey to fisheries of the three fishes named, or rather to the three sizes indicated which may be characterized respectively as the small, medium and large-sized members of the tunny group, we find that the most important fishing localities are situated around the Maldive Islands, in Japanese waters, among the islands of Polynesia, along the coasts of the Mediterranean, in the Bay of Biscay and the waters off the Californian and Mexican coasts. These require separate attention for the reason given above.

I. BONITO-FISHING IN THE MALDIVE ISLANDS

The Maldive Islands are a little-known archipelago of innumerable coral islands of atoll form, rising at most but a few feet above sea-level; they lie well to the south of India and just off the steamer track from the Red Sea to Ceylon. They are virtually independent, owning but shadowy allegiance to the Government of Ceylon, which takes the form of an annual tribute of fine mats and other products of the islands. At the same time a return present is expected, and the Maldivians would be disappointed if it were not of greater value than their own, so, in effect, there is little doubt that the islanders regard themselves as allies rather than vassals of the British power. No European representative of the suzerain resides in the islands; the Colonial Government abstains from all interference in the islanders' home affairs except in the rare case of some serious malpractice on the part of the Sultan or of unrest among the people over the succession to the throne.

The people are a quiet race, Muhammadan by religion, fishermen by calling. Fish of many kinds abound, but it is the bonito that is the end and aim of all serious fishing in the islands. This handsome and most useful fish is a near relative of our common mackerel. In form it is tubby and more rotund than its relative, in fact an aldermanic mackerel. Its corpulent bulk is attired in a close-fitting, resplendent livery of steely blue and white, smooth as satin and apparently scaleless, the scales too minute to be noticed except under a lens. Like the mackerel it is of a gregarious nature, roaming the ocean in great shoals in search of the small fishes on which it preys.

In the eyes of the Maldivians all other fishes are of insignificant value as compared with the bonito. To them this fish and the coconut are the mainstays of life. The bonito season is harvest time; the period of prosperity and greatest activity. Special boats are built for the fishery, long, beamy, graceful craft, fine of line and of shallow draft as befits vessels that have their home in coral-infested lagoons of little depth. As seen at Minicoy the hull is stoutly built, open except for a short decking at each end, and is divided into a number of compartments by means of six or seven cross-partitions or bulkheads. The prow rises high, curving gracefully upwards into a tall, snake-like stemhead not unlike that of an old Viking ship which, indeed, the boat as a whole closely resembles (Text-fig. 24). The afterdecking extends outwards over the quarters into a wide platform, shaped like the expanded wings of a butterfly; from this the actual fishing takes place. A single pole-mast is placed fairly well forward; as in many of our own fishing-boats, instead of being stepped permanently in position, the butt end is pivoted between two uprights, the tabernacle as it is curiously named in sailors' parlance; this permits of it being lowered at will, when it rests in the crutch of a short upright post fitted near the stern. The rig of the larger vessels is a strange combination of fore and aft and square sails. A high rectangular mat sail, the head laced to a yard, is hoisted on the foreside of the mast, while abaft, on the same spar, is set a fore-and-aft mainsail, laced to a gaff but without a boom. Not infrequently this mainsail is of thin cotton. The combination of pale brown mat squaresail and white cotton mainsail is picturesque, but to a sailor has a strangely unhandy appearance. In the hands of the islanders the rig works satisfactorily. Considerable taste is shown in the details of painting and carving. While black and yellow form the usual colour scheme used in the decoration of the hull, the rudder-head and the tiller are often simply but effectively carved in elegant symmetric pattern, picked out in two colours.

Before setting out for the fishing-grounds small fishes, for use as live bait, have to be collected. These are caught in the lagoon in a baited square of netting extended on four poles, one attached to each corner, put out from the side of a boat. The outer margin is lowered well down and ground bait scattered over the place. When the small fishes have gathered to the feast, the net is suddenly lifted and the fishes taken out (Pl. ix, fig. A). The catch consists of two principal sorts, a small one like a minnow and a larger one about the size of a sardine. Until required, they are imprisoned in substantially constructed wicker cages of sub-globular form, some $5\frac{1}{2}$ feet long by about 3 feet across and about $3\frac{1}{2}$ feet deep. The

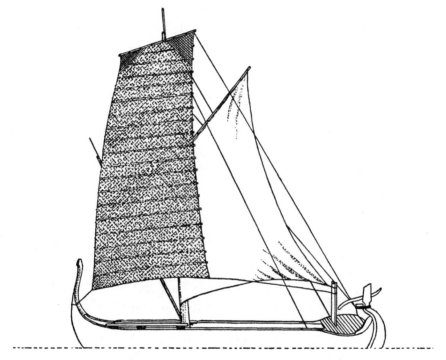

Text-fig. 24. A Maldivian bonito fishing-boat.

mouth is left open but when fish are put in, a net is spread over it, to prevent sea-birds from gormandizing on the contents at their leisure. Each cage is anchored out in the lagoon, buoyed up by two stout baulks of light wood, one on either side. In this manner small fishes are kept alive for 5 or 6 days, awaiting the advent of favourable fishing conditions (Pl. x, fig. A).

To accommodate the live bait aboard the fishing-boat two compartments are fitted up as live wells, one immediately forward of the mast, the other just abaft it. Each has from four to six plugged holes in the bottom. Just before sailing a supply of live bait is transferred to these two live wells and the holes being unplugged, continuous streams of water spout inwards. This inrush would speedily swamp the boat were it not that two men are set to work to keep pace by bailing, with the inrush. By means of perforations at suitable and varying heights in the intervening bulkhead the inflowing water is conducted to the after compartment where the two bailers are located. In this way the water in the wells is constantly renewed and thereby maintained in a fit condition to keep alive the stock of little fishes for use as bait.

Each boat carries a large crew all equipped with short rods save the steersman, the two bailers, four splashers and three or four boys to manage the big mat sail. Each rod is a bamboo about 6 feet long with a line of the same length armed with a barbless steel hook, brightly silvered, the shank broad and flat and curved to resemble as near as possible the shape of a small fish.

Once a shoal is sighted all is frenzied but silent excitement. The boat is headed for it and all available hands seize their rods and crowd upon the after-platform. One of the bailers ceasing work, takes up a position just aft of the mast and begins to sling live bait overboard right and left as fast as he can, dipping them up in twos and threes with a little saucer-shaped hoop-net, 7 or 8 inches across. At the same time two men crouching on either side of the stern platform splash water with all their might, using long-handled scoops made from the flower spathe of the coconut, partly cut down and tied to one end of a light wooden handle. This is a measure of economy; the bonito have to be gulled into the belief that a large shoal of small fish are about and without the splashing the amount of live bait thrown out would be insufficient to carry through the deception successfully. As it is, the combination of this splashing and the fall of a few fishes into the sea every few seconds is enough to bring the hungry bonito dashing excitedly toward the boat. The men become as excited as the fish; flogging the water with their 'tight' lines they dash the hooks wildly among the rushing fish. In their blind eagerness the bonito take live bait or hook indiscriminately. Those that make the wrong choice find themselves suddenly lifted out of the water by main force and swung inboard at the end of a line. With a deft dip of the rod the fish is unhooked and sent slithering between the men's feet into the well of the boat. Often enough the shoal take fright for no apparent reason after a terrific onslaught of a few minutes' duration and disappear as quickly as they came (Pl. ix, fig. B).

Fast and furious is the game while it lasts; often enough the catch of each man averages one a minute; with the fish biting freely and shoals abundant, 2 or 3 hours suffice to load up the boat with a catch of 600 or even 1000 fish.

When the boats return in the evening the fish have to be shared out between the boat-owner and his crew, the owner taking twenty-one in the hundred as his fee. Each man having received his share takes it home and hands it over to the women of the family. What is not wanted for immediate consumption is cured by a highly complex procedure that involves boiling, smoking and sun-drying, identical in all essentials with that practised in Japan, where, too, the same method of attracting the bonito by means of live bait and the fishing with bare hooks is followed.

After being beheaded and cleaned the fishes are split down the back into two halves, each being again divided into two, lengthwise. These fillets are washed in two changes of water and then undergo a prolonged boiling. The next morning they are laid on shallow trays and placed over a fire of smouldering coconut husks or whatever other fuel may be handy. When thoroughly smoked the fillets are dried for some days in the sun until they look and feel like little billets of dark brown mahogany. When considered sufficiently hard, these are stored in bags but if they have to remain on hand for a considerable time before shipment, they must be turned out for further sun-baking if the least sign of mould should make its appearance.

This cured fish forms the chief wealth of the Maldivian islanders, their most valuable export. It is shipped mainly to Ceylon and in the fair weather season a little fleet of tubby Maldivian cargo carriers is usually to be seen rocking at anchor near the landing jetty in Colombo harbour—beamy, shallow hulls painted a dingy red, the cargo space covered with a penthouse roofing thatched with plaited coconut leaves.

The curious dried product goes by the name of *Mās mīn* or *mās*-fish in Ceylon; it forms an essential ingredient in some of the countless varieties of curry made by the Sinhalese for their own particular delectation. The curries supplied by native cooks to their European masters are, at the best, emasculated concoctions, appetizing though they certainly are. For some occult reason 'Master' is supposed by the butler and his satellites to require quite a different preparation of curry to the savoury smelling messes which they would supply to an employer of their own race. Possibly the explanation is that to do so would entail an expenditure of more time and trouble than they consider necessary. And it is curious that this should be so for the fact is that it was Europeans (the Portuguese) who strengthened the native curries of Ceylon and India by the addition of cayenne pepper, and introduced various kinds of flesh into more general use. It is therefore not to be wondered at that some of the most skilful preparers of curries are the wives of Indian and Sinhalese Christians descended from the old-time proselytes of St Francis Xavier and other devoted missionaries of the sixteenth century.

II. CATCHING AND CURING THE BONITO IN JAPAN

In 1907 I made a lengthy tour of Japan to learn what I could of Japanese fishing methods in general and of their pearl-cultural practice in particular. Outwardly courteous as their officials usually were to properly accredited visitors in those pleasant times, there had been no difficulty in obtaining an introduction to the most influential fishing-boat owner in Yaizu, a noted centre of the bonito fishery. So one afternoon saw me decanted by the local train at the railway station just outside that town.

Intimation of my coming had preceded me. A smiling police officer in spotless white uniform, washing the usual invisible soap in cotton-gloved hands was on the platform to meet and conduct me to the inn recommended for my accommodation. He was overpoweringly polite and most solicitous for my comfort, bemoaning the fact that the best inn they had was a poor place indeed and that I would probably find it lacking in all the comforts I was accustomed to. Such a courteous reception was gratifying, but withal there was more than a lurking suspicion that I was under surveillance, and that I was to see just so much and no more.

The town, little more than a large village, consists of a long straggling main street, giving off narrow lanes filled with shabby wooden houses, often mere shacks, tenanted by the fishermen, net-makers and fish-curers who make up the working population. A high sea-wall protects the low-lying town from the fury of winter gales; in bad weather and when not in daily use the fishing-boats, many of them of large size and heavy build, are dragged through an opening left in the wall into shelter on the landward side. Here, if they are to be laid up for some time, a stout thatched roofing is put in place, protecting the unpainted woodwork of the vessel from the drenching downpours common on this exposed part of the Japanese coast.

On the day of my arrival the weather was stormy and wet, and few boats were out. One only, but of the largest size, came in that evening. It arrived just as the sun was sinking dull and wan in a murky, gloomy sky. For some time she lay at anchor well out from the shore, while preparations were being made on land to beach her through the raging surf. Before long a crowd of seventy or eighty men and boys were assembled; paper lanterns began to send flickering signals to those aboard, indicating the place to bring her ashore. On a given signal, anchor was weighed and she began to drift shorewards. While yet some distance outside the surf, a man dropped overboard and swam ashore to inquire whether the huge live-bait floating basket had been moved, as the crew had not been able to find it in order to return to it their unused live sardine bait. Getting his answer, he turned and fought his way back through the boiling surf to his boat, although the information he carried was now too late to be of service. Meanwhile, some of the crowd of men and boys ashore had brought out a number of hurdle-shaped skids or 'way frames' over which to drag the boat; others had fixed in position in the sand high up beyond high-water mark, four huge, wooden, single-fluke kedge anchors, with tackle fitted. As the fishing-boat drifted closer in, several of the crew jumped overboard and brought ashore, after a hard-fought battle with the surf, a stout hawser, made fast to her bows. Coming in, stern first, her head was kept straight, pointing seawards, by men hauling to windward, on the line brought ashore. Excitement mounted high and intense, for in spite of long experience, the task of bringing to land a heavy craft as this through an angry surf must always involve risk and danger; the usually calm and deliberate Japanese demeanour changed; the crowd became a mob of raging demons shouting and rushing wildly about; hustle and noise were the order of the day, but in spite of the din and seeming confusion, everything went eventually with a swing and well-ordered movement. As the boat's stern touched bottom, shore men rushed into the surf and hooked on a big single-sheave block to each projecting end of a stout bar, which passed through the stern-post of the ship, side to side. Simultaneously a hurdle skid was pushed under her keel when the next roller lifted it off the pebbles. The jostling, shouting crowd, frantic with excitement, were already hauling on two stout hawsers which led to intermediate blocks, to which those that passed to the stern blocks hooked on to the boat were made fast. The other end of each of the two hauling ropes was made fast to one of the four kedge anchors up the beach, while the free end of each of the ropes reeved through the blocks at the stern of the boat was made fast to one of the two remaining kedge anchors. With three sets of men working, one putting greased skids under the keel as the boat moved slowly up the beach, another hauling on the ropes going to her stern, and the third keeping her head straight by hauling on the line made fast to her bow on the windward side, the boat was through the surf and out of the water in a surprisingly short time—the result of disciplined activity. Once out of the water, and lightened of her great sweeps and other heavy gear, the boat was dragged high and dry into shelter through a gap in the sea-wall. This boat had been out fishing for bonito and had brought back a moderate catch.

Large sailing-boats are necessary in this fishery for the bonito is a pelagic fish; the shoals seldom come inshore, so the boats have to go far afield to find them. All are caught with rod and line, necessitating a large crew. To complicate matters, the bonito must see live bait or it is useless to hope to catch it. Hence the boats must be seaworthy craft, and of sufficient size to carry from twenty-four to thirty fishermen with a complement of attendant boys, and be fitted with two live-wells for the living sardines used as bait. These wells are large rectangular compartments with openings in the bottom to admit sea-water when live fish are being carried. When empty, plugs are fitted in the openings.

The bait consists of sardines caught inshore; pending fishing requirements they are kept in globular baskets made of fine bamboo wickerwork, about 5 feet in height and 6 feet across at the widest part; these are anchored in the sea to straw-rope net-bags filled with pebbles and are buoyed by two long and very stout bamboos lashed one on each side of the mouth (Pl. x, fig. B). When a boat is ready to set sail for the bonito fishing-grounds, a supply of living sardines is transferred from these store-baskets to the live-wells, where they are kept alive by a constant influx of sea-water through the holes in the bottom which have been unplugged, and guarded by a stout screen of fine netting; other holes are arranged to form exits for the overflow.

Arrived on the fishing-grounds, a sharp look-out is kept for shoals, for the bonito swims high in search of the schools of small fish on which it preys. When a shoal is sighted, the boat is headed for it; live bait is thrown out to attract the fish, and all hands line the low bulwarks, armed with short bamboo rods with very short lines. Bonito are usually in a state of ravenous hunger; once attracted round the boat, it matters little whether the brightly tinned hooks are baited or not; the greedy fish take anything that shines provided there be living fish thrown out in sufficient numbers to deceive them. With luck the crew soon catch their requirements and head for home.

Great quantities of bonitos reach the markets in the fresh condition, for besides being excellent when cooked, the flesh when raw and perfectly fresh is esteemed one of their greatest delicacies by Japanese gourmets. If my own experience be any criterion it would be wise for the European visitor to refuse this delicacy; persuaded by a Japanese friend, I swallowed a mouthful with difficulty and threatening nausea; over my condition during the ensuing 3 days it is desirable to leave a veil.

The greater part of the bonito catches is turned into a cured product, to be seen everywhere in Japanese food shops, but I defy the uninitiated to recognize it as cured fish. To all appearances the pieces exposed for sale are fragments of very ancient and much discoloured mahogany or teak; drop a piece on the cobbled ground, and it behaves as a chunk of hard wood; cut it with a knife and it does not belie the first impression. Actually, when needed for cooking, it is shred with a sharp knife, the shreds being an ingredient in several kinds of soup.

How is this curious article produced? To receive an answer, some patience will be needed, for there are many stages in the process. As I saw it carried through at Yaizu, operations began at 6 a.m. on the fish brought in by the boat which arrived the evening before as already described. The curer with fine courtesy (which I would not expect to receive in our own country!) delayed commencing operations till I arrived in answer to a messenger's summons.

The fish were in tubs filled with water in which floated blocks of ice. One operator lifted them one by one from this tub, and after beheading and eviscerating them, threw them into another tub again filled with iced water. A second operator slit the headless body of each fish into two halves and removed the backbone and fins. Afterwards these halves were divided lengthwise into two fillets, making four for each fish.

The fillets were next packed on edge in shallow circular bamboo trays, with perforated bottoms, and boiled in a deep copper, in which the trays were superimposed, for about 40 minutes, cold water being added occasionally to make good the loss by evaporation.

After boiling had continued a sufficient time, the trays were removed and dipped in a vat of cold water to cool as quickly as possible. When cold, the blistered skin and any adhering fat and bones were rubbed off. After this they were smoked for a prolonged period over a wood fire. Although they become hard and dry by these means, a great deal of very careful treatment is still required; like tea, cocoa and several other of our common foodstuffs, the smoked bonito has to undergo a process of fermentation before it is ready for market. The first stage consists in placing the smoked fillets in a dry box, till they soften slightly, when they are submitted to an elaborate trimming process. This is delicate work, requiring a long apprenticeship. Fortunately, like so many other small industries, it is usually carried on in roadside booths, open to the public gaze. Several men were at work, when I watched the procedure, in a side street at Yaizu. Each had at least a dozen knives of slightly different shape lying on the bench beside him. Some had the point bent to one side and others had it brought to an acute triangular point. Two whetstones lay handy on which the worker sharpened his knives at frequent intervals. The smoked surface of the bonito fillets is whittled away very carefully indeed, extremely thin shavings being removed; all hollows and cracks are scraped out with scrupulous care. After this thorough cleaning, the cracks are filled up with a paste made from waste fragments. Finally, the fillets are laid out in the sun for 1 or 2 days to dry thoroughly. Each piece takes 10 minutes to clean and I was told that an operator can do only sixty pieces in a day, working 10 hours a day.

Surely they are now ready for market? Far from it. They are next filled into closed boxes, until a blue mould develops, when they are dried again in the sun, and the mould brushed off. Again re-boxed, a second growth of mould appears, said to be white this time. On its appearance the pieces are sun-dried for a day and re-boxed, without the mould being brushed off. This treatment is repeated three or four times till no fresh mould appears—the sign that the fish are ripe and may be sent to market.

In Yaizu old Japanese customs still held their ground. On my evening prowl around the town, a brightly lighted window in an otherwise darkened street drew me forward till I stood before the open slats that filled the wooden window frame, a sort of Venetian blind. Inside, a rectangular well, filled with steaming water, occupied the centre of the floor, a low partition crossing it midway. On one side a crowd of men and boys—on the other of women and girls—mostly stark naked, were popping in and out of the heated water of the bath, or sitting cross-legged chatting about village affairs and the latest gossip.

And back in the primitive little hotel where I lodged, the bath-tub was an iron cauldron, a 'copper' such as is used for boiling clothes. As for furniture, it was limited to a nail on which to hang the bather's kimono, and a stool—4 inches high—on which he must attempt to sit the while the attendant maid rinses off the lather following an application of soap after a sufficient sojourn in the 'copper'. Thereafter he might again have a dip in the water, but it was early impressed upon him that all soap must be removed before a return to the bath. Let him not forget that Japanese courtesy extends the first use of the bath to the stranger within the gates, and that a dozen or more people have to bathe in the same water before the day is ended—the maid-servants last of all when the day's work is over.

But to revert to that little stool. How inconveniently low it was! A little awkwardness and how apt it was to tip over and send the would-be sitter over on his back—an extremely undignified position!

Alas! the kindly spirit of Old Japan has become a false quantity to-day, consequence of the vaunting ambition of the military chiefs who ruled the nation and who, in their blind folly were intent upon the pursuit of the hateful light of that *ignis fatuus*—the overlordship of Asia and the Pacific.

III. BONITO-FISHING IN POLYNESIA

When Europeans began to navigate the great South Sea, discovering group after group of its myriad islands, the chase of the bonito, smallest species of the tunny section of the mackerel family, was one of the characteristic methods of fishing then in general operation; this method consisted essentially of rod-fishing with a barbless hook attached to a brightly gleaming pearl-shell lure.

Throughout Polynesia the rod continues to be the favourite device for capturing the bonito. Both the rod and its tackle are highly specialized; to understand how the fish are landed it is necessary to give some details of the canoe and the fishing gear. Some of these vary considerably between the different groups, but these variations are in no wise important except as regards the design of the canoes employed, an indication that any paddling canoe is suitable for this work if built on lines fine enough to permit of swift pursuit when a shoal be sighted.

It is among the islands of Western and Central Polynesia that this fishing has been most fully elaborated—especially in Samoa, the Society group, the Tokelau and the Ellice groups. Of these, I believe the canoes and implements in use by the Samoans to be the most typical. For this reason and because I made a lengthy stay in Upolu, in Western Samoa, in 1925, I shall begin with a description of the dainty canoe used there and of the tackle required for this particular fishery.

The Samoan bonito-canoe, the *Va'a alo*, is a lovely example of boat carpentry, the finest in Polynesia. Anyone can fell a tree, cut off its branches and hollow out the log to make a common fishing-canoe. But the building of a bonito-canoe calls for exceptional skill, for it is built up of numerous lengths of planking—'patches' as they are called—raised upon a basal keel-piece, laid in one piece, 25 to 50 feet in length.

These 'patches' are each of more or less conventional size and form as each has a specific position to occupy when placed in position; their size varies between 18 inches and 5 feet in length. In dressing each 'patch' a vertical flange or ledge is left projecting along each edge on that side which is to be the inner surface of the finished canoe. As the patches are got ready for assembling, the flanged edges of each are bored at short intervals with holes corresponding with holes on the opposed flange edges of the patches which are to be its immediate neighbours. Then, after smearing the edges with breadfruit gum, the opposed flanges are 'sewed' together with sinnet, twine made from fine coconut fibre. This sewing shows only on the inside of the boat; the outside is rubbed smooth and it needs a keen eye to detect the joints. A canoe thus constructed is perfectly watertight and possesses a large degree of resiliency, a useful quality on a coast where coral heads abound in the lagoon within the encircling reef.

The fishing tackle consists of a long rod, carrying from two to six short lines, each armed with a pearl-shell lure. The rod is usually from 12 to 18 feet long, in one piece save for the spliced-on short butt, 18 to 36 inches in length. In Samoa and the Society Islands, a tough, short-jointed mountain variety of native bamboo is preferred for the rod proper, but in the smaller reef islands the tough boughs of various trees have to be utilized. Before the opening of the season the utmost care is taken to ensure that every part of the rod is sound; no accident is more dreaded than the breaking of a rod when swinging aboard a large fish—the sharp splints of a bamboo cut sharp as any razor.

Round the splice a piece of old fish-net is wound and secured. Into this the hook-points of the fish-lures are caught when not in use.

The hook attached to the end of each of the fishing-lines, which are about 6 inches shorter than the rod, is really a lure plus a bone or tortoise-shell-hook tied upon it at one end. The body of the lure is made from a section of the shell of the black-lip pearl-oyster, cut at right angles to the hinge, the whole shaped and arranged as shown in Text-fig. 25, and decorated with a double-ended tuft of fine feathers or fibre threads attached behind the hook. Success in fishing depends upon the use of the correct choice of a lure. The bonitos, eager to gorge themselves on a shoal of any of the small fishes upon which they are accustomed to feed, have an instinctive distrust of any lure not resembling in colour the fishes in the particular shoal being pursued. Hence the need to have several lines in reserve, each with a shank of distinctive colour or colour shading. When one fails to attract a strike, another line with its lure is set free and tried, and this is repeated until one is found to prove successful.

In Samoa two men form the crew of each bonito-canoe; in other islands, as in the Ellice and Tokelau groups, a crew of three is the rule; four are sometimes carried to ensure speed when in pursuit of a shoal.

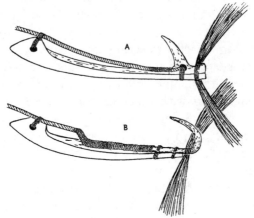

TEXT-FIG. 25. Two examples of Polynesian bonito hooks.

When they set out from the beach the master-fisherman occupies the aftmost thwart with his rod or rods resting on the outrigger, fitted outboard always on the port side. A forked stick, upright on the forward outrigger boom, receives the rod-head and prevents it from rolling overboard.

Every likely fishing-ground is known. Steering towards the selected one, direction is kept by the aid of cross-bearings from prominent features on the coast—a giant of the forest, a hill peak or even a conspicuous house; the men paddling steadily along keep a keen look-out for sea-birds following a shoal of small fishes fleeing before the onrush of a pack of pursuing enemies, bonitos, albacores and dolphins more particularly. From time to time the forward paddler stands up to scan the sea in every direction; should he sight birds circling and whirling in confused flight, he signs to the rod man who rises to decide if the omens be favourable. Should the circling flock be composed of terns and boobies, this means usually the presence of bonito and if an occasional frigate-bird be seen hovering above, the signs are satisfactory and conclusive. All is now bustle and repressed excitement; the men paddle furiously to reach their quarry. As the canoe approaches the shoal, the expert at the stern lifts his rod from its rest, detaches the hook of one of the fishing-lines from the net wrapped around the butt and rests the rod in the sloping half-socket present at the fore end of the short after-decking, at the same time slipping its butt into a stout rope-ring hung and braced below the thwart whereon he sits. Then he picks up his paddle and both men, heartened by the promise of a coming fight, press forward towards the shoal in a final spurt.

As the canoe reaches the fringe of the shoal, the lure should now come into action. The length of the fishing-line is just enough to keep its glittering pearl shank on or close to the surface, lightly skipping from wave-crest to wave-crest. It usually proves an irresistible attraction to the greedy bonito. If it makes a rush for the lure, the fisherman at the stern, sitting with his buttocks touching the rod, senses the pull immediately this happens; he casts his paddle down, swings round, steadying himself by a left-hand grip upon a short bar lashed across the angle made by the thwart with the port gunwale, he seizes the rod with his right hand and swings the hooked fish inboard against his breast or abdomen. With his left hand he knocks the fish off the barbless hook or else disengages it by a dexterous jerk of the line; frequently the fish is already flicked off the hook as it is whirled aboard (Pl. xi).

If the canoe is paddled well into the mass of the shoal and the fish are striking freely, the fisherman, if expert enough, will lift the rod from the rest, and standing up, rest the butt against his groin and bring the fish aboard so rapidly that it has been said that two fishes may be on their way into the canoe at the same time. Every instant counts; the movements of the shoal are unpredictable; they may sheer off at any moment. Before this happens, given good luck and the skill born of long practice, any number up to forty or fifty fishes may be taken—a fine catch for one man to make within the space of a few minutes.

Before the Polynesian islanders became Christians, many and varied were the taboos enjoined and the traditional ceremonies followed. To-day, while much of the old superstitious usage has vanished, the enthusiasm of the men for this madly exciting sport remains as strong as ever. No blood runs so sluggish as not to course wildly with excitement as the fish are whirled aboard in a frenzied fight against time and the erratic behaviour of the shoal.

No live bait being carried, the forward paddler is accustomed to splash water with his paddle towards the trailing and skipping lure in the attempt to imitate the wild rushing and leaping of little fishes in frightened flight before their enemies.

Expert fishermen take the utmost pride in the care of those pearly-shank lures that have served them well; some even provide separate pockets for them in a flannel roll carefully packed away in a cedar-wood box. An expert cutter is able to make shanks of very diverse colourings and markings, so an old fisherman may amass quite a large assortment from which to choose. Of these, some are special favourites because of their frequent successes; the fortunate owners of shanks of proved worth are, however, reluctant to show their treasures to others lest they should be begged for by friends; a refusal would contravene the basis of Polynesian etiquette.

To the practical advantages of possessing the attributes of colour, iridescence and attractive markings naturally inherent in successful lures made from pearl-shell, must be added the gradual accretion of *mana*, that peculiar and mysterious spiritual quality begotten of success and long-continued usage by an expert; lures used by clever fishermen absorb this strongly, according to Polynesian belief, and this is further increased as season follows season in continuity of great achievement. Such lures are objects beyond price and are treasured accordingly—the most precious of heirlooms if son follows father in the fisherman's calling.

From this short account of the bonito rod-fishery as practised in the Indo-Pacific area, there emerges the problem of the place of origin of the method as used from island to island, from the Maldives to Japan, and from Japan to the utmost limits of Polynesia. The use of the barbless hook in conjunction with a rod and short line is common to all, as is also the collection and use of small live fishes for ground-baiting if we include the *tira* method of fishing for albacore next to be described (*q.v.*). Cultural diffusion is indicated definitely and the focal point of dispersal would appear to be Indonesia, at the time when the proto-Polynesians sojourned there, the while they were developing their characteristic fishing methods.

IV. CRANE- OR 'TIRA'-FISHING FOR ALBACORE

This fishery, dead and gone for a score of years, is one more example of the amazing fecundity of invention in fishing devices so often characteristic of communities dependent upon the sea as the reservoir whence they procure an essential item of their food supply.

'Tira'-Fishing, as it is commonly termed in the Society Islands, required the employment of a double-canoe, each hull a dugout built on the lines of the old-time travelling canoe (*tipairua*), with the sides of the larger ones raised by the addition of a broad plank sewed vertically upon each edge of the two dugouts.

A plank several feet long and about 20 inches wide projected horizontally forward over and beyond each bow to form a platform on which one of the crew stood while fishing was in progress. The hulls were generally somewhat unequal in length; in one of the last, a small example measured some years ago, the larger was 24 feet long, the smaller 20 feet. The two were connected by two cross-booms at a distance apart of about 5 feet, the smaller hull invariably on the port side. The forward boom was long enough to project 18 inches outboard of each canoe in order to give a purchase for the side-stays of the 'crane'. According to Nordhoff (1930, 141–53) to whom we are indebted for an account of the operations aboard the last *tira* that went fishing:

> The fishing gear consisted of a long, compound fishing-rod or 'Crane', originally called *tira* (literally 'mast'), but in later times termed *purau* (so named because it is made from a branch of *purau*), 25 to 36 feet in length according to the size of the canoe. This was bifurcated about a foot from the distal end and to each of the short divergent branches thus given off, a fishing line, rather shorter than the *purau*, was tied. Athwart the four gunwales between the fore boom and the after end of the head platform, a short cylindrical bar (*rio*) was laid, its ends projecting a few inches beyond the canoes on each side. To the after side of this, at a point between the two hulls just outside the port gunwale of the starboard or larger hull, the fishing crane was lashed some little distance from the butt, which rested under and against the lower side of the fore boom when the *purau* was lowered into the fishing position. Three stays were attached to the fishing crane about eight feet above the *rio*; two of these, the side stays, were led to the projecting ends of the fore boom. The third formed a fore-stay attached below to the head of the starboard hull, and of a length carefully adjusted to permit raising the fishing crane when required, until it was almost but not quite vertical, when the stay checked its further movement. Besides these, a strong back-stay was attached to the *purau* a short distance below the point of bifurcation, the other end passed aft to men at the stern of the canoe. This back-stay was a specially soft rope made from the inner bark of the *purau* to save the pullers' hands from abrasion.

Ellis (1829, II, 296–7) says that a bunch of feathers was fastened to the end of each of the crane branches to simulate the presence of the sea-fowl that follow the course of a shoal of small fish when pursued by predatory large fishes.

Between the two hulls, made fast to the cross-booms fore and aft, was a live-fish car, a broad, canoe-shaped basket, 8 to 12 feet long, 2 feet deep and about a yard across. Its base was made of a length from the bottom of an old canoe; on this were built-up ends and sides. The ends were blunt, upturned and covered in, leaving a large median opening. In this car was carried the supply of live bait, consisting of young red mullet (*Mulloides auriflamma*), called '*uma*.

When the canoe reached a fishing-ground where albacore were known to lurk, the captain, with a scoop, began to throw out the live bait sparingly and slowly till the albacore began to rise in response. As soon as any fishes were seen, one of the two short fishing-lines, ready armed with a large barbed metal hook (anciently it was of pearl shell) was baited and thrown overboard. At the same moment the crew began to paddle astern, so that the bait was trolled along the surface in a life-like manner. The instant a fish made a rush and took the hook, the men aft jerked the crane upwards by means of the lifting backstay, thereby swinging the fish aboard into the grasp of a man stationed on the port head-platform. The two fishing-lines were used alternately.

When the fishing was over, the empty live-car was hoisted aboard and carried athwart the two hulls, as otherwise it was an impediment on the homeward run.

These double canoes were the property of a number of men and women working in co-operation; one man would own the starboard hull, another the port one, a third the fishing crane and so on; the women caught bait. In 1925, when I visited Tahiti, the last *tira* canoe lay rotting on the beach.

V. THE TUNA FISHERIES OF CALIFORNIA

In the waters off the west coast of California and Central America two commercial methods of fishing the five fishes[1] classed in American parlance as 'Tunas', occupy the field. One relies for success upon the use of a huge purse-seine, the other upon rod-and-line fishing after ground-baiting (chumming) with live fish.

1. Purse-Seining

Purse seines of relatively enormous size and strength are operated with the specific object of capturing the blue-fin tunny (*Thynnus thynnus*), the species which gave our own rod-fishers exciting sport in the North Sea in the years immediately preceding the recent war.

This pursing method calls for no special comment; in principle the net is operated in the same general way as any other purse-seine, except that the power-boats in use in the American fishery are of highly specialized design. Their length ranges between 70 and 80 feet, the beam 18 or $18\frac{1}{2}$ feet, with the tendency always towards an increase in size. All are powered with Diesel engines varying from 100 to 250 horse-power. Out-standing features in their design are a turntable at the stern to facilitate handling of the nets, a power roller fitted on the counter, useful in reducing the labour of hauling the net, a derrick pivoted at the foot of the mast, and a crow's nest perched atop of the mast.

The nets run from 275 to 350 fathoms in length with a depth of 28 to 34 fathoms. The mesh varies according to the species fished. If for bluefin and yellow tunny, the mesh at the top of the net is 6 or 7 inches (stretched); if for the smaller skipjack and the bonito proper, the mesh is reduced to about $4\frac{1}{2}$ inches.

[1] These species are: bluefin tunny (*Thynnus thynnus*), yellowfin tunny (*Neothunnus macropterus*), albacore (*Germo alalunga*) and two bonitos, *Xarda chiliensis* and *Katsuwonus pelamys*; the last-named goes by the name of 'skipjack' in America but in Britain is the species meant when reference is made to the Atlantic bonito.

2. The High Seas Tuna Fishery

This commercial method of fishing is a development from the Japanese high-seas method of capturing the bonito by means of rod and line used in conjunction with ground-baiting. By its capture of great numbers of valuable fish in this way it represents a rare and most unusual combination—commercial practice wedded to a sporting method of fishing, as I hope to demonstrate.

The boats, powerfully engined, run from 70 to 140 feet in length, according to the particular work they favour; for the catching of the yellowfin tunny and the skipjack, in localities distant from their base, large vessels fitted with live-bait tanks, refrigerating apparatus and insulated holds are necessary, whereas if fishing be sporadic and conducted in waters near home, boats of 70 to 80 feet in length are found adequate and economical.

The larger boats scour the high seas from California southward to the equator and the Galapagos Islands in search of shoals of the yellowfin tunny and the striped bonito or skipjack—fishes of similar habits and the same distribution, and both marketed ashore as 'tunas'.

The fishing gear consists of a stout bamboo pole, a line 6 feet long, made up of a 3-feet length of heavy cotton line and a wire trace nearly as long, armed with a barbless hook having the shank embedded in a short brass tube filled with lead, the whole concealed within a brush of white feathers. Alternately, if live bait be put on the hook, the feather lure is dispensed with; in no instance is a barbed hook used.

The small fishes intended to serve as live bait are kept in a tank on deck near the stern; the water is maintained wholesome by a continuous circulation of fresh sea-water, pumped in from outside. Supplies of bait fishes are obtained by netting in any well-stocked bay within easy reach of the expected fishing-ground. This live bait is indispensable; without it the voyage would be a failure.

Fishing is done from a narrow platform, termed the 'racks', made of steel rods or tubes, hinged outboard to the guard rail, but capable of being folded up against the bulwarks when not in use. A knee-rest, about 18 inches high, is fitted on the outside of the platform rail.

When a shoal of fish is sighted either by surface disturbance, the leaping of the fish or the excited hovering of birds overhead, the 'racks' are swung out and held horizontal by chain stays. Nearing the shoal the engines are slowed and some bait from the tanks is thrown out. Using a small hand dip-net a few fishes are ladled out and cast overboard to attract the bonito or tunny. If they are biting, they rush upon the bait, a tornado of hurtling bodies; soon as way is checked, the crew clamber overside upon the racks, armed with one- or two-pole gear according to the size of the fish in the shoal. Each man stands with one knee braced against the low rail above the outer side of the rack, the other leg held taut against the hull behind. The heel of the fishing pole rests against or just below the groin in a pad-rest slung from the belt around his waist. Holding the pole near the end with the left hand, the fisherman grips it about shoulder height with his right. Firmly planted in this attitude he lowers the tip of his pole till the lure and hook reach the water. Then, moving the pole lightly to and fro, the feathered striker skips lightly along the surface, tempting the hungry fish to believe that a live fish is leaping frantically from the waves in terrified flight.

All this time live bait continues to be thrown overboard by one, or even by two men if the boat is manned by a large crew, and if it is seen that the fish are biting, taking live bait and feathered lures indiscriminately. When a fish strikes, the fisherman leans backwards and, with the advantage given by the fish's tempestuous rush, lifts his prize from the water and swings it aboard. A deft flick of the line, acquired from long practice, disengages the hook as the fish hurtles through the air, flying inward to fall upon the deck. Without an instant's delay the lure is returned to the sea, ready for the next fish. When the fish are biting well, they fall aboard in an endless stream, so fast and furious is the play. A few minutes of wild rushes may, however, cease abruptly, the fishes shooting away for no clear or obvious reason. When the rush continues for 10 minutes or more, the catch made is measurable by the ton.

Fishing with hooks baited with small fishes is resorted to only when the unbaited lure fails to catch the fancy of the capricious tuna. Catches so made are small by comparison, for much time is lost by the need to re-bait the hook frequently and also because the captured fish is not so quickly and easily freed from the baited hook as from the lead-weighted lure.

So long as the fishes are of moderate size, bonito or skip-jacks, single pole-rods are used; with the larger kinds, the albacore and tunnies proper not yet fully grown, two men combine to fish conjointly with a single working line suspended by a swivel from a ring to which a shortened line from each fishing pole is similarly attached. Perfect co-ordination of effort is needed (Text-fig. 26).

If full-sized tunny be about, weighing from 250 to 350 lb. or more, two-man power may prove inadequate to land the fish and three-pole and even four-pole teams may become necessary in order to swing the huge fish aboard. How this is accomplished is difficult to realize, but the cold fact remains that by practice and co-operative team-work it does get done. Four men co-ordinating their muscles to the collective work of guiding their respective rods, skipping the lure in life-like fashion on the surface of the sea, and timing the exact moment, after the fish has struck, to heave it from the water, swing it over the ship's rail and finally to jerk the hook from its mouth—surely this is an outstanding example of man's ability to devise means to meet an unusually difficult fishing situation.

But the supreme test is when the shoal consists of mixed species of several different sizes. Expecting a fish of 10 or 20 lb. and then to hook one of ten times this size taxes a fisherman's skill and strength sometimes to breaking-point, with the result that gear is broken or lost or the man himself may go overboard to flounder amongst the rushing fish until he may grasp a rope and be pulled aboard.

Text-fig. 26. The two-rod fishing gear used on the Californian coast in the bonito and tunny fishery.

VI. THE EUROPEAN TUNNY AND BONITO FISHERIES

1. Trolling in the Bay of Biscay

From the many fishing harbours dotting the western and southern coasts of Brittany, and particularly from the picturesque old port of Concarneau, famed for its sardine fishery and canneries, fleets of trim sailing craft, ketches and yawls set out during the season from June to November inclusive for long-distance fishing cruises in the Bay of Biscay in search of the Falstaffian albacore (*Germo alalunga*) commonly called *thon* or tunny and of its smaller relative, the bonito (*Katsuwonus pelamys*).

Gaudy colouring of the hull and sails is characteristic of all these tunny boats; the hull may be red, green or blue, picked out with ribbons of white, often with the sails of discordant, non-matching hues; even these may be inconsistent—the mainsail, mizzen and headsails all of different colours.

Every boat is furnished with two supple fishing-rods of monstrous length, pivoted one on each side of the mainmast, which they overtop by several feet. When in action they are lowered to the proper angle, about 30° from the horizontal, by tackle from the masthead and are steadied by stays running forward from their outer ends.

To each great fishing-rod, six fishing-lines are attached at regular intervals apart. Two or three others are streamed astern from the counter. To each of these lines a copper-wire trace is fastened, its end armed with a stout double hook, concealed within a maize-straw lure, fluffy and pale yellow in colour, with tufts of horsehair added to increase its resemblance to some of the small fish on which the bonito and albacore feed. Tunnies, albacore and bonito are the greatest gourmands among fishes; everything is grist that comes to their mill. Bright and shimmering objects are irresistible; when the two great fishing-rods are lowered, their lines trailing in the water with the lures skipping lightly from wave to wave, the ravenous fish lose no time upon investigation; darting recklessly upon the lures, they swallow the hook concealed within the lure, to be hauled ignominiously aboard, without any attempt to play them.

When killed, gutted and washed, the fish are hung from poles resting in trestle-racks amidships.

The origin of this Biscayan fishery is of comparatively recent date, introduced by the fishermen of La Rochelle and Sables d'Olonne just over half a century ago. News of the success of the new venture spread quickly and many other ports entered the field in competition. Concarneau, Douarnenez, Groix and Etel occupied the leading positions as tunny-fishing ports when the recent war began; a few crews escaped with their boats to Cornish ports, and others, with German guards aboard, were captured by our patrols.

The Bay of Biscay having been put out of bounds for fishing by our naval authorities, these boats were practically useless for any other fishery for none is power-engined—an essential to-day for any large boat that goes fishing in British waters.

2. Butchery in the Fishing Pounds

Europe. In the Mediterranean, tunny of large size are abundant; the principal method of capturing this and the related species which also abound, is one dating far back in time. Certain bays, headlands and islands along the coasts of North Africa, Portugal, Spain, France, Italy, the Adriatic, the Aegean, the Sea of Marmora and the Bosphorus have long been recognized as stations passed periodically by the tunny shoals in their seasonal migrations between the Atlantic and the Black Sea. In these favoured localities alone can the tunny be fished with commercial success.

The time-honoured method is to intercept their progress by setting up long lines of anchored nets of wide mesh. Following these guiding lines the fish pass into a series of net-walled chambers and find themselves eventually in a terminal enclosure, pound or corral. After entering, another length of netting is hauled into position, closing the entrance gap.

This net-walled pound is a veritable chamber of death; the Sicilians aptly term it the 'slaughter house'; men, in barges, are lined along its walls. The killers crowd the gunwales and begin wholesale massacre. The great fishes, red-blooded like ourselves, panting, snorting and jostling frenziedly, surge madly within the slowly diminishing space, for the crews have begun to haul in the flooring-net beneath the fishes. When sufficiently crowded together, the men, maddened with blood lust, begin to haul the fish out of the water with evil-looking sharp-pointed, hook-headed implements—a form of gaff—throwing them into the bottom of the barges where fishermen, the marine equivalents of the matadors of the bull-ring, thrust and stab the wounded monsters until the holds become horrible shambles, blood turning the bilge water into crimson slush. Blood, blood, is everywhere, bespattering everything and everyone engaged in this orgy of butchery.

JAPAN. On the Japanese coasts, wherever conditions are favourable, pound nets for tunny, albacore and bonito are numerous; they are constructed on the same basic principle as those of the Mediterranean, apart from minor differences due partly to long-established custom and partly to the economic conditions which had long prevailed in the fishing community when I toured the fishing ports of Japan. Instead of the rectangular chambers familiar in the Mediterranean, the Japanese favour a rounded or elliptical shape; another peculiarity is the Japanese custom of working each chamber as an independent entity, the property of a single individual or of a family group working in association. A fishing station may consist therefore of a number of independently operated pounds connected chainwise end to end, with their number limited only by the breadth of workable water extending off shore.

According to the fishery laws of Japan, the owner of each section or individual pound, is bound to put his property in working order in good time for the opening of the fishing season. Omission to do this entails forfeiture of all rights, for failure causes the continuity of the series to be broken and leaves a gap through which the fish are able to escape. A rental is paid to the government for the right to erect and use one of these pounds, but the tenant enjoys fixity of tenure so long as he conforms to the specified conditions.

The older type of pound is built of fencing, made of bamboo lattice-work filled in as necessary with reeds, or straw. At frequent intervals this is supported by stout posts driven deep into the sea-bottom, the whole anchored by guy ropes to large stones. In the more modern pounds, as the head ropes of the nets are adequately buoyed by empty casks, drums, logs of light wood and bundles of buoyant bamboos, posts are dispensed with and the number of anchoring cables, placed on both sides of the walling, are correspondingly increased in order to maintain the head ropes in their proper position.

In the chain of pounds which I visited at Himi, a prosperous east coast fishing port on the Noto Peninsula, the outer section, extending far into the sea, comprised a series of five roomy albacore pounds, the landward end joining a shallow-water series of four sardine pounds. All were of elliptical form in plan, with the entrance to each at the shoreward end of one of the long sides.

The sardine pounds were of similar construction but much smaller and usually with a trapped second and smaller chamber at the rearward end of the first or entrance chamber. A long leader from the shore connects with the wall of the pound nearest inshore.

On the closed side of each albacore pound a look-out boat is anchored, with a thatched crow's-nest erected at the summit of a tripod support (Pl. vii, fig. B). On the opposite or entrance side, another boat is stationed at one side of the opening, the crew ready to raise a barrier of netting lying ready on the bottom in order to bar the exit of the fish whenever the watchman signals from his perch in the other boat, that fish have entered the trap.

In some pounds the netting of the walls extends as a flooring across the bottom, forming a continuous bowl-shaped net; when this is present, the net is gradually hauled up till the area occupied by the captured fishes is so reduced that the work of gaffing them out is greatly facilitated.

Apart from the fish sold fresh or sent to a cannery, the flesh is cured by boiling, smoking and drying in manner similar to that already described as practised in the Maldive Islands, but refined and more elaborate, with the result that the product is of a distinctly superior quality.

VIII

BAITING FOR CROCODILES AND ALLIGATORS

I STOOD before the shrine of an Indian village god, a tiny cubical building barely 6 feet every way, surmounted by a low dome. Whitewashed stucco covering the old walls, splashed here and there with red prints of the open hand, made it conspicuous from afar, standing as it did in the deep shade of a lofty, wide-spreading banyan tree that formed a dark green setting to the scene. In the front wall a doorway, without gate or barrier, permitted the deity to be seen dimly in the gloom of the windowless interior. Powerful he might be but not in his looks lay power; he or it, as you prefer, consisted of nothing more than a black, grease-incrusted stone with the upper end daubed red and yellow in crude suggestion of human features. Garlands of faded flowers, disordered by the wind, encircled this image; fragments of others lay at the foot, mingled with tiny clay lamps to hold the oil of oblation when the attendant priest lights them in honour of the god. The shrine was empty of all else save for a little image carved out of stone, barely a foot high, that could just be made out to be a conventional representation of the good-humoured elephant-headed Ganapati, or Ganesha, god of good fortune—most loved of all the gods of India, for is he not the bestower of all prosperity and riches in this life? Others may be of higher rank and be more powerful and dignified, but the homely, smiling 'Belly-god' as the villagers are fond of terming him, is not worshipped in awe and fear as are many of the other gods in the Hindu pantheon.

Outside, planted upright in the ground, stood a rusty trident, the emblem of Siva but here probably of different import; hung on spikes driven into the wall at the side of the doorway were several monstrous double fishing-hooks, 8–9 inches long, together with a large number of small hooks arranged around circular plaques. Such curious votive offerings, for the large hooks were clearly of this character, were difficult to understand seeing that the shrine belonged to an inland village in the very heart of India, fully 150 miles from the nearest sea where sharks are found; I could think of no other purpose for which they could be used except in shark-fishing. I appealed to the villagers for an explanation and from them I learned the following story:

The god in this shrine has no distinctive name other than *Thundil-karar*, 'the Hook-God'. He is the special protector of the fishing caste, although only a minor god among those worshipped by the villagers at large. Chief of the duties of *Thundil-karar* is the safeguarding of his devotees from attacks by crocodiles. These ugly saurians are plentiful in the River Cauveri nearby and are more than usually dangerous because the principal method of fishing in use lays the fishermen peculiarly open to attack. No boats are found on these upper reaches of the river although coracles are sometimes used. To capture the *hilsa*, a large kind of herring which ascends the rivers of India in immense shoals in order to spawn after the manner of the salmon, the local fisherfolk float downstream when the fish are 'running', supported on a short block of wood across the chest. Each man is armed with a large net mounted on an ovoid frame having a very short handle; this he holds immersed in front of him as he floats. Whenever a fish strikes the net, the man instantly raises it and takes out the fish which he strings on a cord tied round his waist. Sometimes a hungry crocodile takes toll, for the fisherman has no means of defence.

The friends of the victim, overwhelmed with grief, are firmly convinced that because of some neglect on their part the god has withdrawn his protection. A special and elaborate festival in his honour must be arranged. At it, offerings are made by a low-caste man—no Brahman will officiate—and a sheep is slaughtered, sometimes fowls as well, in order that the anger of the god may be appeased and that he may once more defend them from the death that lurks in the river. Vengeance, too, is sought and vows are made to ensure the god's help. Thereafter, with lightened hearts, confident that all is well once more between their god and themselves, they set to work to prepare the means for their enemy's destruction.

The village blacksmith turns to and beats out a great two-armed hook, an exact replica in shape though not in size of an old-fashioned ship's anchor minus the stock; each fluke is doubly barbed. A short but stout rope is also made out of coir yarn; to one end is fastened a buoy consisting either of one or two nodes of giant bamboo or of a block of light, buoyant wood; to the other end are tied scores of thin cotton cords, 6 to 7 feet in length and these in turn are made fast to an iron ring or shackle at the near end of the shank of the anchor-shaped hook.

While smith and rope-maker are busily engaged upon their tasks, someone goes off and catches one of the ownerless pariah dogs that swarm about these villages. When all is ready the men troop down to the quiet reach of the river where they believe that their enemy has his lair. Here they drive a stout forked stake into the mud a few feet from the edge of the river. It is planted in a slanting position, the forked end inclined towards the river. The crocodile is to be angled for and the dog is to be the bait. After the dog is killed, the legs are cut off and the two-armed hook inserted and concealed within the body in such a way that its presence will not be suspected. The buoy is carefully arranged in the fork of the stake so that it will be dislodged and become free whenever the rope connecting it with the bait be pulled. The length of this rope is also adjusted to ensure that the bait shall hang a few inches above the mud just beyond where the water laps the bank. When the lure has been completed to the satisfaction of the headman of the caste, the crowd disperse. A watcher is posted out of sight but nothing is expected to happen for some time, most likely not until the bait begins to diffuse an odour grateful to the depraved taste of a crocodile.

Sooner or later, provided that *Thundil-karar* has been adequately propitiated, the crocodile sniffs the air appreciatively and proceeds to investigate. Following the scent he soon sights the bait. A little while is spent in reconnoitring the ground, for crocodiles are suspicious creatures; nothing stirs, so, feeling satisfied, the reptile makes a quick rush, a snap, and presto! the bait has disappeared into the capacious maw. At the same moment the buoy falls out of the fork with a thud, sometimes landing on the snout of the animal. Startled, he lashes round and plunges in a flurry back into the river. The trouble instantly increases. The dog is a dainty morsel, just high enough to give the crocodile the thrill that delights a gourmet, but what of this stuff sticking between his teeth? He tries to cut it through and free himself of the annoying tangle and this he could easily do with one snap of his jaws were the strands twisted into a compact rope; as they are all separate like a mass of loose yarn, a few may be severed but never enough to allow him to get rid of the beastly thing. The crocodile retires in disgust to his lair not recking of the buoy on the other end of the rope; this floats on the surface, indicating to the watcher on the bank the course taken by the prospective victim and the spot where he elects to rest.

The villagers take no action. Were they to do so the effect would probably be to relieve the crocodile of his trouble, for if he wished he could at this stage manage to disgorge the undigested morsel. He must be left in peace till it be judged that sufficient time has elapsed to ensure the digestion of the bait. As soon as this has proceeded far enough the double hook concealed in the dog's body is set free within the reptile's stomach. Should he now try to eject it, the barbs catch either in the wall of the stomach or in the gullet; seldom indeed does he manage to get rid of it.

The villagers are presently given the signal. A few of the hardier spirits, usually near-relatives of the dead man, wade and swim toward the buoy floating near the crocodile's lair; seizing it, they bring it within the reach of the others who tail on to the rope with all their might. A veritable tug-of-war ensues. Should the crocodile be of exceptional size he puts up such a fight that it taxes the combined strength of everybody to haul him out of the river. Then the killing! While the experts rain death blows, the rest shriek and dance with joy and excitement, belabouring and abusing the carcass to their heart's content.

The last scene is the presentation to the god of some of the viscera. The fatal hook is also dedicated to him and added to those already decorating the shrine.

Such in substance was the tale told by the villagers; none could tell anything about the history of the method; their fathers had taught it to them and *Thundil-karar* had always lived in their village. 'Can your honour not see how very old the temple is?'

Actually the method is probably as old as human civilization itself, dating back to the time when early man began to find how advantageous it was to combine the forces of several families for the pursuit of the common good. In the Nile valley 2400 years ago a variation on the Indian method was already old and in common practice, for we find Herodotus telling us that the Egyptians 'bait a hook with a chine of pork and let the meat be carried out into the middle of the stream, while the hunter upon the bank holds a living pig, which he belabours. The crocodile hears its cries, and, making for the sound, encounters the pork, which he instantly swallows. The men on shore haul, and when they have got him to land, the first thing the hunter does is to plaster his eyes with mud. This once accomplished, the animal is despatched with ease, otherwise he gives trouble.' (Book II, ch. 70.)

One of the minor consequences following the tidal wave of Muhammadan conquest that engulfed Christian Egypt in the seventh century was the virtual cessation of pig-rearing; no longer dared the convert to Islam bait his crocodile hook with a chine of pork; instead, as we learn from Leo Africanus who travelled in Egypt about 1515, a live sheep or goat served as a substitute. In the words of John Pory, who did Leo's African *Travels* into English in 1600:

> The fishers binding a strong and large rope unto some tree or post standing for the nonce upon the banke of Nilus, fasten unto the end thereof an iron hooke of a cubite long, and about the thickness of a man's finger, and upon the hooke they hang a ramme or a goate, by the bleating noise whereof the crocodile being allured, cometh foorth of the water, and swalloweth up both the baite and the hooke, wherewithal feeling himself inwardly wounded, he strugleth mightily and beateth the ground, the fishers in the meane time pulling and slacking the rope, till the crocodile falleth down vanquished and dead: then they thrust him in with certain darts and javelins under the shoulders and flanks where his skin is most tender and so make a quicke dispatch of him...of these beasts I saw above 300 heads placed upon the wals of Cana [*Qena*], with their jaws wide open....The Egyptian fishers use to cut off the heads of crocodiles and to set them upon the wals of their cities.

(The custom last mentioned still survives, for in 1929 I saw several crocodile remains ornamenting house fronts on the outskirts of Omdurman.)

A variation on this procedure recorded by Wilkinson (1841, 235) as in use in Egypt in the early part of the nineteenth century is almost identical with that employed in India on the Cauveri river. This time a dog is the bait used, but instead of having a mighty hook embedded in its interior, the dog is tied to a stout stick, sharpened at both ends; such a gorge is quite as effective as a hook, for when digestion sets it free from the attached bait the tension on the rope, as the crocodile endeavours to escape, causes the stick to turn at right angles and to embed its sharp ends in the walls of the stomach or the gullet.

In Bengal a method akin to that described by Leo Africanus is employed at the present day; it makes clear details whereon Leo is obscure. When a crocodile is seen in the neighbourhood of a bathing ghaut, a long rope is brought out and to one end is fastened a wisp of jute having hundreds of strands; this free end of the rope is armed also with a three-way barbed hook. A stake is fastened in an inclined position in shallow water to serve as a fishing-rod. A loop of the long rope is then lightly secured to the end of this stake and so arranged that the bait, frequently a living puppy, hangs a foot or so above the surface of the water with the prongs of the hook between its legs. The other end of the rope is fastened to a tree on the bank. When all is properly adjusted, the villagers retire to a distance and watch developments. Attracted by the yelping of the puppy the crocodile investigates and seldom fails to take the bait. Unable to bite through the wisp of jute strands, he struggles vainly to escape, for the barbs of the hook are firmly embedded in his stomach. His agony is short; the villagers swarm down to the river and drag the struggling animal to land where it is quickly despatched.

An almost identical method is used in South America. Waterton in his delightful *Wanderings* tells how the Indians of British Guiana form a four-pronged hook out of four tough pieces of hard wood a foot long, about as thick as the little finger, and barbed at both ends; these are tied round the end of the rope in such a manner that if the rope be regarded as the shaft of an arrow, the sticks would form the head, with four barbed ends pointing backwards. This contrivance is baited with the flesh of the agouti, the entrails being wound round the rope for about a foot to protect it from being easily bitten through. The arrangement of the fishing-rod from which the bait is suspended is identical with that in use in Bengal, but in this case the bait is not a living, yelping puppy; instead, the Indian beats loudly upon the empty shell of a land tortoise. Waterton was told that this is done to let the alligator know that something is going on; the Indian means it as the alligator's dinner-bell (Text-fig. 27).

Of quite a different type is a diabolical method of dealing with these brutes much favoured by vengeful Bengali mothers who have had a child carried off by a crocodile. According to A. J. Reynolds (1932, 159), the bereaved parent, intent upon making the punishment fit the crime, buys a couple of kids; one of these she slits open; after eviscerating it she fills it tightly with unslaked lime and then stitches up the opening.

Having got ready the stuffed kid in this way, she takes its living companion down to the river, to the place known to be the haunt of the crocodile.

Here she tethers the kid to a stake just clear of the water and leaves it. The disconsolate kid, frightened and unhappy, begins to bleat. If the crocodile be anywhere about he hears this and sets out to investigate the noise, hopeful of another banquet. The moment he shows his ugly snout above the surface, the woman rushes down to the live kid and rescues it, cleverly substituting the stuffed one in its place. She returns to her hiding place among the bushes with the live kid in her arms. By twisting its tail, she makes it voice still more pitiful cries, again attracting the crocodile. Seeing nothing suspicious, he slithers ashore and makes a rush for the stuffed

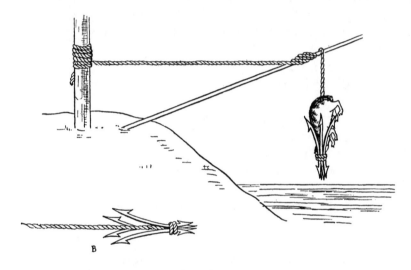

TEXT-FIG. 27. Method of hooking an alligator in South America.

kid. Hurriedly swallowing it he slips back into the water to digest the tit-bit at leisure. Nothing happens till the gastric juice of the reptile's stomach dissolves skin and flesh sufficiently to bring the unslaked lime into contact with this fluid. The slaking of the lime that follows causes agony greater than if the animal had swallowed live coals; the wretched beast dashes hither and thither in its misery, lashing the water into foam as the lime burns through the walls of its stomach. The death struggle quickly comes and in a last effort to escape from its sufferings it flings itself on the bank. Not satisfied with compassing its death, the villagers wreak their vengeance on the quivering carcass, hacking and mutilating it with savage fury till it loses all form and semblance—a mangled mass over which the vultures and the village dogs squabble for hours.

In Sarawak and North Borneo the method of catching crocodiles is essentially the same as that followed in Egypt, Bengal and South America. A stout wooden gorge is embedded in the carcass of a dead monkey (a dog or even a fowl will also do) at the end of a plaited rattan rope, many yards long. When a crocodile seizes the bait, the men who are on watch follow and eventually drag the crocodile ashore. There they proceed to pinion his legs securely. While this is being done, the crowd address their victim in eulogistic phrases, but as soon as his legs are safely bound down, they howl at him and deride him in abusive terms for his foolish credulity. Then they rip his belly open to look for human remains, eventually hewing him into pieces (Ling Roth, 1896, 1, 447).

On the mainland, in the Malay Peninsula, the fisherfolk of Perak substitute an iron bar in place of the Bornean wooden gorge; otherwise the procedure is identical. (*The Field*, 22 January 1938.)

Two other methods of slaying members of the crocodile family deserve record, although in neither instance is a baited hook required.

The first is one mentioned in an old Spanish *History of Mexico* by Clavigero (1788, 1, 384); no attack could be simpler but the attacker required the courage, adroitness and skill of a Spanish bull-fighter or disaster would befall him. The idea was to gag the brute with a gorge. As Clavigero writes:

The fisher presented himself before the alligator, carrying in his hand a strong stick sharpened at both ends, and when the animal opened its mouth to devour him, he thrust his armed hand into its jaws, and as the alligator shut its mouth again, it was transfixed by the two points of the stick. The fisher waited until it grew feeble from the loss of blood and then he killed it.

The other simple way of destroying crocodiles is one practised in Madagascar by the Betsimisaraka, who entertain such a horror of these creatures that they endeavour to propitiate them by every means within their power. They address them respectfully and at a certain spot in the river known to be a favourite haunt of one of their kind, large pieces of beef are thrown in from time to time, often daily, while a goose or some fowls are special tit-bits occasionally offered as a sop to satisfy the voracious appetite of the arch-enemy. But if these means fail to gain his goodwill and to induce him to abstain from attacks upon his benefactors, the villagers know how to take adequate reprisal should he be so ungrateful as to kill or maim anyone belonging to the village. A ball of dried flax is covered with a coating made from thin slices of beef, skewered or sewn together. This is dropped into the water near the lair of the enemy. In due time the savoury odour of the decaying meat guides the crocodile to the new offering. After the lure has been swallowed, the fluid within the beast's stomach causes the flax to swell, and eventually death from this obstruction occurs. The carcass is then drawn to land, amid great rejoicing, and treated with every mark of contempt; eventually the body is thrown upon a fire, a burnt offering to whatever deity the villagers revere (Little, 1884, 104–5).

IX

CATCHING AND CURING THE BOMBAY-DUCK

The Bombay-duck does not sport feathers as everyone is aware who knows anything about a real curry as opposed to the miserable counterfeit concoction of the untravelled European chef; it has a body encased in a sheath of delicate scales and is, indeed, a fish, though to look at it when it appears on the table to give relish to our curry, it has much the appearance of a fragment ripped off the dried flesh of an Egyptian mummy.

Few Europeans ever see it in the living flesh or undergoing the primitive curing given it before being shipped to Bombay, the world's emporium for this delicacy. It is found in greatest abundance off the Gujarat and Bombay coasts, and more particularly off the wide and shallow entrance to the Gulf of Cambay. Diu Island, an important outpost of the Portuguese when they were the lords of the seas and coasts of India, is one of its greatest fishing centres; in the season, October till April inclusive, scores of large fishing-boats from the Portuguese seaports on the Gujarat coast go there to engage in the Bombay-duck fishery.

These boats are trim weatherly craft, of about 20 tons register, built of teak throughout, and intended primarily as cargo carriers. They are, indeed, the finest wooden vessels plying on the coasts of India; formerly their dimensions were much greater, the shipwrights of Gujarat and Bombay frequently building boats up to 100 tons and possessing skill adequate to the construction of much larger ones, now, alas! no longer required. It is worthy of remembrance that many a stately king's ship and stout East Indiaman was built in the Bombay naval yard in the spacious days of John Company by the same class of shipwrights as those few surviving in Gujarat.

In the construction of the smaller craft we are here concerned with, the planking is most ingeniously fastened together by a system of double-tongue and groove jointing. The grooves and tongues are fashioned by the shipwright by means of a curiously dumpy adze; he disdains the use of lines and gauges, depending entirely upon his eye as a guide. Before any plank is fitted permanently into position, the upper edge of the next lower strake is smeared first with a coating of red ochre and then with another of gum damar boiled in oil, over which is spread a thin layer of raw cotton.

In their rig these boats are single-masted, hoisting the local form of lateen sail. Except for a short decking at each end, they are open, but when engaged in fishing the waist is decked over with a temporary flooring made of split bamboos on which the men drowse and sleep during the hours when they lie to their net, awaiting the turn of the tide. The crew of each boat numbers from seven to nine. By religion the majority are Hindus, by caste Machchis or fishermen, a community despised by high-caste people, a condition which has been of the greatest assistance to the missionary in his efforts to convert this class to Christianity!

They are decent, quiet folk, who put into everyday practice a sound and common-sense form of socialism; among the crews there are neither masters nor servants. Every man of them has his own appointed duties and the produce of their common labour is shared equally among the men in each crew. Each man brings two bag-nets, together with the necessary gear of ropes, buoys, floats, etc. The owner of the boat or the man who hires it on behalf of the venture, receives an equal share with the others as his remuneration. For this he has also to maintain the boat in perfect sailing order. So long as she is on the fishing station, all subsistence expenses, the cost of food and drink and so forth, are defrayed from a common fund, the net profit being divided at the end of the season.

They are a lithe, muscular, sun-scorched crowd. Burnt a dark shade of brown, exposure to sun and sea-spray dries their skin so thoroughly that it is no uncommon sight to see them make some simple calculation, perhaps a rough reckoning of the day's catch and its value, by scratching the figures upon the skin of the thigh, a sliver of wood or even the finger-nail serving as pencil. Figures so made stand out white and conspicuous and are easily read upon the dark skin (Pl. XII, fig. A).

The essential appliance used in fishing is an enormous bag-net. If the water be comparatively shallow as off the Bombay coast, say up to 8 fathoms, each net is secured by four short ropes to two huge posts driven deep into the sea-bottom. The nets are conical in shape when extended; they average 150 feet in length with a circumference at the mouth of 250 feet. The meshes decrease gradually from 4 inches square at the mouth to half an inch or less at the cod end. To the latter is attached a 7-foot length of netting which serves as a funnel for emptying the net into the boat after opening the cod end.

Off Diu, where the greatest catches are usually made, the water is so deep that stakes cannot be used and the nets have to be extended by means of four long bridles attached to two piles of anchoring stones, placed about 45 feet apart. Each pile consists of twenty great rectangular sandstone blocks, each about a hundredweight or more in weight, with a hole at the centre for the passage through of the stout rope which ties them together. They are curiously made ropes, for each of the stout strands is made up of twisted leaflets of the date palm wrapped round with strips of the leaf of another palm, the palmyra or toddy palm.

When the piles of anchor-stones are laid out at the beginning of the season, two palm-leaf bridle ropes, about 7 inches in circumference, are made fast at the lower ends to each pile of anchor stones. One of each pair of bridles, longer than its fellow, is buoyed by a large log of light wood, while a strong cord runs also from this buoy to the free end of the second rope.

To set the net, the ends of the four bridles are taken aboard and attached at equidistant points on the circle of the net's mouth; to keep it distended, a barrel-float and two wooden buoys float up the upper section of the net's mouth and serve also to locate its position. Nets are overhauled and emptied before the turn of the tide, either at the end of the flood or of the ebb, and reset at the beginning of the ensuing ebb or flood as the case may be (Pl. XII, fig. B). One boat generally works several nets, either two or three when they are set to stone-anchors, four or even more in the case of staked nets. In the traffic-crowded waters in the vicinity of Bombay, these stake-nets are a standing menace to shipping and this necessitates great care when navigating during the hours of darkness.

A strong tidal current is needed to maintain the nets in distended working order; during neap tides, from the 7th to the 11th, and from the 22nd to the 26th of each lunar month, the current being too slack for this purpose, the nets are detached and taken ashore for repair and, when necessary, for barking.

At the end of the season the anchor-ropes are cut away close to the stones and utilized the following season as lines on which to hang the fish while drying. The stones are too heavy to be removed and so are lost to the fishermen at the end of each season.

As the piles in use are fixtures and as the shoals cannot be counted upon with certainty to be found in one particular depth, each crew generally lay out heaps of anchor-stones at two different depths, one at 3 to 5 miles from shore, the other 6–8 miles seawards, according to the depth of the sea at the place where they are fishing. The cost of these stones is a heavy annual expense. Those who can afford to employ timber stakes are under much heavier initial expenditure but when once set up, they last for years.

The *bumla*, as the Bombay-duck is called in the vernacular (its scientific name is *Harpodon nehereus*), is a gregarious fish, hunting for food in enormous shoals, the prey consisting of prawns and other small crustaceans. It runs from 7 to 9 inches in length; the body is cylindrical, pale and almost translucent in appearance when alive, its flesh soft and flaccid in consistence.

Its voracity is vouched for by the wide stretch of its jaws, armed with strong, needle-like teeth, well fitted to seize and hold fast its prey.

If the bag-nets happen to be set in such a way as to lie athwart the path of these shoals, huge catches are made, but alas! no care is taken to prevent damage to the fish and everything is straightway emptied from the net and slithered into the bottom of the boat; the little *bumla*, a few inches long, higgledy-piggledy with giant *ghōl* (*Sciaena*) weighing 40 to 50 lb. each. A second and sometimes a third catch may at times be emptied on top of the first caught fish and it may be any length of time up to 20 hours before the boat returns to port, so eager are the men to catch everything possible when shoals are passing in exceptional abundance. When this happens the first caught lots become tainted and unfit for food long before they reach shore.

Neither salt nor ice is ever used either afloat or ashore in the treatment of the *bumla*. Such as are deemed fit for curing—and the curer interprets this condition most liberally—are sorted into baskets by women and rinsed in sea-water by the simple process of a deft rotation of the filled basket to and fro in the tide for a minute.

To dry them, the fish are hung in pairs astride worn-out and discarded anchor-ropes stretched between upright posts, the under-jaw of one thrust through that of the other, the long sharp teeth acting as retaining barbs (Pl. xiii, fig. A). For market they are packed in large flat circular bundles, 24 to 30 inches in diameter, each containing about 2000 fishes. According to the size of the fish, so the bundles vary in thickness and diameter; thin fishes are said to be better flavoured and more delicate than the larger and thicker ones.

Pieces of old netting are used to secure the bundles which have no other covering and are therefore exposed to contamination of all sorts. Much as the Bombay-duck is esteemed by Anglo-Indians (old-style!), it is questionable if it would be such a favourite were they to see the crudity and lack of cleanliness characterizing its preparation. However, what the eye does not see, the heart does not grieve for, and it is as well to remember that it is only of recent years that the preparation of several items relished in our own cuisine has been above suspicion.

Well-prepared *bumla* in first class condition is a deservedly esteemed savoury, but it scarcely deserves comparison with the equivalent dainty so greatly relished in Northern France and the Channel Islands—the toothsome *caplin* brought home from the Newfoundland banks by the cod-fishing fleet of picturesque sailing-vessels hailing from the northern ports of Brittany.

Just as the immense shoals of *caplin* serve to attract multitudes of cod to the Newfoundland banks, so do the myriads of *bumla* serve as an attraction to the great *ghōl*, the magnificent golden-mouthed Corvina (*Sciaena aquila*), which here on the north-west coast of India follows the shoals of small fish into certain favoured bays in exactly the same way as it does on the north-west coast of Africa, where, in Levrier Bay under the lee of Cape Blanco, is one of the greatest and most historic seasonal fisheries in the world—the annual resort for four months in the year of a great fleet of Spanish fishing schooners from the Canary Islands.

An interesting accessory industry of the Indian fishery is the preparation of the swim-bladders of certain fishes, those of the *ghōl* being the most valuable, for export as 'fish-maws', the raw material from which isinglass is manufactured. These bladders, after soaking in sea-water to wash off blood and dirt, are dexterously ripped open in an ingeniously simple manner; a long, slender knife of razor-like sharpness is hinged at the top of a groove in a long tapered cone upon which the bladder is drawn in the same way as a glove finger upon a digit. When laid open by levering the knife upwards, the vascular lining membrane is peeled off by hand, leaving the connective tissue wall of the bladder snowy white. Thereafter it is dried in the sun on horizontal sheets of coconut-cord netting raised on poles a few feet above the ground.

These Hindu fishermen are very superstitious and sacrifice to local deities for success and safety at sea. The most celebrated shrine is that of Madhvar Devi, on a bold and dangerous headland near Diu. Here has been erected a tiny four-square shrine (Pl. xiii, b). The goddess is represented in low relief on an upright slab within. A little skirt of faded Manchester cloth is hung across the image, just above the waist; the rest of the figure is daubed thickly with many successive coatings of vermilion paint. The fishermen sacrifice goats and fowls before the shrine and lay small portions at the foot of the image, thereafter taking the offerings to their camp to eat! No accredited priest takes the simple service which is carried through by one of the older men; the killing of the sacrificial animal, the sprinkling of its blood before the goddess and the smearing of a little vermilion upon the deity's face is sufficient ceremonial. Such sacrifices are made at the beginning of the fishery season and whenever a long spell of bad luck has been experienced.

In time of danger at sea, Hindu sailors and fishermen act precisely as do men of like profession in the Mediterranean; they vow an offering to the deity of their home shrine if their prayers for safety be answered. Those of one little port in South India when in danger of shipwreck take special precaution to impress on their protecting goddess the earnestness of their vow; they wrap a rupee, the usual offering, in a piece of cloth and nail it to the mast.

The superstitions of Indian seafaring folk are, indeed, a fruitful field for study; they believe as a rule in the evil eye and mark their boat in diverse ways with a view to neutralize the malignant influence. Most common perhaps is where, among orthodox Hindus, the symbol of the central deity of their cult is employed—the three horizontal bars denoting the worship of Siva being the most common (Hornell, 1946, 273).

X

THE GREY MULLET TAKES EVASIVE ACTION

The habit common to several species of grey mullets of leaping from the water to surmount an obstacle in their path is one that set the early fishermen a difficult problem to solve if they were to obtain good catches of these fishes, a matter of the utmost importance to people living on the banks of estuaries and backwaters, for grey mullets are usually the most numerous of the fishes found in these waters. The solutions found successful in present-day practice make an interesting study; although all are based upon this habit of leaping over obstructions, the methods of overcoming the difficulty are curiously varied.

The most common of these devices is the 'veranda-net', so called because it forms a horizontal platform or veranda upon one side of a vertical wall of netting. This type of net is used extensively in the Eastern Mediterranean, particularly in the great coastal lakes or backwaters of the delta of the Nile, and thence introduced to various places east and south of Suez, whereof Mauritius is notable for the extensive use of this net. The Japanese have also adopted this method with great success.

In Palestine it is a prime favourite of the fishermen on account of the great success it achieves in the pursuit of two most elusive species of grey mullet, the *mouksal* and the *kabban* (*Mugil chelo* Cuv. and *M. cephalus* L.). To capture these fishes, the usual practice is for two boats, starting from the same point, to encircle a shoal by shooting around it a small-mesh light seine-net, 150 fathoms or so in length with a depth of 3 to 6 fathoms, corked above, leaded below. One boat makes a half-circle to the right, the other a half-circle to the left. While they are doing this, two other boats rapidly lay out in the same manner along the median section of the seine a special form of trammel (*m'battan*); this is a threefold net, having a median wall of small-mesh net placed between outer walls of very large mesh; to keep it extended when shot, it has light reed or bamboo poles fastened across it, the ends attached respectively to the opposite margins (head and foot) of the trammel, which are neither corked nor leaded. The poles, each about 9 feet in length, float the net horizontally on the surface of the water, so that when one margin of the net is tied here and there by slip knots to the head-rope of the seine, it forms a threefold platform or veranda at right angles to the vertical wall of the seine (Pl. XIV, figs. A and B).

As soon as the first pair of boats have completed the shooting of the seine in a circle, they anchor after passing one another in order to overlap the ends of the net which they hold. When the shooting of the horizontal veranda-net is also complete, with one margin attached to the head-rope of the seine, the second pair of boats pass between the two stationary ones into the space now enclosed. While some of the crews of both pairs of boats remain aboard making all the din and turmoil possible by shouting and by splashing with their oars in order to terrify the fishes, others jump overboard and while swimming and diving begin to draw together the foot-ropes of the two halves in order to prevent the fishes from escaping underneath. If the net is shot in shallow water, this is not necessary as the seine boats' crews lessen the circle by hauling the greater part of the net aboard.

Alarmed by the noise and splashing, the mullets begin a wild stampede, endeavouring to escape by leaping the head-rope of the seine. When they do this, few make such prodigious leaps as enable them to clear the platform of the horizontal trammel; the great majority fall upon it, where, after a fruitless and frantic struggle, they become entangled in its loose threefold layer of netting. From this they are picked out by the fishermen in the attendant boats.

The nets used in this method of fishing are called in Palestine *tiweek*. Their use is restricted to the day-time; each requires the service of twenty-eight men, seven each in the two boats that shoot the seine and seven others in each of those that shoot the horizontal net.

Although two pairs of boats are required to operate the *tiweek* net to the best advantage, smaller nets may be set by a single pair of boats, one shooting the seine and the other the horizontal trammel.

In Mauritius this type of net-fishing has been brought to a high degree of development and refinement, with several variations in the details of its operation. On one occasion I was present at a specially extensive series of fishing operations in a reserve within the reef on the south coast; fourteen boats participated and when the great length of the seine had been shot and the veranda-net attached, pandemonium broke loose! The men in the boats struck the gunwales with sticks and beat the water with their oars, whilst a crowd of men who jumped from the boats into the water did their utmost to make still greater noise. Soon the shoal of mullets enclosed within the net began to dash wildly towards the far side of the encircling net, where the veranda-net was laced to the middle section of the seine. For a few minutes the air was alive with scores of mullet frantically leaping over the head-rope of the seine. A very few escaped, the rest, falling short of safety, landed on the platform of treacherous net, there to flounder and splash in unavailing effort to escape, till at last, energy exhausted, they lay gasping or supine, tangled in the treble meshing. A few landed on the gunwales of the attendant boats and some with a desperate despairing wriggle managed to tumble overboard into safety.

After the first wild rush, the pace slackened; odd groups of fish from time to time took their jump for freedom, generally losing it. Meanwhile, by clever tactics the seine-boats, while hauling aboard further lengths of the net, gradually moved the entire net into a favourable position in very shallow water. By this time all the jumping mullets had made their leap; the fishes which remained enclosed belonged to kinds of fish that do not jump. To catch these, a small net was brought within the circuit of the seine-net and its foot-rope drawn under the huddle of fishes that remained. By clever manipulation of this net the fishes were brought to the surface and slithered over the gunwale into one of the boats.

Variations in the details of operating this net are numerous in order to adapt them to the varying physical conditions prevailing locally and with regard to the number of boats and men available; sometimes more intricate in the working; sometimes rather simpler.

FISHING RAFTS. When on fishery duty in Malta in 1931 I came across a most effective device based also upon this leaping habit of certain species of mullet. Locally it goes by the name of *kannic*. It has the great advantage from a fisherman's viewpoint of being inexpensive to make and operate.

It consists of a large raft-like structure composed of canes (*kasal*) bound together to form a rectangular float of considerable size, varying with the width of the place where it is to be used. When ready it is placed across the entrance to a creek, where it is anchored by the four corners. From the side turned towards the head of the creek, a vertical wall of netting is suspended.

One or more boats having previously passed up the creek beyond the *kannic*, these, upon receiving a prearranged signal, are rowed noisily towards the raft, the men beating the water, splashing frantically and shouting with demoniacal fury.

Any mullets present rush down the creek in fright, till they find their path obstructed by the wall of netting hung from the raft of canes. This net they leap over, only to land upon the surface of the raft whereon are piled loose masses of straw and the branches of trees; in these the fishes become entangled and prevented from leaping further.

So destructive is this device that it is one of those which are discountenanced by the fishery authorities.

An almost identical manner of 'fishing' is common in Bengal for the capture of the species of mullet called *Mugil corsula*. This mullet, which has become completely naturalized in the fresh waters of the Gangetic plain, is one of the commonest and most highly esteemed of the fishes found there. Unfortunately it is exceedingly shy and very difficult to catch by ordinary fishing methods, whether these be nets or lines. So the ingenious Bengali fishermen have devised a form of floating raft, margined by some bright object, of such a deceptive appearance that the mullets are induced to leap from the water and to land upon the floating structure behind.

Of the several variations of this method of fishing, the commonest is the *chāli* or *chānchi*, a rectangular float of reed matting, made from the *nāl* reed, measuring from 20 to 30 feet long and 3 to 4 feet wide. It is floated flat on the water with a row of the white leaf-stems of the plantain attached along the two long margins. These serve the immediate purpose of keeping the raft afloat and, later, of inducing the mullets to leap from the water. The float is towed by one man by means of ropes attached to the two corners of one of the long sides, while another follows in the wake of the raft. When a shoal of mullet is seen, the *chāli* is towed to the bank and the second fisherman by beating the water drives the fish towards the net as they come near it; the gleaming white surface of the plantain stems frighten them and they essay to escape by leaping over them. Those that do, fall upon the matting, where the first fisherman gathers them up.

A variation of this reed-mat float is adapted in the Murshidabad district for use in conjunction with a boat. Usually it is considerably broader than the one above described, its dimensions being generally some 28 feet by 8 feet. It is stretched and supported by bamboos tied along its length. Attached along the hinder side, supported by sharp upright pieces of bamboo is a narrow net, 4 inches in height. To each corner of the opposite side of the mat, which is the one facing the boat, is tied a long rope buoyed by shola floats at intervals. A second long rope without floats is next tied to the end of each of these float ropes, completing the trap. The mat raft now floats at a considerable distance from the boat, parallel with it. The passing of a shoal of mullets is then awaited. When one appears swimming within the space enclosed by the two long ropes connecting the raft and the boat, each of the two ropes is passed to the opposite end of the boat to bring the floats close together. This and the noise made by the men aboard the boat frighten the fish; with skill in manœuvering the rope the shoal should be headed towards the raft when many will leap upon it. The marginal net prevents the fish leaping off and the mat may either be drawn to the bank or to the side of the boat and the fish removed by a landing-net, after being knocked on the head with a bamboo stick.

The same method, employed at Muzaffarpur, shows considerable variation in detail. The raft is here made of jute stems rolled up for a couple of feet at either end to form a low barrier to prevent the fish swimming off the mat. For the same object and also to stiffen the raft, bundles of reeds are bound along the longitudinal margins, the whole forming a shallow rectangular tray, some 24 feet long by 7 feet wide. To each end of the mat raft on one side is attached a long rope with shola floats as in the Murshidabad form. It is also operated similarly.

The most highly elaborated form of this raft-trap is where the raft is much narrowed and attached in a sloping manner along one side of a canoe having this side cut down almost to the water's edge. The raft, or rather screen, which may be 20 feet or more in length, is not more than 18 inches wide, and is supported by a number of transverse bars of split bamboo projecting 8 inches towards the canoe to form a rough hinge arrangement in conjunction with a bamboo pole lashed along the length of the canoe. This screen, made of jute stems, is let down obliquely till its outer margin is a few inches submerged. On moonlight nights, mullets swimming near, possibly attracted to it by the white gleam of the bleached jute stems, become scared when they come against the screen, and try to leap it, only to fall within the canoe. This method, called *chota sirkī* at Muzaffarpur, is one very commonly employed throughout Mongolian countries. The Burmese, Siamese and Chinese all make extensive use of it, varied only in detail. In Bengal, the Binds, found chiefly in the districts of Malda and Pabna, specialize in this *chāli* system of mullet-fishing, attaining wonderful dexterity in the manipulation of the different varieties of these scaring devices.

The principle embodied in the use of these mats is also employed frequently in conjunction with the barring of small water courses—drainage channels, narrow creeks and the like—with a view to catch fish both going upstream when the rains begin and on their return when they are over. A common plan is to throw up a bund or dam across the stream, leaving a narrow passage in the middle. This is barred by a strong bamboo screen which permits water to pass but not the fish. A boat or a raft is moored on the side of the screen opposite that from which the fish are approaching. Finding their passage barred, those species that jump, essay to leap the barrier and in so doing fall into the waiting boat or upon the mat raft. At night a light or torch is burned in the boat to attract the fish. Sometimes, as in Malda, when a greater space for the passage of water is necessary on account of the strength of the current or the greater volume of flowing water, the earthen bund is replaced by a long stretch of screens behind which a curtain-like net is hung above the water-level between two rows of poles, into which the fish jump.

Apart from Bengal, we find closely related variations employed throughout many lands in the Far East. The Chinese, Burmese, Siamese and Annamites all make use of the idea. The basic principle involved is the employment of a device which will ensure that certain fishes of the Grey Mullet family shall attempt to leap clear of a suspected obstacle; failing in this, they fall into the trap provided. Among the peoples named, the main feature of all the variations of the fishing method under notice is the use of a downwardly inclined attachment fitted outboard upon one side of the fishing-canoe, with the outer edge partially immersed with the intention of inducing fishes to leap from the water. The attachment is generally a broad board, painted white; sometimes it is a frame of wickerwork, decorated with leaves, designed to frighten any mullet which may happen to encounter this fearsome contrivance.

In the lands mentioned, this fitting is often reinforced in one way or another, in order to render the device more effective. One addition is the erection in the canoe or boat of a low wall of netting supported upon a number of uprights on the side opposite that where the painted board is attached. This netting blocks the flight of any fishes which otherwise might succeed in jumping clear. Another is to fill the bottom of the boat with branches or small bushes, to ensure that fishes falling into the boat may become entangled and so prevented from attempting a last desperate leap to freedom.

One man suffices to operate a fishing-trap of this nature. Standing at the stern he paddles his little craft obliquely across what he considers is the probable run of the fish; the boat with its whitened board slatting up and down, in and out of the water, throws the surface into noisy turmoil; this and the gleam of the ghostly board dazzlingly lit up by the moonbeams (moonlight nights give the best fishing results) confuse and frighten the mullets whose run is disturbed. In their endeavour to escape the threatening danger they leap wildly out of the water, purposing to jump clear of the obstruction. If their leap be powerful, the low barrier-net on the off-side frustrates their attempt, causing them to fall back into the boat, there to flounder helplessly amid a tangle of branches and twigs.

Although in common use in parts of China and Indo-China, few descriptive accounts are available, owing in some measure to the fact that this method of fishing is pursued normally by night, when the European is taking his rest. Gudger (1937) has collected many of the descriptions available; among these, the most curious supplementary addition is that figured by Lindeman (1881, 244) from Annam. Here we find the fisherman using a long 'rake', projecting obliquely, outwards and forwards, from the stern. This 'rake' is armed with long bamboo tines, frayed into a bunch or brush of feathery splints at the outer ends. The noise of the splashing caused by this broom-like device as the boat or canoe is urged forward, scares the mullets and turns their course towards the boat; already greatly alarmed, the sight of the strange white side-board reflecting the moon's bright rays, turns their fright into frantic terror and impels them to leap blindly forward to escape the fancied danger—a fruitless endeavour.

In Tonquin, during nights when moonlight is feeble or absent, a flare is sometimes used to attract the fish towards the fishing-boat, and come within the baleful influence of the 'mirror board' as the painted plank, inclined downwards to the water, is sometimes called.

Strangely enough a trick almost identical with the Chinese sloping-board device is to be found in Africa, among certain fishermen on the Congo (Burrows, 1898). These men employ a wide hurdle-like fitting hinged along one side of their canoe, instead of a painted board. Its width, however, is so great that the men find it difficult to collect any fish which may strand themselves on its outer section. To overcome this disadvantage a rope is attached to each outer corner of the hurdle. Then, whenever a travelling shoal of mullet has attempted to overleap the obstacle, the two men who form the crew haul on the corner ropes, thereby raising the outer edge sufficiently high to ensure that a jerk or two will dislodge any fishes stranded upon the surface and send them hurtling into the cavity of the canoe.

But it is in South India that this strange fishing device attains its most effective development. There in the southern backwaters on the west coast of South India (Cochin and North Travancore) I have seen a highly specialized form of this Bengal device, called in South India *changapayikkal* or *changodam*.

To operate it, two long and very narrow dug-out canoes of equal length are required. These are connected in such a way that the hulls diverge forwards from the stern (Pl. xv). This is accomplished by means of two connecting poles; one of these is placed athwart the bows, the other crosses the sterns immediately in front of the steersmen. As the forward pole is 12 feet long, and the after-one only 8 feet long, and as they are lashed by their extreme ends to the canoe hulls, the bows are held apart rigidly at a distance of nearly 12 feet whereas the sterns are less than 8 feet distant from one another.

A net extended outboard upon seven sticks slanting upwards and outwards, runs the whole length of the outerside of each canoe. Each of the extending sticks is about 54 inches long; of this, about 18 inches are inboard, leaving a length of 36 inches to project outboard at an angle of about 25° from the horizontal. The netting, usually measuring about 30 feet in length, is tied to the projecting sticks both at the foot and at the head in such a way as to bag slightly between each pair of sticks. These are spaced apart from $3\frac{1}{2}$ to 4 feet.

As a low freeboard is desirable, several spadefuls of sand are placed in the bows and also amidships of each dugout; none is required at the stern as here the weight of the man who forms the entire personnel of each canoe is sufficient for the purpose. Stakes are next placed athwart each canoe just below the gunwales and these are loosely laced together by a network of thin branches.

Finally, a long dragging device made up of short pieces of chain connected by lengths of rope, is stretched from bow to bow of the two dugouts, of length sufficient to form a slack semicircle reaching back to abaft amidships between the two dug-outs. To keep it in position a cord runs from the centre of this rope-chain to the centre point of the connecting pole at the stern of the canoes.

When the canoes are loaded and manned, the gunwales are depressed close to the water. In this condition they are paddled or poled slowly along the backwater in places where mullets and prawns are expected to be plentiful. The purpose and utility of the chain sections in the drag-rope then become apparent. The clanking of the links and the disturbance caused by their rough passage over the bottom frighten the fish, which leap wildly into the air; some fall into the canoes where the tangle of branches hinders their escape by a fresh leap; others, which take longer jumps, land on the sloping nets disposed along the outer sides of the canoes.

This method of fishing is of comparatively recent introduction, dating, it is locally said, from about the beginning of this century. The person who introduced it had probably received inspiration during a visit to Bengal, Burma or the Malay Peninsula, where analogous methods are in use.

Dimensions, etc.

Hull of each canoe length from 28 to 30 feet; beam, 18 inches; depth, 9 inches.

Number of transverse ridges (*munnikal*) left when hewing out the hull and answering in function to ribs, 12; they are spaced apart about $2\frac{1}{2}$ feet. Thwarts, 4.

Length of net when fitted, 27 feet; width, 30 inches.

A connecting-link between this Indian device and the much simpler Chinese method is described by Gray (1878, II, 293). In this a stone is suspended, pendant at the end of a short rope hung from a point about mid-length of the boat. As the paddler at the stern urges his craft forwards, the suspended stone occasions such disturbance in the depths as to scare whatever mullets are about. Terrified by the racket the fish rise to the surface; there, perceiving the ghostly white board gleaming threateningly in their path, they attempt to escape by leaping over it. Alas! this is seldom successful; the distance is too great for most of them, the failures falling instead into the well of the boat to become the reward of the fishermen's craft.

To determine the centre where this curious system of trapping fish had its origin, we have only to consult its geographical distribution to find the answer. There is little if any doubt that it owes its invention to the fertility of the inventive faculty anciently characteristic of Chinese mentality, the fount whence flowed so many pre-inventions of many discoveries and technical methods perfected in later centuries, such as the whole technique of the silk industry and of the manufacture of porcelain, together with such useful aids to navigation as the mariner's compass, the drop-keel or centre-board and a host of other aids to human progress and comfort.

Whether any of the occurrences of the Chinese trapping device mentioned above as being met with in Indo-China, India and Africa in some modification or divergence are entirely of local and independent invention is beyond our knowledge to determine. Chinese contact is adequate to account for the presence of some form of the device in Bengal, as of course is also the case with its occurrence in all parts of Indo-China, but doubt arises when we find the method in operation in Africa by a tribe living on the banks of the Congo. Even there, independent invention is very doubtful, for many Indonesians, migrants from Java, and strongly influenced by Chinese contacts, voyaged to Madagascar in the first millennium of our era; these people subsequently sailed occasionally up the East African coast during voyages to Aden. It is probable that they established trading and slaving stations on the African mainland and it is possible that mullet-trapping may have been carried, along with other Far Eastern traits of material culture, far into the interior of Africa by the media of trading expeditions, culture contact and Muhammadan missionary zeal (Hornell, 1934).

Of all lands in intimate cultural relationship with China, Japan alone does not appear to have any related or parallel fish-trapping method; in this instance it may be that the attractions of cormorant fishing outweigh those of the 'canoe-trap'.

XI

NETTING FOR HILSA, THE INDIAN SHAD

In the greater Indian rivers, with the exception of those of Malabar and Bombay where natural conditions are unfavourable, the hilsa occupies an analogous position to that of the salmon in British streams. This fish, the hilsa, strange to say, is a near relative of the common herring, rather longer and considerably deeper and heavier in body. It has many of the attributes of its northern relative, notably a delicious flavour, rich oily flesh, and a multitude of fine bones, troublesome at table to those who do not possess the knack of separating them deftly from the flesh. Like the salmon it is born in a river, passes its youth in the sea and remains there till, with approaching maturity, instinct impels it to return to its birthplace to breed. In its life are more mysteries than surround any other common Indian fish, for we know neither with certainty in what part of the ocean it lives during its immature period, nor the exact location of its breeding-grounds; we have little definite knowledge of the circumstances under which it spawns, and as little as to when the young migrate to the sea or what is the ultimate fate of the spent fish. What we do know is that annually when the floods of summer set in with the coming of the south-west monsoon and the melting of the snows in the Himalayas, the rivers, rushing headlong to the sea in spate, are crowded with great shoals of hilsa coming from the sea to spawn. The breeding-grounds curiously enough have never been located with any exactitude; certainly they are far upstream, for multitudes of unspent hilsa are met with a long way inland, frequently scores and even hundreds of miles beyond the farthest tidal influence. Only mature fish ascend the rivers, fishes running generally from 3 to 5 lb. in weight.

In the Ganges, Indus, Godaveri, Kaveri and other similar rivers of considerable length and permanence, the coming of the hilsa is awaited eagerly by the riverside population; its rich flesh and delicious roe are among the few delicacies these people can look forward to. For a fish so highly valued and widely distributed the nets used are naturally many and varied. Simplest of all is the great hand-net used on the Kaveri. This is wide-meshed and in form resembles the small shankless hand-nets used in rivers to catch prawns—the ovoid frame increased to a length of from 5 to 6 feet. To use this in the deep-river channels which the hilsa frequent, the fisherman carries into the water a short, thick block of light wood; resting his chest upon this he floats downstream holding the great net in a slanting position in front of him (Text-fig. 28). The moment a fish strikes the net, he raises it, seizes the fish, kills it by biting its head and threads it on a cord tied to his waist. Having gone a mile or as far as he thinks fit, the fisherman turns and walks upstream to his starting-point, to repeat the operation again and again.

But the excitement of hilsa-fishing in the Kaveri is as nothing compared with the animated scenes on the Indus, where the hilsa gives employment to hundreds of fishermen the whole length of Sind. The usual device is a development of the Kaveri one. The net used has grown, however, into the form of a gigantic landing net, with a shaft 20 feet long and with a bag much deeper in proportion. Armed with this the fisherman floats downstream, either seated in the bow of a small raft-like punt, or supported by gourds, enveloped in netting and strapped to his back. Or he may, when the fishing reach is short, elect for a third, still more primitive method, and

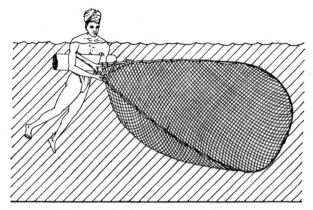

TEXT-FIG. 28. A hilsa fisherman floating downstream on the River Kaveri, supported upon a wooden float.

float down the river balanced precariously over the mouth of a great globular chatty or earthenware pot made for the purpose by the village potter. The net is used as on the Kaveri, but in a nearly vertical position. The hilsa, pushing upstream in vehement haste to reach the spawning grounds, blunders into the net and in spite of the extraordinary agility of this fish, man triumphs, being prepared; a sharp twist of the shaft imprisons the fish in the tail of the net and the fisherman, cautiously shortening his grip, finishes it with a knife and consigns it to the bottom of the boat or the depths of the chatty beneath him; if his support is gourds, a needle is passed through the eyes or the gills and the fish is threaded on a string with the previous victims in tow beside the float.

In specially favourable spots, where the river is deep alongside one bank, the fisherman with his net immersed walks downstream along the shore, adjusting his pace to the speed of the current. In the vicinity of towns both the gourd-float and the chatty are preferred to the punt; they give better results and involve practically no expense. The chatty is considered the better killing method, but where the reach within which the fish are caught is long, the fisherman prefers the gourds—their weight is less for the long weary tramp back to his starting-point.

But whenever the fishing reaches are far from market centres, the fishermen form curing camps and fish entirely from boats. These are veritable Noah's arks, for all save the bow, where the fishing is done, is covered with a light penthouse roof of grass matting whereunder the fishermen, their wives and children live in friendship and amity with a couple of goats, a dog or two and perhaps a cat. Perched on outriggers a number of tame pelicans, fed with the coarser fish taken, may be considered to form part of this happy family; most of the time they pass dozing lightly, an observant eye opening at intervals to make sure that no chance food is missed.

THE GANGES. The hilsa being by far the most important food-fish in the Ganges, and its fishery one that engages the attention of the vocational fisher-castes far beyond any other, it is natural that extremely ingenious and effective methods have been evolved by a race noted for its inventiveness in this art. Of these, three deserve detailed description. These are the *kharki* or *sharki-jāl*, the *shānglā-jāl* and the *kona-jāl*.

The first two are purse-shaped nets with hinged mouths which can be shut instantly when desired; they may be termed clap-nets. The *kharki-jāl* is the smaller and simpler. It has a roughly rectangular bag-net of the same shape as that of the *toni-jāl* of Bogra from which it appears to be directly derived. The widely gaping mouth is attached to two long and flexible bamboos, one representing the head-rope, the other the foot-rope, of ordinary nets. These two hinge together at each angle of the mouth, in the same manner as the two sides of an old-fashioned clasp-purse or of a modern vanity-bag. A vertical bamboo attached to the middle of the lower lip of the mouth passes upwards through a ring at the middle of the upper lip. The net when ready is lowered a few feet into the water by two ropes passing one from each side of the prow of a boat hurtling downstream with the current (Text-fig. 29).

These ropes are attached to the upper lip of the net, one on each side of the vertical bamboo which is held in the hands of a fisherman sitting at the fore end of the boat. A second man steers and if need be paddles. The mouth is kept distended by the first man pressing downwards upon the vertical bamboo. When a hilsa, hastening upstream intent on breeding, enters by chance the wide open mouth of this great purse, the trained touch of the fisherman senses this at once; instantly he hauls on the bamboo, thereby shutting the mouth of the trap. The net is then hauled aboard, the captured fish taken out and the net hung again in the open position over the boat's bows.

This net may run over 25 feet wide, with a length of bag of over 8 feet, the mesh about 2 inches from knot to knot.

The *shāngla-jāl* is a refinement of the *kharki-jāl*, more elegant in form and more delicate and responsive in manipulation. In outline the mouth is semicircular, the two flexible bamboo lips often over 25 feet in length, bent into a deep graceful curve that gives an easy hinging motion when the mouth has to be shut. The bag is rather short, being at most 10 feet from front to back. The two ropes suspending it from the prow of the boat—it is used in the same manner as the *kharki-jāl*—are attached at the hinged corners of the mouth, instead of half-way between them and the centre of the net as in the simpler form. Again the closing handle of the latter is replaced by a long cord. A knot on the rope above the ring in the centre of the upper lip limits the opening of the mouth. A fairly heavy weight,

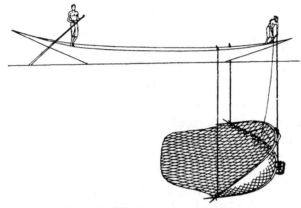

TEXT-FIG. 29. A fishing dingi drifting down the Ganges with its *shāngla-jāl* lowered into position to catch hilsa.

a brick or a stone, is attached at the middle of the lower bamboo lip. All these variations are designed primarily to enable this net to be used at much greater depths than the *kharki-jāl*, which is primarily designed for the capture of fishes swimming fairly close to the surface. Indeed the *shāngla-jāl* can be used at any depth found in the Ganges, as the closing rope may run to a length of 15 fathoms. A fine cord, dividing into three branch lines at its lower end is attached at three points on the upper surface of the net. The other end of the line is held taut in the fisherman's hand; the slight jerk or quiver it transmits when a fish enters the net is sufficient signal—the net is instantly closed by a jerk of the cord. The net is then hauled up and emptied.

When the hilsa season is in full swing the great reaches of the lower Ganges and its main tributaries and effluents—the Padma in particular—are crowded with hundreds of fishing dinghies carrying *shāngla* nets, half of them drifting rapidly downstream with their nets set, the other half sailing or paddling upstream with the nets aboard, the great arcs formed by the bent bamboos of the closed mouths showing like gigantic upturned crescents, as the nets are carried with the mouths closed and the hinged corners upwards.

The third of the special hilsa nets is an extremely complicated form of boat-seine provided with huge bag-shaped pockets at intervals. It is the *konā-jāl*, also called *bhāshā-gulli* in Pabna. It is one of the longest seines used in fishing, measuring some 300 feet in length with a depth between the head-line and foot-rope of 30 feet. It is strongly made of sunn hemp with a mesh of 2 inches, knot to knot. Like nearly all Gangetic nets it is tanned with *gāb*.[1]

Bamboo floats are tied lengthwise to the head-line at intervals of 16 feet, but no sinkers are attached to the foot-rope. Every 30 or 40 feet apart are openings, 12 feet wide, leading into large conical small-meshed bag-pockets, 20 feet in length. The mouths of these are distended by two bamboo poles crossing one another obliquely from corner to corner. The mouth of each of these bags is trapped by means of a secondary funnel-shaped pouch opening inwards and having an aperture at its apex. The tail end of the main pouch is bunched together when in use by a cord-lashing. The net is operated by two boats each loading half of the net aboard. It is shot by the boats across the current and then the ends are worked round so that the operation finishes by enclosing a circular area of water. The hilsa that find themselves within this ring of net, in their frantic struggle to find a way of escape, rush through the trapped mouths of the pockets and become prisoners. They are taken out by undoing the lashing around the tail ends of the various pockets. Like so many other seines, this net is also used as a drag-net; it may also be staked out and employed as a stationary multiple bag-net. It is much used for catching hilsa in winter and spring in the deltaic districts.

Drift-nets and gill-nets are employed chiefly when the rivers are in flood—May to October. At this time the depth of water is too great and the current too strong for the easy or effective employment of seine-nets and drag-nets; hence nets of good killing quality that may be floated with the current are greatly in demand. Of these the most typical and powerful is the great *chhandi-jāl*, which, like the three special nets just described, is employed chiefly to capture hilsa when the shoals are ascending the great rivers in the rainy season. The *chhandi-jāl* is made like all large drift-nets in a number of short lengths, which are tied together into a long fleet when about to be shot. Each piece measures 36 feet in length by 24 feet deep. Twenty-four pieces usually constitute a fleet. The nets are of hemp tanned with *gāb*,[1] and have a mesh of from $1\frac{1}{2}$ to 2 inches, knot to knot. Floats of bamboo or of light wood are used to buoy the head-line at intervals of about 20 feet, while the foot-rope is weighted at similar intervals usually with annular burnt clay sinkers, or fragments of brick. The net can be

[1] *Gāb* is the Bengali name of the fruit of *Diospyros embryopteris*.

adjusted to float vertically at any desired depth. This large net is shot in the evening from one or several of the extra broad boats called *chhandi*, built specially for this method of fishing. When all the net has been paid out, a rope to the hither end of the net is retained in one of the boats and the net and boat allowed to drift downstream. Or the boat may be moored and the net allowed to stream out with the current. The hilsa in their ascent strike these nets and become gilled. Usually the net is examined at intervals of 1 to 2 hours to remove any enmeshed fishes.

XII

FISHING AT PORT SAID

PORT SAID has several picturesque aspects; of these none surpasses in interest that side of her life which is in the realm of the fisherman. Of late years with the steady development of the port and its conversion in part into a fashionable summer resort for middle-class Cairenes, its importance as a fishing centre has grown steadily. To the Italian colony much of this prosperous enterprise is due. First came a few of the picturesque lateen-rigged trawlers that contribute so much charm to pictures of Venice and its neighbourhood in Turner's time and in our own days to those of Chioggia and other fishing ports at the head of the Adriatic. Their numbers gradually increased and if the traveller goes down the Port Said breakwater in the early morning before the fleet leaves for the fishing-grounds, or towards sunset after the boats have returned to port with the day's catch, he may count as many as thirty-two or even more boats, bows on to the wall (Pl. XVI, fig. A).

Seen thus, they look clumsy craft, broad in beam, extremely bluff in the bows and round at the stern, the single stout mast short and stumpy if judged from a yachting standpoint. What the mast lacks in height is made up by the length of the yard of its great lateen sail slung from the masthead, for all these boats are felucca rigged.

The stem rises free 1 foot or 18 inches above the low bulwarks and in some, a diminishing number, its summit is crowned by a mop-head of sheepskin, laid on wool-side outwards. A hawse-pipe is conspicuous on either bow, made prominent by a massive wooden encircling ring-frame, tailed upwards at the after end, so made as to look like a huge fat comma lying on its side. Seen end on and a little way off as these boats sail into port, the conspicuous hawse-pipe ornaments give the bows a queer suggestion of a gigantic cat's face with eyes wide open and unblinking. Curiously enough the Romans actually called the hawse-pipe the *oculus* or eye, for when an opening had to be cut in one bow through which to pass the hawser, it was located exactly at the place where the decorative painted eye had been placed at that earlier period when the anchor-rope passed over the rail instead of through the bulwark.

Many of the sails show traces of having been decorated with gaily painted bands and symbols after the custom prevalent on the Venetian coast. No prettier scene can be imagined than the sight of this little fleet of fishing-boats streaming out in pairs from the harbour mouth into the golden pathway of the risen sun as they set out on their day's work, unless it is a sight of the same fleet lying becalmed in picturesque disorder and with flapping sails when the wind falls just after they have got under weigh. The more energetic get out a pair of great sweeps and, so aided, the lumbering craft begin to crawl slowly towards the open sea where a little wind is hoped for. The toil of the crew in moving the huge sweeps gives the onlooker a faint glimmer of comprehension of the cruel efforts the galley slaves of ancient and medieval times had to put forth in order to send the great war-galleys of old foaming through the sea to attack their adversaries.

These Italian boats work in pairs; hence it is always an even number we see tied up in port. The net they use is the original of the modern trawl, the forerunner indeed of every variety of the beam and otter trawls. Compared with the huge net employed by a steam trawler, this Italian trawl is small and weak. On the fishing-grounds off the delta of the Nile, where the bottom is soft and muddy, the very lightness of the latter net is its outstanding merit; having no heavy weights along the ground-rope, it skims the ooze so lightly that it runs no risk of burying itself and having some portion torn away when being hove in. It is a net particularly suitable to a soft and smooth bottom such as that lying off the mouths of the Po, the home waters of these boats, or as here off the delta of the Nile. Each fishing-boat has a bridle-rope attached to one side of the net's mouth; separating to a suitable distance, the two boats sail on a parallel course, towing the big bag between them and adjusting the spread of their canvas to the speed at which they wish to tow. Their catches appear to be fairly remunerative, but large quantities must be caught, for prices are low. Red mullet, bream of various kinds, gurnards, yellowtails, rays and the like, are among the commonest of the fishes caught, together with great quantities of large prawns and of a magnificent blue-clawed swimming crab, that has passed into the Mediterranean from the Red Sea since the opening of the Suez Canal; some, too, of the fishes and prawns caught are similarly newcomers to the inland sea.

The cutting of the Suez Canal has added materially to the fishery wealth of the eastern end of the Mediterranean, a benefit not dreamed of by de Lesseps when he schemed and slaved for the success of his plans. The blue crab is particularly interesting in this respect for it took 30 years to get through the canal. However, on entering the Mediterranean it found conditions so remarkably favourable that it has increased in a most extraordinary manner. Hundreds of tons are landed at Port Said and on the adjoining coast; it is no uncommon sight to see such large quantities taken ashore from a boat that the only way to deal expeditiously with them is to shovel them with spades into the waiting cart.

These boats do not usually leave port on Sunday, a day devoted to the repair of boats and gear. To clean and paint or repair the bottom, the boats are careened, hove down on their beam ends, alongside and with the aid of their partner boats.

Seine-netting, an Egyptian method as old as the pyramids (Pl. xvi, fig. B), is carried on even more extensively than trawling. Hundreds of men follow this as their daily occupation along the coast, east and west of Port Said. Their nets are of great length, but of moderate width, standing 12 feet deep when in the water. A boat carries out the net, shooting it in a deep semicircle in the usual manner. As many as ten men tail on to each of the hauling-ropes; so long are the net and these ropes that even with this considerable manpower it takes nearly an hour to get the net ashore. Excitement grows as the bunt comes close in; everyone is on the *qui vive* to know if a big catch has been made and a number of lads spring up from nowhere, intent on stealing what fish they can if opportunity offers. Mullet, red as well as grey, some soles, and a quantity of crabs and prawns are the catch to-day; with curses the vagrant boys are driven off to come back again a moment after, like persistent flies to a bald pate. While some of the fishermen overhaul the net and begin to load it again into the boat, others gather up the catch and send it off to market.

The midday siesta on the sands is full of colour; groups sit about drowsing, others gamble with knuckle-bones; the industrious squat mending their nets and some prepare the dark red tanning liquor wherein to dip nets requiring rebarking.

Mullet fishers who erect barrier-nets upheld on long poles, with part extended obliquely over the water to catch those fish that attempt to leap clear of the barrier—the habit of certain species of grey mullet—are occasionally to be seen; they are to be recognized by the load of bamboos carried in their little open boat, for forming the palisade of net (Pl. xiv, fig. B). On one occasion I wished to take a photograph of a couple of these boats as they were being brought alongside the breakwater. My object noticed, the men covered their faces with their hands and leaped hurriedly ashore. They harboured no ill-will, for a few minutes later one of them asked me for the loan of a knife with which to divide a huge water-melon among the men comprising the two crews. And when this had been done, the cool, juicy core, a sparkling honeycomb-like mass of crisp pink cells, glittering in the sun, the luscious tit-bit of the melon, was offered me with smiles—a delicious morsel indeed at midday on an Egyptian summer day.

Of all the fishermen on the Egyptian coast, the most picturesque is the cockle-gatherer, his cockles, however, being the shells of a little wedge-shaped mollusc known scientifically as *Donax*, but which has no common English name, though abundant on many of our sandy shores. This fisher carries a long hand-dredge with harrow-like teeth along the lower edge of its iron frame. Armed with this, he walks backwards in knee-deep water, scraping the sand with his implement, behind which is a short bag of netting to receive the shells dislodged from the sand. To free his hands and give more hauling power, a broad belt of webbing passes round his hips, the ends fastened to the lower part of the dredge-pole.

All these fishermen, whether Egyptians or Italians, are prone to superstition. Allusion has already been made to the mop-heads on the stems of the Italian boats. This is a lingering survival of a custom once prevalent from end to end of the Mediterranean; in its original form, still surviving in parts of Arabia, the skin on the prow was the pelt of an animal, either sheep or goat, offered in sacrifice to a deity for the protection of the boat and her crew. Little by little it has become a meaningless custom, its real significance as little understood by those who practise it as is that of our own field scarecrow to the farmer who puts it up ostensibly to frighten birds—which fear it so slightly that sometimes they built a nest in it!

The harmful power of the evil-eye is widely believed in by all the fishermen; on the Italian boats the horseshoe is favoured, the usual place to affix it being either the forward edge of the stem or a point immediately to one side of this.

Moslem fishermen prefer to protect their small boats by a painting upon each bow of a hand with the fingers making the sign of the horns, either formed by extending the forefinger and little finger and closing the others, or by extending the thumb and forefinger and turning down the others against the palm.

XIII

CATCHING FLYING-FISH OFF THE INDIAN COAST

I HAD long known that an important fishery for flying-fish was carried on in summer off the Coromandel coast of India, between Point Calimere in the south and the city of Madras in the north; till 1922 I had no opportunity to see the actual operations. Fishermen had given me accounts of the method employed and, while I was fairly satisfied with the story in the main as obtained and sifted by a cross-examination that made me feel entitled to the wig and gown of a barrister, some details were still obscure or doubtful.

In the south, in the Tanjore district, the season runs from the end of May to the middle of July, varying in length with the onset and strength of the south-west monsoon rains. As soon as the river floods arrive in earnest, the Rivers Coleroon and Kaveri begin to discharge such an enormous volume of silt-laden water that the sea for many miles from shore becomes discoloured with reddish sediment in suspension; this ends the fishing season, for flying-fish never enter muddy or discoloured water. As the river floods north of Tanjore are meagre in volume compared with those of that district, the flying-fish fishery in the north usually lasts to a later date. In the neighbourhood of Cuddalore, it generally continues until the middle of August, while off Madras, in years when the rains are delayed greatly, it may even extend into September.

Two species of flying-fishes are recognized by the fishermen, a larger called distinctively *thai-kola* ('Mother-Kola') and a smaller one, usually called simply *kola*. The former has spotted pectoral fins and is *Cypsilurus poecilopterus* (C. & V.). It is caught on hand-lines. The smaller species, 8 to 9 inches in extreme length, is also a *Cypsilurus*; its pectorals are notably long and are purplish in colour with a hyaline border. The popular belief is that the larger species is the male and the smaller the female, but there can be no doubt that they belong to distinct species.

The fishing-grounds are situated on the edge of soundings, where the sea-bottom rapidly deepens to the 100-fathom line and beyond. Here begins that wide stretch of ocean characterized by the intensity of its colour, where the green of the in-shore waters changes first to a deep indigo tint merging soon into a dark, forbidding colour that is appropriately named *kala pani*, or 'black water', by the people of India. So long as a voyage is within the green-water belt of the coastal region the orthodox Hindu is content, but to cross the gloomy *kala pani* is a thing he may not do without loss of caste and with the penalties and expenses consequent thereon. From this it follows that the emigration of Indians to Fiji, Mauritius, Natal and British Guiana, which reached large proportions during the second half of the nineteenth century, was restricted almost entirely to Muhammadans and the low-caste Hindu sections of the population.

Like their enemies the bonito and the swordfish, flying-fishes are essentially oceanic fish; they seldom wander shorewards beyond the limits of the *kala pani*; the nearest fishing-ground is never less than 10 miles off shore, and, often enough, fishermen have to go out 15 or even 20 miles before they sight the shoals for which they search. These men possess neither canoes nor plank-built boats; their only craft is the catamaran, a shaped raft made by tying together, side by side, a definite number of logs of wood. Of these there are several types. Most common is one of three logs, manned by two fishermen. Such is useless for the flying-fish operations. A catamaran suitable for this purpose must be roomy enough to carry a number of men, normally seven, and to transport a heavy cargo of fish if the venture prove successful. It must also be able to sail and be of stout construction, for the fishing season coincides with a time when the weather is unsettled, when a storm may suddenly arise, blowing the primitive craft scores and maybe hundreds of miles out of its course. To answer these requirements the deep-sea catamaran is constructed of seven main beams, squared, of light wood obtained usually from Ceylon; each averages from 30 to 35 feet in length. Each log being tapered slightly towards the fore end, the form of the completed craft becomes definitely wedge-shaped in plan after the addition of an elegant upturned prow of five pointed pieces cleverly jointed on to the forward ends of the seven main logs. It must not be imagined, however, that it is just an ordinary raft of triangular shape; in the light of long experience, all its proportions have been carefully elaborated and specialized, making it, indeed, the highest development of the catamaran in use on the Indian coast (Pl. xvii, fig. A). Its logs are all slightly curved, making the 'deck' moderately concave and giving the structure fine lines for skimming over the sea—the draft is barely 1 foot when loaded. Although of such shallow draft and without the vestige of a keel, it is usually able to keep a course without making excessive leeway. Two powerful lee-boards are brought into action when necessary, one placed abreast the fore-mast (they generally step two masts), the other nearly abreast of the steering paddle, 12 feet in length, which in itself is so long and broad as to subserve the same purpose.

The masts are short, raked forward and stepped in shallow sockets cut in the outside log of whichever happens to be the leeward side for the time being. The sails are a form of primitive lateen, the foot controlled by a boom which, however, does not extend forward beyond the mast (Pl. xvii, fig. B).

A fore-stay and a back-stay are present but shrouds are absent, their place taken by the halyards and by a short side-strut to each mast having its foot stepped on the outer log on the windward side; its upper end is lashed to the mast about 3 feet above the mast-socket. Even with these substitutes for shrouds there is always danger of the masts and sails falling overboard should the craft be taken aback by a sudden change of wind; this, however, is of rare occurrence in the case of these flying-fish catamarans, so steady is the wind at the season when these craft are at sea.

The tack angle of the sail is cut off, giving a short luff. By means of a doubled grommet, the sail is hung from the mast-head. Reefing in heavy weather is effected by rolling up the lower part upon the boom; the head of the sail can also be lowered to some extent, as a series of notches are cut at intervals below the mast-head; the yard grommet and stays may be lowered to rest in any one of these. Each sail is provided with a sheet and a vang or guy made fast to the upper end of the yard.

On the morning fixed for our expedition a selected catamaran came alongside the fishery steamer at 6.20, about an hour after the rest of the fleet had set sail; the crew, with characteristic Indian philosophy, had indulged in an extra hour's sleep, for they knew that the steamer, although leaving port an hour later, would still reach the fishing-ground about the same time as their unaided comrades.

The principal dimensions of this craft, by no means the largest of the fleet, give a good idea of their considerable size; they were as follows:

Length overall, 33 feet; beam at the forward lashing, 4 feet; at the after lashing, 7 feet; foreyard, 29 feet long; after yard, $21\frac{1}{2}$ feet; steering oar and the two lee-boards, 12, $10\frac{1}{2}$ and 9 feet respectively.

Giving our catamaran a tow, we had leisure to note the gear carried. The masts and their spars lay to one side of the craft, the upper ends resting on the prow. On the opposite side were three large bunches of two kinds of densely-branched shrubs, each tied to one end of a coil of coir rope; these were the lures intended to attract the flying-fishes. One of these is usually a short branch of the screw-pine (*Pandanus odoratissimus*); the others are bundles of the little leguminose shrub called *Kāvālai* in Tamil (*Tephrosia purpurea*),[1] commonly abundant in waste places. Sometimes the branches of the neem (*Melia azadirachta*) are used if *Kāvālai* is not readily procurable.

The general equipment consists of four short catamaran paddles, thin blade-like and slightly curved, with a beaded edge along one margin to give purchase for a secure grip. Three oars, each with a long blade tied to one end of a pole, a single-fluke wooden anchor with a stone lashed cross-

---

[1] *Tephrosia* is a genus of plants used in many parts of the world as a fish poison. (See Chapter XVIII.)

wise at the butt to form a stock, two dip-nets, several coils of spare rope, some light floats, empty baskets for the fish, a large earthen jar filled with drinking water and a rather inconsiderable bundle of cooked rice. A narrow scoop used in ordinary boats for bailing out water is here carried for the purpose of dashing water on the thin cotton sails; this completed the outfit.

Each of the two dip-nets is made by lashing the short sides of a rectangular piece of netting, $5\frac{1}{2}$ by $4\frac{3}{4}$ feet, to the outer ends of a pair of poles, about 7 feet in length. In use the poles are held parallel to one another with the net stretched lengthwise between.

When we had gone about 12 miles seaward, the sea assumed a deep indigo colour. The depth was 23 fathoms. Our fishermen called out that they descried flying-fish in shoals but not rising in flight from the surface; they asked to be cast loose. It was now 8.40 a.m. Soon afterwards numerous other two-masted catamarans came up; most went farther seawards than our position but several dropped sail and started fishing close by. These were part of the large fleet we had already seen some distance from port when we left anchorage at 6.25 a.m.

The preparations are simple. Sails are furled around the booms, the masts are unstepped and disposed as already described with the fore ends resting on the prow.

The catamaran is now drifting broadside to the wind, the starboard side, on which is the accessory log, being to windward. From this side the men now cast overboard their three bundles of leaves at the ends of three ropes of unequal length; of the set measured, one was approximately 50 fathoms long, the second 30 fathoms, and the third only 10 fathoms. The screw-pine branch was tied to the longest rope, the two shorter ropes carried the smaller bundles, consisting of bunches of *Tephrosia* plants. Each bundle is supported by a small float of light wood, so nicely adjusted that neither it nor the bundle of leaves project above the surface of the water. The catamaran, with its crew standing up, offers some slight resistance to the wind and so drifts more quickly than the leaf bundles which stream away from the catamaran on the windward side.

After adjusting their lures the men patiently await the gathering of the flying-fishes around them. If fish are plentiful, and seen to collect in quantity round any one of the leafy bunches it is drawn very cautiously towards the catamaran with every precaution against scaring away the fishes. Four men in two pairs squat upon the accessory log tied along the windward side of the catamaran, each pair with a two-handled dip-net ready between them. The bush is hauled in so that it comes alongside between the two sets of dip-nets; if fish are plentiful both nets are brought into play and the fishes are scooped out of the sea swiftly and quietly. The outer end of each net is dipped almost vertically into the water, brought up under the fish and then, being raised quickly, the fish slide down the middle of the net into the catamaran where the three remaining members of the crew cram them as quickly as possible into big palm-leaf baskets.

When the lures streamed out from our catamaran were drawn in, the real reason was discovered for the attraction they have for flying-fishes. It is not, as formerly believed, to obtain shade and shelter; it is to find a place suitable for the deposit of their spawn. The proof was plain; the twigs and leaves of the bushes were full of a tangled multitude of tiny colourless eggs provided with innumerable glassy filaments, tough and elastic, attaching them in masses to one another and to the leaves and branches of the plant (Text-fig. 30).

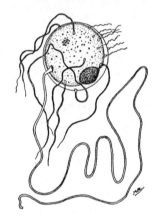

The filaments are of three kinds; first, a single one, stoutest and longest, the egg's main anchoring cable; second, a tuft of from seven to sixteen very tiny ones on the opposite side of the egg; lastly, four to six medium-sized ones mid-way between the first and second kinds. When the eggs are attached only to one another the main and medium-sized filaments are tangled together to form a stout cable of considerable length, from which the eggs project on all sides after the fashion of grapes in a bunch.

I was informed but could not verify the statement that the fishermen sometimes detach the eggs, crush them and throw the resultant mass back into the sea; this is said to attract

TEXT-FIG. 30. Egg of an Indian flying-fish (*Cypsilurus* sp.) undergoing fertilization. The short, sinuous-tailed bodies are spermatozoa; the long filaments are the means whereby the eggs are attached to floating seaweeds.

further numbers of flying-fish which eagerly devour this form of ground bait. That the fish do feed upon eggs of their own species under certain circumstances is certain, for masses of eggs, of the peculiar form described, have been found in the stomachs of some that were dissected at another time.

Floating seaweed, such as the well-known gulf-weed or *Sargassum*-weed, is what the eggs are tangled up with under normal conditions.

In seasons of abundance very large catches are common. Besides being eaten in the fresh condition the fishes are sun-dried, without salt, in great quantities to supply the markets of Rangoon, Penang and Singapore. If adverse winds are experienced on the way home, the catamarans are sometimes so much delayed that their catch becomes putrid and has to be thrown overboard. However, it has to smell very badly before the men proceed to this extremity. Even if 2 days old on landing, they will yet attempt to cure it!

XIV

THE FATAL ATTRACTION OF THE SHADOWS

IN the sea and more particularly in fresh-water ponds and streams, the smaller fishes live a precarious life. They are constantly on the defensive against a host of enemies—predatory fishes, water-fowl and water-snakes, with man himself as the most dangerous of all. Shelter is sought wherever possible among the leaves and stems of water-plants; here small fishes find comparative safety from all except man, dodging pursuit by slipping in and out among the branches of the underwater forest.

Primitive man must have gained knowledge of this habit at an early period in his rise to power, for we find his descendants turning it to their profit in many ingenious and diverse ways over a vast area of the world's surface, particularly in India, China, South-west Asia, and Central Africa. The usual device is to submerge branches and bushes in suitable waters with the object of attracting fishes to their leafy shade and shelter, thereby making easy the task of capturing them in profitable quantity.

'Bush-fishing' as we may term this practice, varies widely in its operation and its details; often it is of considerable elaboration, requiring careful preparation and the co-operation of many fishermen; sometimes it assumes a communal aspect and importance, ending in high revelry. The whole village on such an occasion indulges in the rare luxury of feasting upon an unlimited supply of roasted fish, with the prospect of plentiful food again for the morrow.

In Bengal, in the immense waterspreads that cover hundreds of square miles of low-lying land during the rains, in the innumerable creeks and passage-ways that intersect the Gangetic delta and in the countless village tanks, several forms of fishing based upon the placing of bushes in these waters are practised by the country folk with much relish and profit.

The simplest form of this bush-fishing technique is seen in the fishing of the small tanks and pits found around the peasants' homesteads everywhere in this water-sodden region. During the rains when they are full of water and connected with the general inundation that spreads at this time over the whole land, leafy branches are thrown in. As the water-level goes down after the end of the rainy season, large numbers of all kinds of fishes seek shelter in these pits (*khatis*), induced to do so for the protection which seems to be offered by the mass of branches and twigs they find there. Sometime later the peasants remove these obstructions and catch the fish by hand or by plunge-basket (*polo*). This fishing has considerable monetary importance in the bheel country of Khulna, Faridpur, Bakerganj and the adjoining districts.

Boats not in use are kept submerged to prevent damage to the wood. The interior is often filled with bushes and tree-branches to attract fishes, and then, when a net has been thrown over the boat, it is drawn ashore and the sheltering fishes caught.

In more extensive collections of water more elaborate methods have to be adopted. Three principal variations are in use.

The most elaborate of these comes strictly within the category of net-fishing, but as the other two are those from which this has been evolved, it is desirable to give the description here of all three.

In the simplest form the method is adapted to places where a considerable width of shallow water borders a deep channel; in this case a section of the shallow area, 15 feet or more in diameter, is surrounded with an earthen bund or a bamboo fence, isolating it and separating it on one side from the deeper water; in the barrier an opening about 3 feet wide is left. The space within the bund is then filled with branches of tree. After an interval of 10 to 30 days, large numbers of fishes and prawns, attracted from the deep water without, are found sheltering among the branches. The opening in the bund is then shut, the branches removed, and the water bailed out, leaving the fishes stranded on the mud. This method is practised chiefly by men who are not regular fishermen.

This simple plan of fishing is greatly improved upon by professional fishermen and then becomes one of the most effective means of catching fish employed in this region.

Between September and December, when the waters are subsiding, bushes and branches of trees are piled in suitable spots in a jheel or in some quiet watercourse or creek undisturbed by any violent current. Various kinds of fishes, but chiefly carps and chitals (*Notopterus* spp.), together with the larger prawns, resort to the shelter of the piled-up bushes called collectively *jāg*, *dal* or *kāthās*. As the flood subsides, the rapid growth of water-weeds—filamentous algae and the like—forms a dense felting over the tops of the branches, rendering the shelter increasingly attractive to the fishes and prawns; the smaller among them find much to feed upon among the branches where diatoms and minute crustaceans swarm in multitudes.

To catch the fishes sheltering among the bushes two methods are in use according to the depth of the water. When it is less than 4 feet deep, the place where the bushes are is surrounded by a screen made of reeds or split bamboos laid parallel with one another and roughly woven into long lengths by means of twisted grass or fibre. The width or rather height of the screen, for it is planted edgewise on the bottom, supported by poles at intervals, is about 4 feet. As soon as the 'surrounding' operation is completed, men enter the enclosure, throw the bushes out and secure the fish by means of hand-nets.

Screens are also used in similar manner to enclose areas of shallow water where water-weeds are in profusion.

This kind of fishing requires the co-operation of several men who usually keep two heaps of branches in the water from October to July, when this method of fishing becomes impossible owing to the floods that accompany the onset of the monsoon. They fish one of these heaps each week, in the intervals working areas where no branches have been placed. This gives each shelter a fortnight's rest.

Much more elaborate means are requisite when the water is deeper than 4 feet, with a correspondingly large increase in the number of fishermen. The preliminary operation of forming heaps of branches and bushes is the same as before but on a larger scale; a longer interval is also allowed from the date of depositing branches in the water.

The beginning of March, when the subsidence of the floods has sufficiently reduced the depth of water around and over the bushes, is considered the proper season to begin fishing. By this time, too, the maximum number of fishes have crowded within the shelter, and have become generally of fishable size. The first operation is to fish the surrounding water with a circle of cast-nets. This frightens the remaining fishes into the bushes or *kāthās*, which are then surrounded by numerous lengths of a special form of wall-net tied end to end. The length of this enclosing wall of netting depends on the height and area of the *kāthās*; for large ones as many as ten or twelve sections are joined together, each about 26 feet long with a height of 17 feet. The net is held upright by the head-rope being tied to a circle of poles driven securely into the bed of the jheel or stream and projecting several feet above the surface of the water. The pieces of netting are made specially deep (wide) to permit the lower edge, heavily weighted with elongated earthen sinkers, to rest in folds on the bottom and the upper edge to be carried aloft several feet above the water, to prevent the alarmed fish from escaping by leaping the barrier. After the pieces are laced together, with the exception of an opening in the netting at one point, the fishermen enter the corral in a boat at this place, and after closing the opening behind them, set to work to clear away the mass of branches. This they do by breaking it up and throwing it piecemeal over the wall of netting. When the bottom has been made thoroughly clean with the help of bamboo poles with hooks on the ends, a matter of considerable trouble as the men have also to dive to make sure that all the pieces are removed, the boat is cautiously taken outside, two men being left behind. These dive to the bottom and draw the sinkers attached to the foot-rope on one side of the enclosure as far as possible towards the other side. The same course is followed with the sinkers of the other side, so that the bottom of the corral is covered with two layers of net. Divers now lace these overlapping layers together, and then the men in the attendant boats draw up the centre of the net, driving the fishes to the side of the net, when they are emptied into the boats, or the whole net may be detached from the poles and hauled ashore to be emptied at leisure.

As usual this net has a diversity of names in the different districts. In Nadiya it is generally known as *kumhār-jāl*, as the potter, *kumhār*, is essential to the working of this contrivance owing to the need to weight the foot-rope with a great quantity of earthenware sinkers.

In the sea, bush-fishing is beset by difficulties unknown in riverine and deltaic waters; nevertheless there are two localities where it is carried on upon a considerable scale.

One of these is off the Coromandel Coast of South India. Here a peculiarly ingenious method may be seen, especially off Madras, if some of the catamaran fishermen when they go afloat take with them their *madi valai*, or 'handkerchief net' as we may term it, from its four-cornered square shape. But before it can be used the fishermen have to set their lure. This consists of a long coir rope bedecked with closely set strips of palm leaf (*olai*) nipped between the strands. The lower end is anchored in several fathoms' depth by means of a stone, or much more frequently on this sandy coast, a great mass of fibrous turf. A log of light wood serves to buoy and mark the upper end. To work the net so that it will capture the fishes that hover in the shade made by the bedecked rope, four catamarans are needed. Each takes hold of one corner of the net, two in front and two behind. Those in front let the corners they hold sink to a considerable depth by means of bridle-ropes let down to the required length; the two behind have their corners hauled high up. In this way they advance upon their lure-rope, paddling against the tide with the net between them, oblique in the water, its lower end well in advance of the upper (Text-fig. 31). As soon as the net strikes the lure-rope, which it does low down, the men in the two catamarans in front haul in the bridle-ropes with might and main; on their quickness depends much of the success of the operation. As the forward ropes come in, the lower edge of the net rises, and in doing so erects a barrier to the escape of the fish that were sheltering amongst the olais. The edges of the net are quickly bunched together and the fishes crowded into the centre of the net. The operation is facilitated by the drift of the current causing the anchored rope to stream with the current and so directly into the net as it is drawn along against the current.

In Palk Bay, lying between India and the north of Ceylon, a kindred method is employed, but in this case great bushes and even entire thorn-trees (babuls) are anchored on the sea-bottom. Periodically these bushes are surrounded by nets and the sheltering fishes captured. In the case of small bundles of branches, when the net is closed in all round, divers go down inside and bring the branches to the surface and then, by pulling, overlap the lower edge of one side of the net over the other, so that the fish are herded into one place and captured. This done, the pile of branches is re-anchored and left for several days longer to permit a further lot of fishes to gather in their shade.

Much more elaborate is the procedure when whole thorn trees are put down. These the divers cannot raise, so after a deep wall of net has been placed round three sides of one of these trees, a bag-net is arranged on the fourth or open side, with its mouth facing the submerged tree and its wings overlapping the end of the wall-net that completes the circle. Several divers now swim round the tree and gradually drive the fish from it into the bag-net, which is then closed and hauled into the waiting boat with its catch of fish.

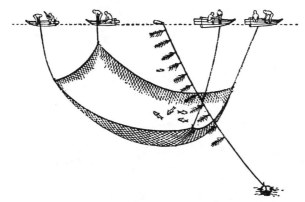

TEXT-FIG. 31. Diagram showing how the *madi valai* is operated.

In China related methods of fishing are in operation; greatly variable in details, all conform to the same basic idea of luring fishes to seek refuge among bushes and branches placed purposely in ponds, lakes and waterspreads. Some of these are described by Thiersant (1872, 166).

It is, however, to the negro fishermen of the Central Sudan that the palm must be given for the development of this species of fishing to the highest degree of complexity and efficiency. The best examples are found in the basin of the River Benue, one of the principal tributaries of the Niger. The Battas of this region are exceedingly clever fishermen, keen and ingenious in their methods; of these, bush-fishing is perhaps the most outstanding, for in it their procedure is a marvel of foresight and patience.

As described and figured by Monod (1928, 265–6 and Fig. 55) this fishing device owes its great success to two main factors, (*a*) the provision of places of pleasant shelter to the fishes, and (*b*) the 'taming' of these fishes by a regular course of feeding over a prolonged period.

The work begins at the time when the water in the river starts to fall; the fishermen place a large quantity of leafy branches over a considerable area of the bottom in reaches of the river suitable for this purpose; as usual this procedure is designed to furnish fishes with the shady retreats they appreciate so greatly. The time to do this is when the flooded banks of the river begin to show again and sandbanks to appear here and there.

A little while later the men build a small platform on piles among the bushes; the next day one of them returns with some food for the fishes. Any village waste will do—a few handfuls of millet-sweepings for example. This is fed to the fish by trickling it into the water from the platform. This feeding becomes a regular daily routine; to give notice of feeding-time

TEXT-FIG. 32. Ground baiting of a bush-filled enclosure on the River Benue, Cameroons.

and to call upon the fish to assemble, the fisher slaps the water with his hand. This signal becomes well known in a short while, and is answered promptly by the fishes. To please the palate of any that may prefer plant food, special dainties are provided, such as the juicy shoots and young leaves of plants of the melon family.

This treatment goes on for about one moon; at its end the bush-littered area is surrounded with a wickerwork palisade except on the side adjacent to the deep water in the middle of the river; here a wide opening is left (Text-fig. 32).

The building of the fence makes no difference to the fishes; they continue to assemble and partake of the generous droppings from the fishermen's platform. They suspect no treachery! During a further two moons the daily repast is provided with regularity.

The climax occurs towards the end of the third month from the beginning of operations. The idyll is about to change to tragedy. One fine morning the almoner fails to appear; instead, the river bank is covered with a swarming mass of people in a hilarious state of unusual good humour. All the village has turned out and many strangers are present.

Among the foremost of the crowd are some carrying baskets full to the brim; their contents are soon being emptied into the water, as the bearers wade out among the bushes. Are the fishes being given a last and glorious repast? Alas, no; instead of food, it is a pulp made from the bark of a forest tree, a species of *Balanites*, the most powerful fish-poison known to the people of the Benue basin. Soon the poison begins to do its deadly work; the stronger and more resistant fishes attempt to flee—all in vain, for the opening to the river has been closed. Stupefied fishes begin to float up, and to catch the remainder the fishermen lift out the bushes and branches and net the fishes that are sheltering there.

The day's work ends with a feast of fish grilled on rods over fires lit on the river's margin—an orgy of gluttony. What cannot be eaten, or stored for future use, is sold to the Fulbe traders who have gathered around like vultures to a carcass.

XV

FISHING FOR OCTOPUS, CUTTLEFISH AND SQUID

THE octopus, although a mere mollusc, has brain-power greater than that of the average fish. It is a wary creature, strong, crafty, and up to many subtle tricks to capture the crabs which are its favourite food or to evade the attacks of enemies. As a consequence, fishermen, who value it as their most killing bait, have to devise super-stratagems, if they are to succeed in catching it in the quantity they require for the baiting of their lines and traps and as a tasty addition to their own diet, should they belong to one of the so-called Latin nationalities.

Occasionally it may be taken with comparative ease. On coasts with a considerable tidal range as has the north coast of France and the Channel Islands, the low water of spring tides lays bare the snug retreats where some of these creatures crouch, awaiting the return of the flowing tide. Fishermen and others make holiday on these occasions, searching rock pools and hide-outs under boulders for octopus, crabs and other dainties not usually taken without special gear. Often the presence of an octopus in one of these retreats is betrayed by an accumulation of broken crab-shells, disposed in an untidy heap before a hole under a boulder. The shore-hunters are armed with gaff-hooks wherewith to haul the occupant out; if it is an octopus, the fisherman turns its body inside out, forcing gills, heart and viscera out through the wide opening of the branchial chamber, 'turning its cap' as the fishermen say.

In the Pacific, in the Cook Islands and other Polynesian groups, the octopus is hunted by divers who carry two sticks, one with a pointed end, the other armed with a gaff-hook. They search for likely holes among the rocks of the sea-bottom, poking the pointed stick into every likely one. If an octopus is at home, he resents this intrusion and wraps his sucker-beset arms around the stick. Then the gaff is brought into play and with its big hook embedded in the quivering body, it is easy to drag it forth and to 'turn its cap' exactly as is done on the French coast.

Another trick practised in the Cook Islands is this: the diver takes down a handful of slaked lime tightly gripped in his left hand, and empties the lime within the entrance to the suspected lair. Any octopus that may be in occupation is so distressed by the powdered lime diffusing through the water, that he issues forth, to be caught and killed (Burnett, 1911).

But the most distinctive trick employed by the Polynesians to deceive the octopus is the rat-lure. This is currently believed by the islanders to

FISHING FOR OCTOPUS, CUTTLEFISH AND SQUID

be based upon the myth which tells of the feud existing between the octopus and the rat caused by the ungrateful and scurrilous taunts of the rat after it had been saved from drowning by the octopus, which had given the rat a ride to safety on its back. Few fishermen in Central Polynesia are without one of these lures. This consists of a cone-shaped stone about 3 inches long. Two oval sections cut from the back of a big cowry shell, such as the brown-spotted *Cypraea tigris*, are tied upon one side of the stone to form the back, with a length of palm-leaf midrib tied upon the other or belly side, and long enough to project beyond the apex of the stone —its hinder end—to a distance of 4 or 5 inches. This represents the rat's tail. Every day that this lure is used, a number of freshly cut narrow strips of tender green coconut leaf are tied on at intervals, to make the tail look more realistic! (Text-fig. 33.)

Thus complete, the end of a fishing-line is made fast to the cord frame around the stone, at a point as near as possible to the centre of gravity.

When taken out to a place known to be a haunt of the octopus, the lure is lowered quietly to the bottom and moved slowly along; by varying the direction of the pull, it is made to progress with a dancing motion; according to the fishermen, the octopus, as soon as it sees this rat-like thing intruding upon its domain, is beside itself with anger, remembering all the rat's gross insults; furious, it rushes out and seizes the rat in deadly embrace, intent upon its destruction! When this happens, the fisherman either dives and seizes the octopus, or, more usually, he hauls the lure and the clinging octopus to the surface, alongside the canoe; so determined to kill the hated rat is the octopus that the fisherman is able to gaff it before it has time to relax its grip and make its escape.

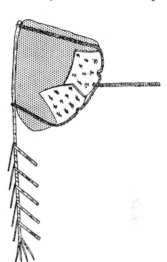

TEXT-FIG. 33. A Samoan example of the 'rat-lure' used to catch octopus in Polynesia.

Another widely distributed method of capturing octopus of small size depends upon their well-known predilection for dark cavities wherein they may lurk, awaiting opportunity to pounce upon any unwary crab that may pass. In Italy and in Japan a large number of small unglazed earthenware jars are tied at intervals to a long line, and laid on the bottom till the next day when the fishermen lift them and extract all octopus that may have taken possession of certain of the jars.

In Italy the jars (*lancelle*) are dumpy in shape, with a handle at each side of the narrow neck to give purchase for attachment to the rope connecting the various jars. In Japan the jars are oblong with long and narrow necks, without handles.

Oblong basket traps, rounded at one end, and made of fine wicker-work are also used in Italy for the same purpose. These have a funnel-shaped mouth at the broad end, with strong grass or cane splints arranged around an opening at the apex or inner end of the funnel. These offer little resistance when forced from without, but close together immediately against any attempted exit. As with the jars, these traps are attached singly at intervals to short branch lines given off from a long main rope.

Sometimes, as in Malta, the octopus is taken with a jigger armed with three or four hooks.

But it is at the southern end of Palk Strait, between India and Ceylon, that the most curious trap is found. The octopus there are mostly of

TEXT-FIG. 34. A small species of octopus numerous on the *Zostera* beds in Palk Strait, South India, ×¾.

small size; they abound in the weedy shallows and are in keen demand by line fishermen, for the flesh is firm and not easily pulled off the hook; their odour too is tempting beyond measure to the fish sought to be captured (Text-fig. 34).

To capture them, long lines are prepared having some hundreds of short branch lines tied on at intervals of 5 to 6 feet. To each a large *Pterocera* shell (*P. lambis*) is attached, the apex and 'fingers' being first broken off (Text-fig. 35). These lines are laid upon the bottom and when lifted next morning many of the shells are tenanted by little octopods that have sought concealment therein.

Every village on the Indian mainland fronting this part of Palk Strait possesses these octopus-lines and the quantity of octopus thus caught is very great indeed (Pl. xxxii, fig. B).

The number of shell-traps on one of these long lines usually runs to upwards of 800. The crew of a line-fishing canoe consists of five men, and each of them, when he joins, brings five or six short lines, each armed with twenty-five to thirty shells, say a total of 150 to 160 per man, or a grand total of twenty-five to thirty short lines; these when joined together give a long line carrying from 700 to 900 shells in all. They are laid in a depth of 2½ to 3 fathoms of water, one end buoyed by a large wooden float.

The fishermen credit the adult octopus with a vast amount of sagacity; among other clever tricks told of them is that when they enter an empty shell, they are careful to close the entrance with a shell or a piece of stone as a screen against their enemies. They are also said to sham death when they realize that they are finally cornered, but I cannot vouch for the truth of either story. Another favourite trick is to eject a cloud of inky fluid from a sac within the body. This diffuses at once and forms a dense dark cloud—a smoke screen! Under this cover the octopus frequently escapes.

The octopus is by far the most intelligent of the cephalopod mollusca, and it seems an absurdity to class it with snails, whelks, oysters and cockles; in one sense the name of 'Devilfish' sometimes given to it in England seems justified. If several octopods are watched in captivity and if they are at home in their surroundings, the cleverness of the creatures in stalking their prey and their cruel rapacity in tearing their victims into pieces are uncanny and quite devilish. I have watched an octopus on the prowl sliding stealthily over the bottom with all the skill of a highly trained intelligence; every bit of cover is made use of and even the colour of the bottom is imitated for concealment. It is a master of camouflage; passing over yellowish sand the dark body tints of the octopus fade and there is nothing but almost imperceptible movement to betray its presence.

TEXT-FIG. 35. Shell of the five-fingered chank (*Pteroceras*) used in South India as an octopus-trap, ×½.

Anon it crawls over a mass of brown weed—dark tints return in a flash and once more the animal is indistinguishable from its background. This ability to make lightning changes in its colour disguise is due to the colouring matter in its skin being contained in tiny sacs controlled by minute muscle fibres. If the muscles contract, the pigment spots grow and expand, giving dark tints to the body; if they relax, the spots close to pin-points, and a greyish yellow pallor suffuses the body. Crabs are the chief food of the octopus, but it will often open bivalves and in the tropics it manages to kill and devour large-sized cowries; fish are occasionally caught by the cruel, snake-like arms.

CUTTLEFISH (*Sepia* spp.). The habits of cuttlefish differ widely from those of the octopus. Instead of living a hermit's existence in holes and crannies, they are gregarious by nature, moving about in shoals. In places where they are known to appear regularly at certain seasons, they are fished for with nets, usually seines; otherwise they are taken singly by means of some deceitful contrivance.

One artifice commonly practised by the Provençal fishermen of the south of France is to employ lures made of cork or light wood, 5 or 6 inches long, with pieces of mirror-glass showing on one surface. The shape of the lure varies; some are oval, or square, others are crude representations of the cuttlefish itself and yet others are boat-shaped. The cork or wood is usually painted white to make it conspicuous. The pieces of silvered glass are inserted between two layers of cork or wood, subsequently fastened together. The Provençal term for this kind of lure is *supeirollo*. No cuttlefish seems able to withstand the attraction of its painted wood and bright mirrors when it comes within the focus of its eyes; it clutches the bright bauble and is forthwith hauled to the surface and killed.

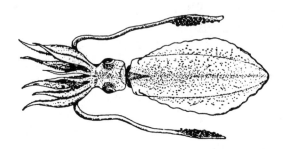

Text-fig. 36. The common squid, *Loligo*, ×½.

Still more ingenious is a lure employed in Malta. This makes use of the sexual attraction exerted by the female cuttlefish upon the ardent males of the same species. A female cuttlefish is sought for by the fisherman; when found she is tied or sewn to the end of a length of line. Thus 'baited' the line is trailed slowly behind a boat with enough line paid out to ensure the bait being close to the bottom. A sudden increase in the weight at the end of the line indicates the arrival of a male; so intent is he upon holding on to his captive that he allows the line to be hauled in and himself brought to the surface, where he meets an untimely end. The same tactics may be repeated several times with the same female; my informants state, however, that the attraction becomes inoperative after half a dozen experiences (Hornell, 1931, 19).

THE SQUID (*Loligo* spp.). As with the cuttlefish, the squid (Text-fig. 36) moves about in shoals; this gives opportunity to capture them in nets. Apart from this method, the usual one is by means of some form of the jigger. In Malta, various forms and sizes are in use; the most common one is a cylindrical leaden sinker, armed at the distal end with a circlet of closely set barbless hooks, with the points curving upwards.

In the north of Ceylon and on Rameswaram Island in Adam's Bridge, jigging for squid is practised chiefly for the requirements of the individual fishermen, who sun-dry any surplus they may have. To fish in this manner the fisherman erects a small look-out in shallow water. The main portion of the structure consists of a stout branched bough of Y-shape, the stem embedded firmly in the sand; across the ends of the two arms, which project several feet above the water, a strong pole is lashed to serve as a rest for the fisherman. A quantity of leaves are piled around the foot of this stage to attract the squid; the fisherman when ready seats himself on the cross-bar armed with a slender pole 12 to 15 feet long and terminating in five or six stout jigger-hooks arranged in a circle (Text-fig. 37).

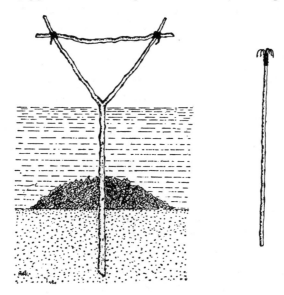

Text-fig. 37. A common squid-fishing device in use in the north of Ceylon. On the right is the jigger used to hook the squid.

Watching the bottom intently, with the jigger-head hidden among the leaves, the fisherman waits till he sees a squid approach to investigate the heap. As soon as it comes within range he cautiously moves his jigger into a favourable position and, with a deft jerk, imbeds the hooks in the squid's body and lifts it from the water. The reason why the squid seeks shelter amid the leaves set as a lure is, on the part of the female, for the purpose of finding a suitable object on which to attach the gelatinous candle-like cylinders in which the ova develop. The male frequently follows the female at this time, so sometimes both fall victims to the fisherman's jigger.

This method of fishing is generally carried on in the morning, the fisherman occupying his look-out for 4 or 5 hours at a stretch. At Ariyakundu there are usually nearly one hundred of these squid machines in operation during the squid season.

XVI

TRAPPING DEVICES

I. DELTAIC AND FRESHWATER FISH-TRAPS

To find ingenuity at its maximum in the invention of devices for trapping freshwater fish, we must go to the low-lying deltaic regions of India towards the head of the Bay of Bengal; the people of Bengal, Orissa and Ganjam, with those of the Kistna and Godaveri deltas, have brought this branch of fishing to the level of a fine art. To describe a tithe of their clever inventions would require a large volume to itself.

The idea of a cage-like trap, easy to enter but difficult to leave, is the principle adopted in the vast majority, modified in a hundred different ways. The framework is usually formed of fine screen-work made of slender slips or splints of bamboo, separated by narrow interspaces and bound together by strands of fibre obtained from the Palmyra palm.

These traps vary widely in shape from conical and cylindrical to rectangular or box-shaped. The majority have one or two openings, rounded or slit-shaped, defended by a *chevaux de frise* of inwardly projecting bamboo splints that yield readily to the entry of any fish that attempts to push its way in, while offering no means of exit to the prisoner within.

Most primitive of all is the separation of some shallow area of water from connexion with the main body, by the simple method of throwing up a low earthen bund between the two and then emptying out the water by bailing, so that any fish present are left behind stranded. The villagers may also wait till the surrounded shallow water dries up of its own accord, and so save themselves the labour of bailing.

Such fishing is seldom productive of anything but small fish. To catch larger ones and in greater quantity, screens made of slender bamboo rods, woven into long lengths by a few widely separated lines of jute string or even grass, are employed to separate and surround the area to be fished. These screens, called *chachi*, *pāti* or *garāi* in Bengal, are made in lengths of 30 feet or thereabouts, with a width of 3 to 5 feet. They are used in a variety of ways. In tidal waters, an area of shallow water may be surrounded by a long length of screen at high flood. When the water ebbs, all the fish present are stranded on the bottom or are floundering in shallow pools, where they can be caught by hand or by the open hand-trap (*polo*) to be described later. The mouths of shallow tidal creeks that dry at low tide may be similarly cut off during flood tide by a wall of these bamboo screens. In the jheels these screens are freely used to cut off large shallow areas The enclosed space is then divided into small enclosures by throwing up earthen bunds. Each enclosure in turn is emptied of water by bailing until the fish are all stranded. A specialized method of using this bamboo screen is for a band of fishermen to take a long length of it to a tank where it is placed in the water in a V-form; the fishermen in two parties extend themselves outward in a line from the end of each arm of the screen, beating the water and gradually converging. In this way the fishes are driven within the open arms of the V-screen. As the men close in upon the opening, the two arms are brought together. The sides are next advanced cautiously towards one another till they almost touch. From the small space thus formed the massed fish are taken by net or by hand alone. In Cuttack this trap is termed *salwa* or *pulti*.

The only snare commonly employed is the baited spring, called variously *barra*, *kāi-barsā*, and *dātiā* (Rangpur). It is set freely in inundated paddy fields, the favourite resort of the climbing perch (*koi*). This fish aestivates in the mud and with the rains emerges to resume a semi-amphibious life in shallow weedy waters. It is one of the commonest food fishes in Bengal and Bihar; being pleasant eating and esteemed as highly nutritious, its life is a continuous struggle against the wiles of man. The baited spring is one of the chief dangers it has to encounter. This little device is nothing but a strong flexible splint of bamboo pointed at each end. A short fine cord tied about its middle connects it with a cylindrical float made from a joint of the *nal* reed (*Pseudostrachium polymorphum*). The bait used is generally a grasshopper. To set the spring the two ends are bent till they nearly meet, when the two ends are adjusted delicately within the strong chitinous body of the insect. Hundreds of these little snares, pendant from their reed floats, are often set in a single paddy field. The unsuspecting *koi*, seeing a tempting morsel, seizes the bait; as its jaws come together the ends of the bent bamboo splint spring apart within the mouth or throat, forming an effective gag impossible to get rid of. When fishing for *sōl* and *gazāl* (murrel), grasshoppers, cockroaches and small frogs are used as bait. These snares are set in the evening and the victims gathered in the next morning.

This device is probably a modification of the gorge, a product of man's ingenuity dating back probably to the palæolithic age; if this be the case, we have here a survival in modified form of the progenitor of the modern fish-hook.

Of fish-traps proper, the simplest and most primitive is the human hand itself, searching along the sides of boulders or in shady nooks of an overhanging bank. Even yet this is a far from unproductive mode of fishing given the needful skill and knowledge of the habits of certain fish. But on a muddy bottom hand-fishing is difficult and some accessory mechanism had to be invented to prevent the fish slipping away while the hand searched for it. Wicker hand-traps were the result. The most primitive form is that of the truncate cone open at each end—the plunge-basket. This type is common throughout the length and breadth of India and is the one whence come all of the many form-varieties found in Bengal. A typical *polo* or *tāppu*, as it is generally termed in Bengal, varies from 2 to 2½ feet in height (Pl. XIX, fig. A). The lower aperture which is made as wide as can be conveniently operated has a diameter of about 24 inches, whereas that of the upper is made just sufficient to permit the hand and arm to enter comfortably—5½ to 6 inches. The frame of the ordinary Gangetic form is made of split bamboo supported internally by a number of bamboo hoops. The laths of bamboos used in construction, about 3 feet in length, are first split into three or four narrow splints to within a few inches from the end. The undivided extremities are bound around the mouth hoop very firmly with a closely set series of loops and knots, while below, the narrow rods into which the lath was split being pulled asunder slightly, are kept apart at the proper distance by being tied with jute fibre to the series of bamboo hoops which are placed within at regular intervals, each succeeding one increasing in diameter towards the bottom. The lower ends of the bamboo splints project a few inches beyond the lowest hoop in order to enable the trap to be pressed down into the mud and so give it a firm grip and prevent any imprisoned fish from escaping by burrowing under the edge of the trap. The *polo* is used only in quite shallow water, not exceeding 2 feet in depth. The fisherman wades into the water, generally of some partially dried up bheel or tank, continually dropping the trap into the water and pressing down the wide mouth into the muddy bottom with his left hand, while with the right, passed in through the narrow upper opening, he gropes around in the mud for any fish that the trap may have covered. The end of the dry season when the jheels, bheels and tanks are drying up, is the season for *polo*-fishing. The owner or lessee of a drying-up jheel will then call up the neighbouring villagers to combine to clear it of fish. They are called together by the blowing of a conch trumpet (*sankha*); men, women and children, sometimes numbering hundreds, respond to the call. Working methodically in a closely set line, they traverse the bheel from end to end, capturing many fish as they go, and herding the rest into a dense shoal at one end, where the final slaughter takes place. In a few hours even an extensive area of shallow water will be, apparently, wholly despoiled of fish. Few of even the smallest fish escape but some of the deep burrowing species, particularly murrel and pankal (*Mastacembalus pankalus*) may go deep enough to be overlooked. But they do not escape, for when the fisherfolk have done, numbers of Bagdis and kindred people crowd to the place and throw up a low earthen bund partitioning off a large area. This they proceed to drain by bailing. In a few hours the bunded part of the bheel is empty of water and then all set to work to clear it of the fishes lurking deep in the mud. First come the men in a close set line each with a pronged fork, the *anchra*, in his hands; with this they fork over the mud, dragging out struggling fish from below much as a farm labourer forks out potatoes. The women and children follow behind groping in the thrown-up mud for the smaller fishes. Having cleared out one area, another is drained and the previous procedure repeated till the whole bheel has been worked through.

The truncate cone, the primitive and most widely used form of the plunge-basket, is frequently modified considerably in shape, according to local fancy and custom, into a bell-shape, sometimes high and elegant, sometimes depressed and squat. The shape is controlled by varying as required the relative diameter of the hoops, to which are attached the bamboo splints that radiate downwards from the narrow upper opening (Pl. xix, fig. A).

Several transitional forms connect the conical or bell-shaped *polo* with the scoop-traps properly so called; such are the *chāk-jāl* and the *tura* of Pabna.

The *chāk-jāl* is clearly a development of the *polo*, the bamboo cone being replaced by a net-bag suspended tail end up by a loop cast over the apex of a conical frame made by tying three or four bamboos together at one end and attaching the other end of each at equidistant points to a wide hoop of halved bamboo. The mouth of the net is laced around the circumference of this mouth hoop. It is used like the *polo*, but after it has been pressed down into the mud, the loop at the tail end is cast loose, permitting the trapped fish to rush into the bag of the net. The *chāk* is then tilted over and turned mouth up, the fish falling into the tail end. It has advantages when fish armed with poisonous spines are being trapped, but taken generally it is a less effective instrument. A closely related contrivance is in use in Africa in the shallows of the River El Beid, an affluent of Lake Chad (see p. 52).

The *tura* is particularly simple in construction. A length of fairly thick bamboo is taken and split into a large number of long narrow strips to within a few inches of one end, which is kept entire to serve as a handle. Then, as in the *polo*, the rod-like strips are spread till a long narrow conical form is assured; in this position they are secured upon narrow internal hoops of progressively larger diameter from the undivided butt to the wide mouth which is securely distended by a stronger hoop. It is used to catch mud-living fishes; it is operated like the *polo*, but as it is without an opening at the apex to admit the hand, it has to be up-ended with a scoop-like motion to lift out any fish caught.

The *chāk-jāl*, both actually and figuratively, leads into a blind alley. No other trap or net is derived from it, whereas the *tura* appears to be the parent of all the scoop-traps in existence. It leads directly to the *nui*, *beloin*, or *gānj* and thence to the bamboo form (*honchā*) of the lave-net.

The central form of the *nui* and *gānj* is a cylindrical scoop open at one end and brought to a closed eccentric apex at the other; a bamboo rod runs along one side and projects beyond the closed end to form the handle and give purchase in tilting and lifting it. Some of these scoops are straight, others more or less curved in the form of a cornucopia. The fisherman holds the free end of the bamboo rod in his right hand, his left grasping a loop of cord, or of cane attached to the same bamboo close to the open mouth end. Holding it thus the fisherman presses the open end slantwise against the mud and pushes it cautiously along till the bank is reached or till he thinks some fish are caught, when the scoop is gently raised and any fish removed. A usual size is about 20 inches in length with a mouth diameter of about 12 inches.

A much larger form of scoop is the *honchā*, which is essentially a primitive form of lave-net, where instead of meshes of thread or cord being employed to make the scoop or bag part, fine bamboo mat-work is substituted. Two principal types are seen in the country of the lower Ganges. In the first a rectangular piece of open-meshed bamboo mat strengthened along the margin by a strong strip of the same material, is bunched up into a scoop-form by two adjacent corners being brought together (Pl. xix, fig. A). Across the wide rectangular mouth thus formed, a bamboo pole is attached, passing from the centre of the base upwards to the apex, beyond which it projects to form a short handle. This gives what is essentially a primitive form of push-net as used in shrimping on sandy coasts in Europe. It is indeed frequently used in similar fashion. But the characteristic Bengal method is for the fisherman to press the scoop down with its lower margin in the mud and with the mouth turned towards him, and then to tramp and splash about in the mud, disturbing any fish that may be there and driving them into the scoop, which he lifts suddenly from time to time to examine.

A still closer approximation to the lave-net is where the scoop is given a rigid mouth frame, composed of a triangle of bamboo. This is always used in the manner of a push-net and is essentially a primitive form of this net, constructed of simpler materials. If a large *honchā* have the sides flattened instead of being curved, and the handle replaced by a dragging cord or bridle attached to each end of the base of the large triangular mouth, we get the peculiar trap generally called *hogrā*. Filled loosely with leafy branches it is anchored by its bridles to strakes in the bed of a stream where a strong current runs. The mouth is directed upstream. Its leafy interior soon becomes the resort of a number of fishes and prawns seeking shelter and shade, or in some cases to deposit their spawn. Every few days the trap is cautiously drawn ashore and whatever fish are inside caught and removed. It is a very common fishing implement among the ryots in many districts and goes by many local names, *shāgrā*, *shārgā* and *okhrā* in Lower Bengal and *shār* in Dinajpur.

Another device, of extreme simplicity, which utilizes the habit of certain fishes to seek shelter in holes and crannies is the *chunga*. It consists of a single long internode of a thick bamboo, open at one end, and closed at the other by leaving intact the first internodal partition. A number of these *chungas* are placed under water in holes in the bank of a tank or sluggish stream and left there for several days, to attract fish to make their homes in their enticing cavities. The fish most partial to these *chungas* is the eel-shaped *bāin* (*Mastacembelus* spp.) for its usual spawning place is in holes in shallow waters especially when choked with aquatic plants. When the fisherman visits his *chungas*, he closes the open end with the palm of the hand, and lifts the trap to the surface to empty it. It is said that poisonous snakes sometimes take refuge in these *chungas* and hence this system of fishing is considered dangerous. A somewhat similar method is adopted to catch the burrowing *singi* (*Saccobranchus fossilis*) and the *magur* (*Clarias magur*), by placing narrow-necked earthenware jars (Beng. *kalash*) on the bottom of a tank as tempting hiding-places for these fishes.

Of cage-traps the number and variety are endless; to attempt to describe all would result in producing a wearisome catalogue. Fortunately, they fall into a series of types, so only the most distinctive of each will be noticed; it must be remembered then that in each instance there are in addition a large number of related forms, varying in some detail or another.

The trap from which all these appear to be derived is not a cage at all. It is merely a short cylinder of grass or fine bamboo matting that sieves out fry and prawns from some little runnel. For this purpose one end is left open, the other bunched together and tied. It is usually placed in one of the little drainage channels from a paddy field or in an opening in a little dam or *tatti* fence thrown up across a shallow rivulet. Fish fry and prawns that pass along with the current find their way into the trap, and accumulate there till they are removed. An elaboration of this idea consists of the addition of a large funnel-shaped entrance, shaped like a conical *polo*. The open apex is much narrowed by leaving free and projecting the upper ends of the bamboo splints of which the funnel is made. In the primitive form this funnel is separate and not attached to the terminal cylinder; to set up the trap the open apex of the funnel is inserted within the open end of the cylinder and the two jammed in position in the opening through which the water is passing. In this form the fish that pass in have their exit barred by the inwardly projecting splints of the narrow end of the funnel.

The next stage in the evolution of this type is the permanent attachment of the entrance funnel to the cylindrical body. When this combination is reached the utility and fishing efficiency of the design is enormously increased, particularly as it can now be made of stronger material and consequently of much larger size. What was the blind hinder cylinder now becomes the larger and main part of the trap—the body—the funnel diminishing in relative proportion. But as the two parts cannot now be separated to take out the fish caught, a special door is located at the hinder end of the cylindrical body. In the simplest form and where big fish or even tortoises have to be dealt with, the whole of the back wall of the cage forms the door and has to be unlaced from the sides each time the trap is emptied. In others where smaller fishes only are caught, the hinder end of the trap is narrowed down and a portion of the back wall made to hinge down to form a regular door through which fish may be taken out. At the same time the mechanism of the funnel has been improved by arranging the converging bamboo splints at the inner end of the funnel mouth into a more or less complete *chevaux de frise*, easy to pass when going inwards owing to the flexibility of the bamboo splints, but impossible to pass in the reverse direction, as every attempt results in the close interlocking of the splints. Further the opening is no longer central, but moved to a position nearer the upper wall of the trap; the bamboo strips and splints forming the funnel are consequently unequal in length, short above and increasing in length from above downwards. This arrangement adds considerably to the difficulty of egress.

Sometimes these traps attain very considerable dimensions. Of such is the *pāron*, a truncate cylinder which may be 5 feet in length by 3 feet in height. The cylindrical body is slightly flattened at one side—the bottom— to enable it to lie more securely when fixed in position by being tied to stakes driven into the bottom of the river or jheel. It is used to catch large fish and tortoises and is the largest kind of trap used in the Gangetic region. Ordinarily it is emptied once in 3 days, the fish that have entered being taken out by unlacing the whole of the back wall. It is very stoutly built of bamboo strips, having a mesh of 2 inches along each side. The *katya* is another trap nearly as large in general dimensions, but with a smaller mesh (1½ inches) and tapers towards the back to a small door, being used to trap smaller fishes than the *pāron*. To increase further the catching power of these traps vertical leaders of fine bamboo splints, strengthened and kept upright by cross-bars of bamboo laths, are added to guide fishes more quickly and surely to the trap-funnel. In the *pāor*, a large subcylindrical trap of the *katya* type, one of these lateral leaders is attached on either side of the mouth. The trap is placed facing the current, the leaders, often of considerable length, extended on either side. Fish coming downstream encounter one of the leaders and, guided by it, eventually enter the opening at the base of the funnel-shaped mouth and become prisoners. In the *dohāir*, a smaller trap, there is only one leader stretching outwards from the centre of the mouth. It is used near the banks of shallow streams, set facing across the current with its leader stretching outwards towards the other side. It is able to trap fish travelling in either direction—up or down stream—for either way they strike the leader and all those that turn towards the side where the trap is, are usually caught.

Further complication and security against egress is obtained by setting a second funnel-shaped trapped partition, similar to that across the mouth, some distance inwards, thus forming two chambers within the trap. The *kai-chāi* also known as *jalangā*, is a good example of this form. In shape it is a truncate cylinder, subtriangular in section: it never runs large; the interstices of the bamboo splint framework are very narrow, so that quite small fishes and even fry are captured. It usually has a cord carrying-handle on the upper side. A great variety of traps utilizing this idea of additional trapped openings are in use, but they have no special importance and are often extremely local in their range; sometimes even dependent on the whim or particular ingenuity of the people who make and use them.

Nearly all the remaining types of cage-traps may be classed as box-traps, being quadrangular in general form, though frequently with the corners rounded. A transitional form is the *kholson*, a cylindrical trap with truncate ends, set upright on one end. The trapped opening, instead of being at one end as in the forms previously described, extends vertically along the whole length of one side of the cylinder. The walls of the trap turn inwards slightly on each side of the opening from which projects inwards a converging screen of bamboo splints; the free ends of these are fine, sharply pointed and lightly interlocked in *chevaux de frise* manner. Fishes find no difficulty in pushing their way through, so delicate and yielding are the slender interlocking fingers of bamboo; but passage in the reverse direction is practically impossible. The door through which fish are taken out is situated at the top of the trap on the side away from the entrance. This useful trap is used in comparatively deep water with leafy branches extending some distance on each side, partly to attract fishes by their shelter and also to act as leaders. The *chāro* of Pabna and Western Bengal is constructed on the same principle, but with the curves of the *kholson* converted into rectangular corners. By converting the cylinder of the *kholson* into an oblong box with rounded vertical angles at each end, and by putting in a vertical mouth, trapped as in the *kholson*, in each of these ends, the double-ended *choukā* of Rajshahi is evolved.

Another set of more or less quadrangular traps made of finely split bamboos laced together very closely so as to leave very narrow interspaces are used by ryots and villagers to catch prawns and bottom-feeding fry and small fish. Of these the *boichna*, *rābani*, *āntāl*, *doār* and *darki* are typical common forms. The *boichna* is one of the commonest of these traps. It is a tall contrivance standing upright on a long narrow base, rounded at each end. The tall bamboo splint sides that rise from this are strengthened by horizontal bars of bamboo laths, kept apart by a few cross-stays passing from side to side. The upper-side of the trap is ridge-shaped, the sides being brought together and tied to a long ridge-bar of split bamboo, except for a short distance at one end, where the sides are neatly laced together, so that by pulling out the lacing, an opening can be readily made through which the contents of the trap may be shaken out when the trap is inverted. In one side close to the bottom at two or three places, a few of the upright wall-splints are cut away and converted into trapped openings of fine bamboo splints arranged to admit the prawns and small fish sought for. This trap and also the others are set usually with the opening facing the current. In size the *boichna* usually measures from 2 to 3 feet in length by 16 to 20 inches in height with a width of 6 to 8 inches (Pl. xviii, fig. A).

The *rābani* (Pabna, Jessore, etc.) and *doār* are smaller editions of the same type; the *āntāl* has two trapped openings on one side and a third on the other. Frequently several of these traps are arranged in a row; in Chilka Lake large numbers are massed together to form a labyrinth, with one line of traps arranged as a leader running out from the shore to the recurved end of this compound form of trap.

The *dārki* common throughout Bengal, is a rectangular or box form of *boichna*, having a vertical trapped opening, extending the whole height of the trap, placed midway between the usual two semicircular openings close to the lower edge of one side.

Bottle-shaped traps woven of fine bamboo wickerwork, and cones of woven kusha-grass, with trapped mouths, form another and separate minor class. These little contrivances are laid on their side and any small fishes that enter are taken out through the neck opening which is closed when in use by either a little door or some form of plug.

Another type of trap has the form of a blind sleeve, with a diameter in the hinder part carefully adjusted to approximate closely to the average girth of the adult kind of fish sought to be captured. It depends for success on the difficulty which a fish of cylindrical body has in backing out from a flexible tube when it has forced its way so far in that its body exactly fits the cylinder (Text-fig. 38). In form it resembles the rat-traps used by the Azande people of the Anglo-Egyptian Sudan, but is without the terrible thorn armature of these strange rat-traps.

This tubular trap is widely distributed through India, passing south from the Ganges at least as far south as the southern limit of the Nellore district, just north of Madras. From the bell-shaped mouth, it quickly narrows to a long tubular hinder region, 10 to 14 inches in length, of a diameter just equal to that of an adult eel-like murrel (*Ophiocephalus* spp.), the fish which it is designed specifically to entrap. It is made of dark brown palmyra fibre extracted from the butt ends of the leaf-stalks, worked in double ply into a meshwork of netting. This little trap is often to be found, set in scores in any suitable marshy ground such as that bordering a waterspread. Each trap is anchored between tufts of reed or grass, each side of the mouth attached to a short cord or length of strong fibre either to pegs on each side or to adjoining tufts of grass. Murrel are voracious creatures always on the prowl for fish and frogs, and little runways between tufts of herbage constitute their pathways through the marsh. The villagers know of these tracks and set their traps accordingly. Hundreds are set along the margins of the larger tanks when bordered by marshland; their success in practice is remarkable.

A tubular trap of identical form and construction is in use in the Philippine Islands (Aldaba, 1931, 8).

But of all the ingenious contrivances designed for the capture of the elusive murrel, commend me to another Philippine trap, the *baloob*. This should really be included in the category of those contrivances borrowed

TEXT-FIG. 38. A tubular trap used in India to capture murrel (*Ophiocephalus*), ×¼.

by the fisherfolk from the hunter, for it consists of a miniature stockade trap with a drop-door worked by a trigger—a trap built on the same principle as is sometimes used in India to capture tigers.

This small murrel-trap has walls built of bamboo stakes driven well down into the mud, to form a round-cornered oblong; at one end, a drop-door is fitted sliding up and down in grooves made from half bamboos. When set, this door is left in the raised position, held there by a cord connected with a trigger-catch within the pen. The top is roofed in with twigs and dried coconut-palm leaves.

The murrel, eager always to find cover in any quiet shady nook, is attracted towards the entrance by the pile of leaves and branches arranged purposely around the front of the trap; on entering it begins to explore the recesses of this ideal retreat and soon touches off the trigger and becomes a prisoner by the fall of the door.

These traps measure a little over 2 feet in length, with a breadth and height of about 16 inches. As many as two hundred have been counted along the margin of one lake in Luzon.

Extensive fish-weirs or pound-traps are little used in India except in a few backwaters where conditions are unusually favourable. One of these is that at Sonapur in Ganjam. Here, owing to the considerable rise and fall of the tide, huge, semi-permanent pounds are built up of palisading of jungle poles, the intervals filled in by bamboo screens or tatties. Long leaders of converging screens shepherd the fish and prawns to the openings in the outer pound-trap, while others within lead them towards smaller inner chambers where the water is deep and apparently free from dangers. At low tide the pound dries out more or less completely, when the fishermen enter and remove the catch.

In China and Indo-China many of the traps in use are similar or closely akin to those of India; Chinese genius tends to develop the subtilties of the net rather than of the basket-trap for fishing. In Africa also, traps are greatly in evidence in the region of the Great Lakes and in West Africa and the Central Sudan. Being without personal knowledge of the Chinese types, I refrain from any detailed reference or description, and, as is seen above, I have limited myself to a short account of those Indian and Fijian ones with which I am familiar. For descriptions of certain notable African types, see Chapter v.

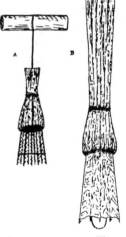

TEXT-FIG. 39. Thorn-lined traps; A, a floating variety used to catch prawns, Fiji; B, another from the Duke of York Group, Bismarck Archipelago, with the thorns completely covered.

Lastly, to describe the floating prawn-trap. Allusion has already been made to the thorn-lined traps used by the Sudanese Azande for the capture of rats. It is therefore of great interest to find the same idea employed in Fiji and some places in Melanesia for the catching of prawns and small fishes.

In Fiji, where I have seen an example in the Suva Museum, it is used as a floating prawn-trap (*ndai-ni-ura*). It consists of an elongated bell-shaped frame made of a number of twigs armed on one side with curved thorns; these are arranged with their points directed backwards from the mouth of the little bell. The upper section of the bell-frame is neatly covered with leafy material, apparently consisting of strips of Pandanus leaves; the lower half of the frame is uncovered, exposing the ends of the thorny twigs. These constitute a formidable circlet of barbed lances, held in position by a cord which makes a turn round each as it encircles them near their thorny outer ends (Text-fig. 39).

To set, the trap is suspended from a short, light, wooden float. Bait is placed within the leafy apex of the bell; the prawn enters to reach it, but is unable to return as the barbs are against it. It is set in quiet water, still pools preferably.

Its length overall is 9 inches, excluding the float.

II. MARINE FISH-TRAPS

These fall into two categories, the movable basketwork kind, and that where the structure is of a semi-permanent character, usually supported by stakes driven into the sea-bottom.

MOVABLE FISH TRAPS. The forms represented among these, usually constructed of basketwork, are bewildering in their variety; attention will therefore be limited here to the traps of three widely separated representative regions: the Italian and Maltese type, the Indian type and the Oceanic type.

(a) *The Italian and Maltese type.* This occurs in great variety of size. The largest have an overall length of about 6 feet. They are built up of a composite basketwork whereof the meshes are made of the cylindrical stems of a rush (*Juncus acutus*), closely hooped with bands of split bamboo. The complete trap has a bell-shaped body, with the mouth, placed at the broad end, trapped by the insertion of a basketry funnel provided with a spine-beset opening at the inner and narrow end (Pl. xx, figs. A and B).

When in use this trap (*nassa*) is lowered to the bottom and buoyed, in one of the places where certain fishes are known to favour. No bait is placed within the trap, which lies upon one side, and yet when lifted scores of fish may be found within.

The traps for small fishes are of several sizes and have differing sizes of mesh according to the fishes they are intended to catch. Unlike the large size already described, the body and the mouth funnel of these traps are woven in one piece; the shape is the same and the wider end, which is the lower end when set, is trapped as in big traps. These *nasse* are suspended at varying distances from the bottom, each hung from a short branch line from the main rope, which is anchored at the bottom by a stone, and buoyed on the surface by cork floats. Additional corks are tied to the rope at intervals to aid in sustaining the weight of the baskets, wherein small stones are placed to keep them in an upright position. Unlike the large traps, these smaller sizes are always baited (Pl. xxi, fig. B).

The moray (*Muraena*), the ugly and vicious eel-like fish so highly esteemed by the Romans of the Empire, is caught in a small, roughly made trap of cylindrical shape, built up out of strips of palm leaves and midribs; one end is closed and the other trapped. The octopus is sometimes taken in this trap.

(b) *The Indian type.* In India, sea-fishing with traps of basketry is limited to the shores of the Gulf of Mannar and Palk Strait. The simplest form is roughly heart-shaped with the corners angular. At the centre of one side a wide aperture leads into a funnel; at its inner end this turns sharply downwards, without any armature of spikes. This trap is used wherever an extensive area of rocky bottom occurs in shallow water.

At Rameswaram, on one of the islands in Adam's Bridge, the fishermen who fish inside the reef fringing the coast, have evolved an extremely elaborate stellate form of this trap, with a roomy side chamber in each of the arms; three and sometimes even five entrances to the undivided interior are provided, each placed in one of the angles between two arms (Pl. xxii, fig. A). The trap is woven either of strips of bamboo or of split withies of babul arranged in a hexagonal meshwork of the same pattern as is used in the cane-seating of chairs. Exceedingly ingenious is the way the men plan the weaving; they have evolved a pattern which allows the whole trap, excepting the funnels, to be made from two sheets of this basket-work; one, the bottom, is shaped to the eventual outline which the trap is to have; the other is more intricate in form as it has to be so shaped that it will constitute not only the upper surface of the trap, but also the sides, by means of flaps and extensions; these have to be so designed and placed that they may be bent in the various directions necessary to form the multiple sides of the finished trap. The lower edges of the sides are laced to the edges of the bottom, and the trap is completed by inserting the three entrance funnels, and lacing them in position (Text-fig. 40, A, B and C).

This done, it remains but to bait the trap and to anchor it in the shallows within the reef by means of stones tied to the sides, or placed inside and there made fast.

The fishermen who use these traps transport them upon primitive catamarans made of any odd pieces of light wood tied together by a cross-bar at each end; their paddle is a 5-foot length of split bamboo.

Traps similar to the simple heart-shape variety of these traps are in use in Madeira and Brazil. Considering that the Portuguese, who form the ruling race in Brazil, are noted for their skill and energy in the prosecution of sea-fisheries wherever they go, and that for nearly a century and a half they were in effective occupation of those places in India and Ceylon where these basket-traps are found, and where considerable sections of the fishing community are Roman Catholics whose ancestors were converted by Portuguese missionaries, it seems certain that this Indian type of basket-work-trap was introduced into South America (and into Madeira) by Portuguese, who had become acquainted with it when serving in India as priests, soldiers or traders (Pl. xxii, fig. B). It is significant that only the simplest design, that most easily constructed, is in use in Brazil and Madeira. The multiple, star-shaped variety seen at Rameswaram requires special skill to shape and weave, more perhaps than a parish priest could command.

(*c*) *The Oceanic type.* Among the numberless islands from Sumatra to Polynesia, the varieties of movable fish-trap are very many and of great range in size and shape. Nevertheless, one dominant and characteristic form is found nearly everywhere; this is the barrel-shaped trap, with a trapped entrance at each end. Sometimes there is only a single entrance, but this is less typical. Some are of huge size (Pl. xxi, fig. A), and some are used in quite deep water, such as those used by Dr Willey in his successful attempt to capture living specimens of the pearly nautilus.

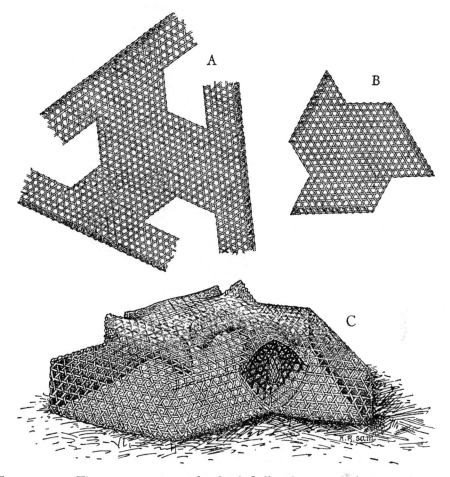

TEXT-FIG. 40. The two components of a South Indian three-way basket trap. A, woven basketry shaped to form the top and sides; B, the part to form the floor of the same trap; C, the trap completed.

When of very large dimensions and of consequent relative lightness they are secured upon a hurdle-like frame of heavy wood, to which they are attached by an arched banding of split rattan or bamboo; the whole weighted by stones lashed on. In most instances the meshwork is of the hexagonal form already noted as usual in the fish-traps of South India.

In Fiji two are in regular use, called respectively the *uwea* and the *susu*. The two are seldom used by the same community; it is either the one or the other. Both kinds are in use in Samoa and possibly derive from Fijian contacts as these types are in common use throughout Melanesia (Text-fig. 41, A, B and c).

The *uwea* type is of barrel-shape, averaging 4 feet long, with the greatest diameter at mid-length of 30 inches. The two ends are of rather less diameter (Pl. XXIII, fig. A). The framework is made from the aerial roots of the smaller mangroves (*Rhizophora* spp.); after the bark is scraped off, they are split and woven into the desired form. At each end a funnel of wickerwork is inserted, the apex directed inwards. In this apex is an

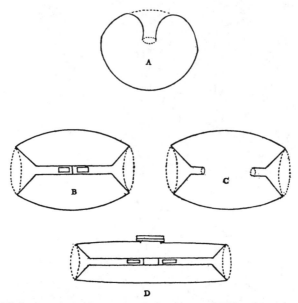

TEXT-FIG. 41. Diagrammatic sections through four types of Fijian fish-traps. A, the *susu* type; B, the *uwea* type of Mbau; C, the *uwea* of Rewa; D, an eel-trap of *uwea* type.

opening communicating with a tubular wicker-walled passage joining the two funnels. In the traps used at Mbau a partition of split rods is placed at mid-length across this passage to block it and on each side of it is a large opening in the wall of the passage. By this arrangement any fish which enters one of the end-funnels and thence continues into the central passage, finds its progress barred by the partition and is forced to pass through the adjacent opening to reach the bait placed within the body of the barrel. Here it has to remain a prisoner until taken out through an opening in the outer wall, closed by a wicker 'door'.

At Rewa the general construction is the same except that the apices of the end-funnels open directly into the cavity as seen in Text-fig. 41, C.

The bait placed within an *uwea* consists of cooked yam and taro, the entrails of fish and broken-up crabs. Besides this bait, fragments of lustrous pearl-shell, bits of cone-shells and of the giant clam (*Tridacna*) were formerly placed within as lures; to-day pieces of broken crockery, preferably white, have replaced the shell fragments, and these are considered much more effective than the old.

When sinking an *uwea* for fish, the fisherman marks its position by a length of bamboo, tied as a buoy, to the end of a line attached to the trap. The trap is left for 24 hours. When the men return the following day in their canoe, instead of hauling it up forthwith, one of them dives to the bottom to ascertain if any fish have been trapped; if the report is favourable, the crew haul up the trap, remove the fish and reset it. This procedure is termed respectively the *rai* or 'seeing' and the *vuevue* or 'lifting up'.

This trap-fishing usually begins at the time of yam-planting, about the month of September and is continued until December, the period when fish are most abundant in the inshore waters of Fiji. During the time when the *uwea* is being operated, the fishermen in old times were accustomed to sleep in the *mbure* or temple; it was taboo for them to sleep with their wives lest the *uwea* should not be filled. Since the people became Christians this taboo has largely fallen into abeyance (Pl. XXIII, fig. A and Text-fig. 41, B).

The second type of fish-trap in common use in Fiji is the *susu*. In form this is a rude counterpart of the British wickerwork lobster pot, a subglobular or spheroidal wicker-woven basket with a wide funnel-shaped mouth, turned downwards, at the summit, through which fish find it easy to pass to reach the bait within, but wellnigh impossible to make the return trip (Pl. XXIII, fig. B).

The *susu* is roughly woven of large mesh, from the aerial roots of the *tiri* mangrove. The large ones have a door fitted at one side for the removal of the catch; the smaller or ordinary sized one, 30 inches wide by 20 inches high, are without a door, the fishermen finding it easier to make a temporary opening by pulling apart the sides of one of the loosely woven meshes.

In Kandavu Island, contrary to the Mbau custom, the operation of this trap, called there *kawa ni ika*, is recognized as among the tasks pertaining to the women; they usually set it in water 4 or 5 feet deep. As the anchoring of the trap is done by heaping stones around it, the woman-owner has to dive repeatedly before she is able to secure it safely. In Kandavu this kind of trap is woven from the stems of the vine, *Pleiosmilax vitiensis*.

Deane (1910) states that the fishing rules in Kandavu regarding the use of the *kawa* are stringent. In the early morning the owner may not spit nor eat before she goes to lift the trap. At no time should she eat prawns or crabs or anything that turns red when boiled. Were she to do so, the inside of the trap would appear red and so terrify the fishes that they would not dare to venture into it.

We may compare with the freshwater devices described in Part I of this chapter the traps used by the Fijians. They are constructed on two different principles: (*a*) those of a narrow tubular form made after the fashion of the Indian murrel-trap (*q.v.*); and (*b*) those based on the *uwea* type with one or two trapped funnel-shaped mouths.

Those in the first category have the warp made of bamboo splints held together, in those for use as fish-traps, by an in-and-out spiral weaving of narrow strips of bamboo, fairly widely woven. In those where the spiral weft is closely woven, eels and prawns will be taken as well as fishes.

The usual manner of making one of these traps is to take a length of stout bamboo, and then to split it carefully into a number of narrow splints, leaving a portion of the bamboo several inches in length unsplit at one end to form the closed terminal end of the trap when complete. In and out of these splints a narrow strip of split bamboo is interwoven in a spiral manner, spaced closely or widely according to the kind of fish it has to catch (Pl. xix, fig. b).

These traps vary greatly in size, from 4 feet to 8 feet in length. The smaller ones in general use measure $4\frac{1}{2}$ feet, with a diameter of 5 inches except at the mouth, where the wickerwork widens to a diameter of 7 to 8 inches to facilitate entry. A trap of this size can be made from a bamboo of $1\frac{1}{2}$ inches diameter, split lengthwise into ten strips united at one end.

For eels and prawns great care is taken to weave the weft so tight and strong that no effort of an eel to squeeze through can succeed. In one of these traps which I examined, the longitudinal ribs, sixteen in number, were split from one piece of bamboo 4 feet in length. It was between $3\frac{1}{2}$ and 4 inches in diameter, with a flaring mouth bound round the edge with a leaf-strip of the screw-pine (*Pandanus*).

These tubular traps are usually placed on the bed of a shallow stream with the mouths directed upstream. A bank of gravel and clay is built on each side and between the individual traps so that the bulk of the stream passes into the mouths—a primitive fishing-weir. When this work is completed, the fisherwomen proceed upstream for some distance and then return downstream splashing and shouting in order to frighten any fish which may be about and so drive them ahead into the open mouths of the traps.

The *uwea* type of eel-trap is similar to the marine form in principle but instead of being wide and barrel-shaped it is cylindrical and has a diameter of only 9 inches at each end, rising to 12 inches at mid-length. Being designed solely to catch eels, the wickerwork is woven as closely as possible. The funnels inserted in the ends connect with a tubular inner passage as in the *uwea*, but instead of one partition at mid-length, there are two, separated by a space of 3 inches, the better to prevent the eels from breaking their way through. An opening left in near the end of each passage leads into the body of the trap, whence escape is all but impossible. To permit the trap to be emptied, a rectangular opening is left in one side of the body of the trap at mid-length, closed by a thick pad of short lengths of mangrove roots, tied down tightly before the trap is placed in working position (Pl. xxiv, fig. A).

FISHING-WEIRS OR POUNDS. This type of permanent or semi-permanent fishing contrivance is widely distributed. In the British Isles many variations occur under the names of fish-weirs, hedge baulks, stop-nets, keddle-nets, stake-nets, etc.; the huge tunny-nets of the Mediterranean represent a highly specialized type. These when typical have all or part of their structure supported by posts embedded in the sand or mud, with the intervals closed by netting or wattle or brushwood (Davis, 1923 and Parona, 1919). In North America fishing structures of related construction are many and diverse.

Other areas where this class of fishing-engines is prevalent are Western India, the Malay Peninsula, the Dutch Indies and the Philippine Islands, where weirs have outstanding importance among the coast population as the means for assuring adequate supplies of one of their staple foods.

This distribution extends eastwards as far as Fiji, where we find the simpler forms of these traps in such number and in such variety as to enable us to understand the origin and course of development of the most intricate contrivance of this most variable of fishing-engines. We find them ranging upwards from a simplicity of design such as is easily constructed and operated by the unskilled women of the village, to a complex of leader fences and trapped chambers that prefigures the plan of the complicated weirs of Europe and North America.

The genesis of this extraordinary series as seen in Fiji is an impounding shallow enclosure of boulders arranged in crescentic plan-form. Similar boulder fences were formerly in use in Australia (Pl. xxv, fig. A), and I have seen the remains of the same kind of semicircular stone barrier on the shore of Coiba Island, now the penal settlement of the Republic of Panama. The next step is the substitution of a reed fencing for low stone walls, followed by the employment of permanent barrier fences supported by stout posts with a pocket-like trap at the centre of the arc, or at the apex if the fencing is in two lines meeting at an angle to one another (Pl. xxv, fig. B). Other improvements were gradually added until we find the better class of Fijian weirs consisting of one or two long 'leaders' of staked reed fencing, which conduct the fishes to one or more heart-shaped cages or pounds; from these the fish find it impossible to escape, for the only way out is by the passage through which they entered and this is barred by the elasticity of the edges of the screens that form the sides of the doorway—they part readily and open upon the least pressure from outside, but on the inner, any pressure applied merely closes the edges more firmly.

The details of these progressive stages in evolution require further description in order to understand their construction and the way they operate.

(a) *Boulder-walled tidal traps.* The method of trapping fish by means of low walls of boulders set out in horseshoe form between tide-marks is undoubtedly one of the most primitive methods of fishing, maybe the very earliest of the efforts of early man to devise a mechanical arrangement for effecting the automatic capture of fishes.

In Fiji it is common wherever the shore formation is suitable; it requires a gently sloping foreshore with easy gradient, so that the distance from high to low water-level may be considerable; this foreshore beach must also be of fairly hard bottom if possible.

Given these conditions the Fijians were accustomed to collect great boulders and to form with these low-walled pens, in which some of the fishes which come inshore with the flowing tide are enclosed and stranded or else concentrated in shallow pools at the lowest point within the pen, when the ebb-tide uncovers the foreshore.

Many of these are still to be seen on suitable coasts; with improved methods and especially since the introduction of European types of nets, no more of these pens are likely to be built. Some are falling into disrepair; even so, the village women still visit them at low tide in the hope of easy captures.

The walls are generally quite low, seldom more than 12 or 15 inches high at the deep or seaward end. In Kia Island they continue to be favoured; several enclose large areas of the foreshore, with walls higher than on the mainland of Vanua Levu—up to 18 inches. In this island they are built at two horizons; one kind for use during spring tides, the other when the neaps are on. Mr George Barker estimates that there are over 3 miles' length of these stone pen walls around Kia, where this art flourishes in old-time strength.

In building a *moka*, as it is called in Fijian, two arms run seawards from just below high-water mark of spring tides, more or less parallel; as they approach low-tide level, the arms bend inwards and approach one another, finally meeting. In some *mokas* this curve is unbroken; in others the wall takes a dip inwards at the centre, thereby forming two small rounded bays.

The walled *moka*, I am told, is the men's *moka* but in practice at the present time, although the men may have built the walls, it is usually the women who collect the catch.

The women's *moka* in Kandavu Island and probably elsewhere, is a pyramid of stones $2\frac{1}{2}$ to 3 feet high. Each woman usually has four or five of these. At low tide she and her friends surround these, one by one, with nets, take out the stones and collect any fishes which have been hiding amongst them. Afterwards the piles are rebuilt in readiness for the next rise of tide.

This method is a variation of bush-fishing, a favourite way of capturing fishes in the shelter of a pile of brushwood placed in a stream or lake for this specific purpose, by the people of Africa, India and China, as I have described in Chapter XIV.

(*b*) *Palisaded fish-pounds.* In this method of fishing as practised in Fiji the long arms of these great traps are among the first objects that attract the attention of newcomers as their steamer approaches Suva.

These engines, the *mba kele* or 'fixed-post fences' function on the principle of intercepting fish during their daily movements along the coast and then of leading them into trapped pens at the apex of two converging fences or 'leaders'. As they are built in shallow water with the pen or pound at the outer end, the collection of the catch is made just before extreme low tide, when the water has almost dried out, leaving the imprisoned fishes floundering in a few inches of water. The fisherman kills the captured fishes with a short 'stabber' or striker (*kenai sua*) made of heavy wood, 21 inches long, sharply pointed at one end. This is used in fish-drives and fish-pens where the confined space forbids the use of a fish-spear (Pl. XXV, fig. B).

The construction of a fish-fence entails much labour and expense. Hundreds of stout stakes, 9 or 10 feet long, must be collected; one end has to be pointed, for these have to be planted firmly in the bottom to a depth of 3 or 4 feet. The rest of the material consists of great lengths of reed screens. These are made of reeds in the round, $6\frac{1}{2}$ to 7 feet long, woven into mat-form of the same breadth after the fashion of Indian tattie blinds; in making them the reeds are laid parallel with one another, and then bound together by four or five rows of lacings spaced about 20 inches apart. These lacings are paired lengths of the flexible *mindri* creeper (*Stenochæna palustris*) woven in and out opposedly round each reed: the thickness of the *mindri* determines the width of the spaces between the reeds; this averages three-eighths of an inch. Only the smallest fishes are able to squeeze through this narrow slit.

When all the preparations are completed, the fishermen plant the stakes, 4 to 5 feet apart, in long, curving lines. When all are in position the reed matting is tied on, forming a barrier to all passing fish. The completed fence is usually in the form of the letter 'J' with the curved section forming the seaward end. Sometimes two rounded heart-shaped compartments, trapped at the entrance, are fitted in the outer bend as pens or pounds, one at the extreme outer end, and one *vis-à-vis* on the opposite side of the bend, just where the longshore arm ends. Text-fig. 42, A and B, explains graphically the lay-out of some common types; Text-fig. 42, A, is the one commonly seen. Various modifications are met with, according to the owner's fancy or experience or in order to meet some local configuration of the shore line and tidal run. Text-fig. 42, A and B shows two of these. The more complicated form in which are two doubly trapped pens is seen in the same series of diagrams (Text-fig. 42, C).

Reed fences have comparatively short lives; they fall in ruin before the first storm of moderate intensity.

In the Tongan Islands an entirely different arrangement of the trapped chambers is characteristic of the fishing-weirs which are numerous in the shallow water within the reef-lagoon on the coast of Tongatabu. In the one examined typical of all, the fencing is erected on a zigzag plan, with a single rounded pound, at the apex of each of the salient angles. Tongan fencing is made of two parallel rows of stakes set upright a few inches apart,

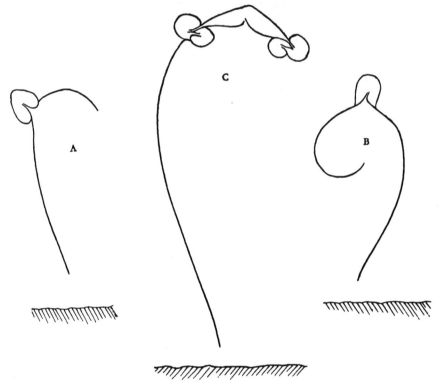

Text-fig. 42. Plans of typical fishing-weirs or pounds, Oceania. A, as used in Vitilevu Bay; B, one seen east of Savu-savu Bay; C, a type with two double pens.

the space between filled in with branches laid horizontally. From the outermost pound a long leader runs slanting towards the shore.

In the Dutch Indies and in particular in Java and around Batavia, elaborate fishing-weirs are many and greatly variable in the lay-out. An outstanding characteristic runs through all, distinguishing them from the Fijian type: this is the striving after symmetry. It might be thought that this occurs as a result of the Dutch love of order and tidiness, but this cannot be, for these traps are built and owned by the native Javanese and Malays. By a curious coincidence these people do have something of the

Dutch characteristics mentioned and this seems to eliminate any suggestion of Dutch influence in the planning of the weirs. In one type, two long curving leaders lead to a single heart-shaped prison chamber; in another a long straight leader leads direct to the centre of the widely open mouth of a very wide and large heart-shaped pen; this leads into a much smaller pen and this in turn into a third and thence into a fourth and terminal pen; both these two last are trapped at the mouth by the close approximation of two inwardly projecting lips which it is practically impossible for fish to force if they attempt to escape. The medial position of the leader permits fishes to enter from either side; it makes no difference whichever direction the fish may be running.

XVII

THE GREATEST EEL-FARM AND EEL-TRAP IN THE WORLD

1. MOSTLY ABOUT GETTING THERE

HIDDEN away in the heart of that vast and dreary system of brackish marshes and lagoons formed in the course of the never-ending conflict waged between sea and river in the widespread delta of the Po, high up on the Italian side of the Adriatic, live a quiet and industrious community of fishermen who cultivate these shallow waters as methodically as the agriculturist farms the stable earth. These people, inhabitants of the ancient city of Comacchio, are descendants of Roman subjects who, driven from their homes by a flood of barbarians from the north in the middle of the fifth century of our era, sought refuge in the recesses of an immense marsh which their skill and industry have transformed through the centuries into a gigantic system of fish-farms without rival in the vastness of its extent and the richness of its produce. Other men of the same origin who fled to the low islands off the coast farther north, turned their attention to manufactures and to trading and thus founded the nucleus of the mighty commercial community that became Venice, a republic of merchants, whose sea-power made her for long years the mistress of the Mediterranean.

Comacchio had no such ambition; it was too busy building dykes and catching fish to trouble about other commerce. To-day it remains unknown to the tourist, a place so far off the beaten track that when I inquired at the chief tourist agency in Venice as to the best means of travelling thither, an astonished clerk admitted that he was not quite sure, although he remembered that a similar inquiry had been made several years ago, also by an Englishman. Consultation of various time-tables showed that it was necessary to travel by rail to Ferrara, thence by steam-tram to the little town of Ostellato, on the western edge of the fish-farm area, where, if I were in luck, a *diligenza* would be found to carry me the remaining 13 miles to Comacchio. But it was doubtful whether I would be able to inspect the fishing operations unless I were provided with a letter of introduction. The help of the British Consul seemed indicated. He proved to be a very courteous Italian gentleman and he very kindly furnished me with a personal letter of recommendation to the Prefect of Ferrara.

In due course I reached Ferrara by noon the following day, where I found the Prefecture to be located in the magnificent medieval castle of the princely house of Este, a huge embattled pile dominating the city as a stately oak overshadows a thicket of brushwood. Up the noble staircase to the Prefect's office; a neat maidservant says the Prefect cannot be seen; some little persistence and a small *douceur* brought the advice to return in an hour's time, when, perhaps His Excellency might be visible.

The interval was easily filled in. My Italian courier knew where a dish of the most delicious and freshly made tagliatelli was to be had, together with a bottle of the best wine produced in the province. Both came up to expectations and when we had done, there was just time for a hurried visit to the fine old cathedral, before returning to the castle. The maidservant had fulfilled her compact and smilingly ushered me into the great man's presence. I explained briefly the purpose of my visit and handed him the British Consul's letter. Taking it in his hands, upside down as it happened, he looked solemnly at it, without reversing it. After a pause, long enough to suggest that he was reading it, he looked up and said: 'This is quite irregular, the English Consul in Venice has no right to address me; this province is outside his area. This request should have come through the Embassy in Rome.' I suggested that it was too trivial a matter for the Ambassador, that the Consul wrote semi-officially and that all I wanted was a recommendation to the officials at Comacchio to further my inquiry if it was in their power. This had no effect. The Prefect repeated all he had said before and added that he could not give orders—the fishery was a private concern and was not under the control of the Government. He could do nothing. Feeling decidedly annoyed, I told him I would return to Venice and report to the Consul that he declined to assist me. This had a greater effect than I expected. The Prefect altered his tune and became less difficult. Still maintaining that he had no power to help me, he promised eventually to send a telegram to the sub-prefect at Comacchio to give me any assistance in his power.

Hurrying away I just managed to catch the noisy little steam-tram as it was leaving on its afternoon run to Ostellato and beyond. It was made up of half a dozen waggons laden with sugar-beet and a couple of passenger coaches filled with sturdy peasants. Outside the city the track, which runs along one side of the highway, skirts a broad canal for some distance and I noted with interest that the industrious Italian fisherman has borrowed from China the mechanical lever dip-net, suspended from the end of a derrick-like arm, operated by a windlass that alternately submerges and raises the four-cornered net.

After the town is left behind, the country extends in level plain, as far as the eye can see. The wide fields are given over entirely to the cultivation of beet and hemp, their boundaries marked out by long, straight lines of tall, stiff poplars. No vineyards are to be seen, but up each tree a vine is trained and its branches led on cords to form a leafy festoon stretching from tree to tree. The time was the end of September and the vintage was on. Crowds of men and women were busily engaged in gathering in the crop, throwing the great bunches of black grapes into huge tuns loaded upon carts drawn by yokes of the most beautiful cattle I have ever seen. Without exception every pair were creamy white in colour, the dreamy, docile eyes looking out from a dark-rimmed setting like the kohl-darkened eyes of Eastern beauties. So like are these oxen to the so-called Chillingham wild cattle of Northumberland that some have suggested that the remote ancestors of the British breed were Italian cattle introduced into England by the Romans.

When Ostellato was at length reached, I did, indeed, find the promised *diligenza* awaiting the tram, but a crowd of bustling countrywomen in voluminous skirts, carrying huge baskets of vegetables, got there first and filled it to overflowing. Was there any alternative? Yes, a burly figure was hailing me from the box of an antiquated and nondescript vehicle that had perhaps been a victoria, in its prime, volubly and insistently soliciting the honour of my patronage. What though the vehicle was shabby and dilapidated and the harness tied together mainly with string, the horse appeared sufficiently alive to serve the need of the moment. A bargain was soon struck, and we prepared to start. Closer inspection showed that the hood which was up was a fixture in that position, so preferring fresh air I disposed my courier inside and clambered up to a seat beside the jarvey. 'Come close to me', he urged, 'the spring on that side is weak; it might break.' Not very hopeful, I thought!

The old fellow was garrulous. Though my Italian is but weak, I managed to get the drift of much that he said. He was immensely proud of having served in Garibaldi's army; this he told me by way of introduction, feeling, I take it, that this would secure him the favour of any Englishman. A few words in praise of his old leader gratified the old man immensely. The Liberator was his one and only hero and it was with the greatest pride that he told the story of how he had been wounded at the battle of Gaeta; he wanted to doff his coat and shirt to show me where the bullet had glanced along the ribs, leaving a long furrowed scar.

When I told him of my futile interview with the Prefect, he roared with delight: 'Oh, so you do not know that he is always fuddled by midday; if you want to get any sense out of him, you must see him in the early morning', was his comment. Parenthetically I must explain that this incident occurred in pre-Mussolini days; the Duce certainly did his best to regenerate Italy and such abuses became evil memories of the past during the heyday of his rule.

Our way lay for the most part along the crown of a broad earthen embankment skirting the northern side of the greatest of the artificial lakes or *valli* made by banking in and subdividing the lagoon area devoted to fish-farming. The wide fields, demarcated by vine-festooned lines of stately poplars, were left behind. In front lay a treeless expanse of dead, stagnant pond and marsh, stretching away without break to the eastern horizon. The time passed quickly; the old Garibaldian at my side, learning of the object of my journey, was now so much my friend that he pooh-poohed the idea of interviewing the sub-prefect for assistance. 'You may be sure the Ferrara prefect has done nothing,' he asserted, 'he just wanted to get rid of you. But never mind, my brother is a *fattore* at the principal fishing station and he will show you everything.' During the rest of the drive when Jehu was not telling me how the eels and mullet are caught in the farms or pointing out objects of interest, he recited long passages from Petrarch, descriptive of the country we were in. Imagine an English cabby or taxi-driver quoting Shakespeare's descriptions of English scenery!

Only once on this long monotonous road did we come across a house—a little inn with a deal table set out under a vine-covered trellis. The wine was thin and the grapes small and poorly grown, but hunger is a good kitchen and both were as acceptable as though they had been of the finest quality.

The great bell of the gaunt grey cathedral of Comacchio was booming out the hour of seven as we entered the city, a place much larger and more important than I had expected. The streets were already empty of people and traffic as we drove up to the solitary albergo, and shops were few and unpretentious. As I was soon to discover the city lives a life all its own, a life detached from the bustle and anxieties of the outside world; it is comparable to a great passenger ship anchored far out from land, visited from time to time by bumboats bringing what supplies are not obtainable from the sea itself. The people are all dependent, directly or indirectly, upon one central authority, which in turn has but a single source of revenue —the produce of its fisheries. These are the property of the Commune and are either worked directly by the employees of the Commune for the common good or else are rented out for a term of years to a commercial firm. The menfolk follow their calling after the fashion of the sea, working in shifts or watches throughout both day and night at fishing stations located on platforms of reclaimed land or ancient islets dotted here and there throughout this huge lagoon region. Relieved at intervals of 12 days for a few days rest with their families living in the city, these men are paid a modest wage supplemented by a daily ration of fish which assures them a standard of living that exceeds that of many classes of workers in Britain. Canals intersect the city in all directions, as in Venice; the people live an amphibious life and much prefer a boat to any wheeled vehicle; the water is their home and the source of their livelihood.

The little albergo proved a pleasant hostelry; it served, and I hope still serves, as the *de facto* club of the town's intelligentsia—the lawyer, the schoolmaster, the local engineer and some business men—who were immensely diverted by the story of my encounter with the Prefect of their province. The food was excellent, for what these country folk do not know about the preparation of *pasta* in its various forms of macaroni, spaghetti, tagliatelli and so on, and of the finny inhabitants of the lagoons, eels, mullet, smelts and bass, is not worth knowing. And who can resist ample indulgence in a good strong wine when the bottles bear the name *Bosco d'Eliseo*, produce of a vineyard on the broad sandspit or *lido* separating the lagoons from the sea? But I have to admit that there was a fly in the ointment, and a large and troublesome one at that; the lagoon marshes breed noisy and extremely hungry mosquitoes; without a mosquito net enveloping the bed, sleep is out of the question!

The way in which the fishing rights came into the possession of the Commune or Corporation of Comacchio is interesting. During the Middle Ages they were one of the chief sources of revenue to the Este family, Dukes of Ferrara. In 1598, Pope Clement VIII dispossessed the Estes and seized both the Duchy and the Comacchio lagoon, and it remained a papal possession until Napoleon seized it in 1797 during his campaign against the tottering Republic of Venice. Being loot which he could not remove to Paris, he wisely sold it to the Commune of Comacchio, which has held it ever since.

Eels constitute by far the chief product of the farming operations, the catch ranging from about 400,000 kilos in a poor season to over 1,000,000 kilos in a good one. The revenue to the Commune when the fishery is rented out is from 120,000 to 180,000 gold lire (lire 25 to the £1 sterling). Most of this is marinated in spiced vinegar and the bulk of the manufacture was sold to Germany and Austria before the war. In the Middle Ages the kegs of marinated eels were carried on pack-horses along the historic road between Venice and Augsburg, the great artery of commerce in those days between Germany and the head of the Adriatic.

II. EEL-FISHING AND EEL-FARMING AT COMACCHIO

The Comacchio fish-culture region at the time of my visit consisted of a series of thirty-seven sections or *valli*, which for convenience I shall hereafter call 'fish-farms'. These lie between two of the deltaic effluent branches of the River Po and have a combined area of about 90,000 acres. To each section is apportioned at least one fishing station where are situated the labyrinths employed to trap the maturing fish, the storehouses for gear and repair material, and the barracks where live the *fattore* or foreman of the *valle* with the company of fishermen under his control. The men live and mess together like soldiers in barracks, a necessity consequent upon the fact that the chief work of the year, the herding of the fish into the traps, takes place during the night. The life is hard but custom and the traditions of centuries render the men passively content, satisfied if

THE GREATEST EEL-FARM AND EEL-TRAP IN THE WORLD 163

they be allowed Saturday and Sunday on alternate weeks to spend with their families at Comacchio.

They struck me as a fine body of men; true handy men they are, for their duties include the supervision of the entry of the fry from the sea during the spring, the repair of the dykes, the weaving of the reed screens, the construction of the labyrinths and sluices and the collection of the mature fish. Repairs to the embankments and fishing stations are executed during the hot season (June to July) when the water in the lagoon is low.

The work of policing is done by a separate staff of over one hundred men who patrol the lagoon in light boats both day and night. Their duties

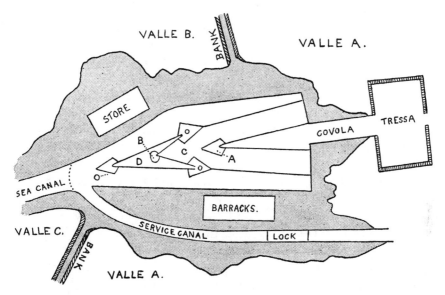

TEXT-FIG. 43. Plan of a labyrinth for the capture of eels and mullet at Comacchio, Italy.

are no sinecure, for the surrounding villages are full of poachers and the area to be protected so extensive—the perimeter of the lagoon is 177 miles!

The various fish-farms are bounded and divided from one another partly by natural tongues of land and chains of islets and sandbanks, and for the rest by artificial earthen banks which convert the islets and miniature peninsulas into continuous embankments (Text-fig. 43). Where necessary the foot of the dyke is reinforced with rows of stakes. The earthwork itself is the sandy mud from the bottom of the lagoon; sedges and grass are encouraged to grow on the slopes and edges to protect and consolidate the surface. The natural chains of islets nearly all run north and south, roughly parallel with the coast; this suggests that they represent remnants of successive and ancient sea-bars, now stranded inland owing to the gradual extension seawards of the land by deposit of silt brought down by rivers, which the prevailing coastal current fashions into a bank running in the same direction as itself. The depth of water is never great in the fish-farms; it generally ranges between 3 and 4 feet, but in times of drought large areas dry out.

The fishing stations are located generally at places where natural islets originally existed. Here one or several canals are cut, connecting the water within the fish-farm with a wide channel on the outer side, leading to the sea. Except for a short period each year when the eel fry are due to arrive in their countless, jostling multitudes, the canals through each islet are blocked at their inner ends by wattled palisades which serve the double purpose of imprisoning the stock of fish within the farm, and of allowing some interchange of water between the lagoon and the sea. A second and more elaborately built series of palisaded screens is set up on the approach of autumn in the form of a trapped labyrinth designed to capture the maturing eels when the awakening of the breeding instinct urges them to leave their inland home and head for the spawning grounds far out in the Atlantic, where alone the European eel finds the conditions suitable for reproduction.

These labyrinths are most ingeniously constructed. Divested of detail, a typical example may be described as a successive series of three V-shaped sets of very stout reed screens supported by heavy timber posts; each has the open base turned toward the inner end of the canal and the apex directed toward the sea. The fish, which comprise mullet as well as eels, enter the second chamber of the labyrinth through a very narrow apical opening in the first with walls that give slightly as the fish press against them, springing back into position after they pass through. When in turn the fish attempt to leave this second chamber, again by a slit-shaped opening at the apex, the species are separated automatically as they pass out; the place where they find themselves is a heart-shaped trap without exit and with walls just stout enough to prevent the mullet from escaping, but not sufficiently thick to hinder the eels, fiercely determined to win their way to the sea, from forcing their bodies through the bundles of reeds. They succeed only to find themselves in a third and terminal triangular chamber having a small trap, also triangular in plan, at each of its angles. The walls of these traps as well as those of the main chamber are constructed in a most massive manner; the reed screen, composed of a number of layers of reed bundles, is from 7 to 8 inches thick, supported by stout piles and secured in place by horizontal baulks of timber. Through these massive screen-walls there is no escape even for the most slippery of eels, possessed though they be with frantic, overpowering desire to force a way to the sea at any cost (Pl. xxvi, figs. A and B).

This so-called fishing of the lagoon continues for a period of three months—October, November and December. Large catches occur only on moonless or overcast nights. When a storm from seaward coincides with the occurrence of such black nights, the quantity of fish that accumulates in the labyrinths is sometimes so enormous that the traps become choked with a solid mass of struggling fish. After one such night over 322 metric tons of fish were taken from them, as much as $64\frac{1}{2}$ metric tons being yielded by one fish-farm alone. Quantities so vast are inconvenient to handle, so, whenever the workers find the fish accumulating too quickly in the labyrinths, they light bonfires at the inner ends of the canals and this has the effect of checking the migration temporarily.

The fishing season had just begun at the time of my visit. Never shall I forget the scene during the emptying of the traps. Standing on the thick summit of the reed palisade, lusty fishermen, stripped to the waist, their bodies glistening with sweat, lunged and twisted great dip-nets among the writhing bodies of the eels imprisoned in the final traps; enough being caught, still greater effort was needed to raise the struggling mass of bronze-hued fishes. Slowly and with assistance the net came up and then what a mighty splashing when the contents were decanted into the store receptacles!

The night's catch, which was but a small one as the season was only beginning, having been stored away ready for despatch to the factory, all hands trooped back to barracks for the midday meal; the men insisted that I should join them—no men are more willing to share their crust with the stranger than the Italian peasant and fisherman—and so delicious was the savour that came from the mess-room that I very willingly accepted the invitation so kindly proffered. The *pièces de résistance* were broiled eels and grilled mullet, fit delicacies as then prepared for the most critical of gourmets, washed down as they were with wine of excellent flavour although it came out of a stoneware jar and had no distinctive name. Bunches of small but luscious black grapes, piled in heaps on the bare table, served as dessert, and then, finally, a little cup of excellent coffee and a small glass of the local cognac. Here, certainly, was no low standard of living!

The next morning was spent at the factory in Comacchio. A barge had just come in filled with a writhing mass of eels all in the characteristic livery assumed when fully adult and ready for their seaward migration. The boat lay in a little basin at one end of a shed where a number of 'headers' were seated before wooden blocks, each surrounded by several baskets. The eels, scooped up by means of landing-nets, were filled into baskets and distributed to the headers whose operations consisted in chopping off the head of the living fish and dividing the body at intervals so as to give lengths of $4\frac{1}{2}$ inches to each. Only at alternate intervals was the body cut right through; at the other points it was merely nicked deeply, to allow the halves of each double section to be folded upon themselves. As the men work they sort the pieces according to size and quality into the various baskets around them. The heads are considered as offal and are sold by the heap to the workers and townspeople at a trifling price.

As the baskets are filled with the severed sections, they are carried to the roasting room where they are spitted and then cooked before roaring fires on open hearths. This room extends the full length of the building; the fires, eight in number, occupy the whole of one side, the spitting tables the other. Between are wooden racks on which the filled spits rest before and after roasting. The spits upon which the double sections of fish are transfixed are iron rods about 7 feet long, provided with an L-shaped handle at one end, so that when hung upon a bracket at either side of the fireplace it may be turned by hand. Eight spits are ranged in vertical order before each fire. The four upper spits are tended by one woman, the four lower by a second; both stand at the right-hand side of the fire as the handles are all placed on that side. These two workers attend solely to the roasting of the fish—to the proper rotation of the spits. Other women see to their placing and removal. The fresh spits with the raw fish are placed on the upper brackets; the lower rows get the greater heat and as they are completed and removed those above are moved down to occupy their places. Wood fires are used; fresh fuel is frequently added to keep them blazing furiously, giving out an intense heat.

As the fish roast a considerable quantity of oil oozes out. This drips into a sloping gutter in front of the hearth and flows along it into an underground tank. Some further oil is also collected from the spits as they cool on the racks which are furnished with wooden troughs at the base to catch the drip. The oil obtained is employed in the frying of smelts. When the roasted eels have cooled sufficiently they are stripped from the spits and arranged in orderly rows in circular shallow baskets which are carried outside and laid in the shade of a wide veranda to finish cooling before further handling.

When the fish have lost all their heat, the baskets are carried to the packing room where the sections are neatly packed into wooden barrels and kegs of various sizes. The lower layers are packed fairly tightly, the upper ones rather less so; when full the barrels are headed up, and spiced vinegar containing a little salt is poured in through the bung. The barrels are left to stand for some time, additional vinegar being added if necessary when the time comes to close the bunghole.

The barrels and kegs are made on the premises. On an average about 22,000 are required for the year's pack. As showing the extensive nature of this trade at the present day, the quantity of vinegar required during the three months which constitute the main fishing season, averages 350,000 litres or 77,000 gallons, all made from local wine.

Marinated smelts are prepared differently from eels as they are smaller and more delicate. Instead of spitting and roasting they are first rolled in flour and then fried in deep oil in copper cauldrons. After frying, and subsequent cooling, they are packed in kegs in vinegar in the same way as eels.

Considerable quantities of the fish caught are also marketed alive, special live-cars being employed to convey them to the towns along the coast and up the River Po. They have the form and appearance of a flat-bottomed lake boat; they are sharp at both ends and are fully decked over. The sides are perforated with rows of narrow slots. There are no bulkheads within and they have but a single square hatch, closed with a sliding cover. These live-cars when prepared to convey quantities of live eels, are corded round with many lashings of rope to enable them to stand the strain of prolonged towage.

Similarly shaped craft but of greater size are employed in large numbers as storage receptacles whenever abnormal catches of eels are made in the labyrinths. If the marinating factory is to be run economically, it is obviously essential that a steady supply of fish shall be available during the working season, hence the value of these great store-chests. A usual size is about 50 feet in length by a beam of 10 feet and a depth of 2 feet. Each fishing station has a number ready in its store shed; in them the eels live for days and even weeks without harm. With such provision the administration is prepared to take full advantage of those notable nights when vast multitudes of eels simultaneously develop an instinct that urges an immediate departure for the sea. In a single night a couple of hundred tons weight of fish may be taken from the labyrinth traps; some weeks are needed to roast and marinate such a quantity; were it not for the use of these store-boats, work would be forced at a wasteful pace and much fish might be lost.

XVIII

POISON-FISHING

THE capture of fishes by means of toxic substances thrown into still waters is so widely distributed throughout the world as to lead us to deduce high antiquity for the practice.

In South America, particularly in the basin of the Amazon, fish-poison is employed more extensively than in any other region. Owing to the prevalence there of this usage and because of the great diversity of plants made use of, botanists have devoted much attention to the subject and nearly one hundred plants have been listed as yielding extracts poisonous to fishes, or capable of causing stupefaction in varying degree. The great majority are the products of plants collected in the adjacent forests, but a few of the more potent, notably *Lonchocarpus nicou*, *Tephrosia toxicaria*, and *Clipadium* spp., are cultivated over a wide area either in small domestic clearings carrying from 25 to 100 plants or in regular plantations of as many as 10,000 stocks. (See Killip, 1930.)

In Europe the toxic qualities of certain species of *Verbascum* and *Cyclamen* have been employed for a similar purpose. To the Greek poet Oppian, who wrote of fish and fishing in the second century A.D., we are indebted for a wonderfully vivid word picture in smoothly flowing verse (*Halieutica*, iv, 658 ff.) of the gradual onset of the stupefaction that attacks fishes following the scattering of pounded *Cyclamen* roots ('sowbread') in pools and streams. The poet must surely have taken an active part in some such exciting scene as that which I watched enacted within a Fijian lagoon, when we find him writing:

> Soon as the deadly Cyclamen invades
> The ill-starred fishes in their deep-sunk glades,
>   ...the slowly working bane
> Creeps o'er each sense and poisons every vein,
> Then pours concentred mischief on the brain.
> Some drugged, like men o'ercome with recent wine,
> Reel to and fro, and stagger through the brine;
> Some in quick circlets whirl: some 'gainst the rocks
> Dash and are stunned by repercussive shocks;
> Some with quenched orbs, or filmy eyeballs thick,
> Rush on the nets and in the meshes stick,
> In coma steeped their fins more feebly ply,
> Some in titanic spasms gasp and die.
> Soon as the plashings cease and stillness reigns,
> The jocund crew collect, and count their gains.

In Africa the stupefying of fishes by decoctions of various plants is both common and widely distributed; the plant most in favour is *Tephrosia vogelii*, used in preference to any other wherever it may be found in abundance, from Sierra Leone in the west, through lower Nigeria, the lower Cameroons, on to Uganda, Nyasaland, Mozambique and Madagascar in the east.[1]

So highly valued is this plant as affording the easiest possible way to obtain a good supply of fish that it is cultivated with this purpose in view everywhere in and around the villages of the high plateau region of the Cameroons lying south of the savannahs of the Lake Chad region.

The leaves are the part made use of, so, when a communal fish-poisoning expedition has been decided upon by the village elders, the people collect great quantities of *Tephrosia* stems and carry them to the place of fishing, where they are stacked in heaps. Groups of men attack these with sharp-edged sticks, cutting the leaves into a green mush. When this is complete, the mush is usually mixed with some stiff mud. If the pool is of little width, men wade in with baskets filled with the mixture and scatter it by handfuls over the whole surface. Should the pool be large and wide, basketfuls are loaded into a canoe to be distributed in the places out of reach of the waders. Five minutes later the smaller fishes rise to the surface, belly upwards. A wild scramble ensues, everybody intent upon reaping what they may of the finny harvest.

If the place chosen is part of a stream, a barrier of interlaced branches is set up at the lower end and basket-traps are sometimes placed there to receive any of the larger fish which retain enough strength to attempt escape from the contaminated area.

But *Tephrosia* is by no means the only poison-plant used in this locality. The pods of *Tetrapleura*, the fruits of *Mimusops djave* Eng. and several other lesser known poison-plants are also utilized, if *Tephrosia* is unobtainable in sufficient quantity. One of these is *Morelia senegalensis*, the use of which extends across Africa at its widest, from Sierra Leone and Senegambia to the Bahr-el-Gazal Province of the Anglo-Egyptian Sudan.

In the flat savanna region of the Cameroons lying within the basin of the River Benue, the leaves of *Tephrosia* are replaced as a fish-toxin by the bark of the forest tree *Balanites aegyptica* Del., reduced to a pulp. This is used by itself in the usual manner as above described and also in conjunction with an elaborate arrangement whereby great numbers of large-sized fishes are induced to congregate by means of a long-continued course of daily feeding within a selected area in the bed of the Benue river, stocked with many tree

---

[1] The use of *Tephrosia* as a fish-poison in Africa is probably due to introduction through contact with Indonesian settlements in Madagascar and, possibly, on the mainland coast itself. This is, indeed, one of the pieces of evidence pointing to the strength of Indonesian cultural influence upon the east coast of Africa in the first millennium of the Christian era.

branches to give shelter to the visitors. At the end of a month the fishermen enclose this area with a rough fencing, leaving open a wide doorway at a point farthest from the shore. Towards the end of the third month the doorway in the fence is closed and the area within is poisoned by means of a decoction of *Balanites* pulp, whereby all the fishes are collected by the villagers without further trouble. (Monod, 1928, 266.)

Among other plants used by Africans for stupefying fishes are: *Randia dumetorum*, employed by natives living on the Upper Nile and in Mozambique; in Natal another species of *Randia* (*R. Kraussi*) takes its place. *Mundulea sericea*, *Lasiosiphon kraussianus*, *Combretum ternifolium*, and the large tubers of a species of Mucuna are also enumerated as yielding fish-poison in Nyasaland. (Bertram *et al.*, 1942, 70.)

Yet another plant, *Raphia vinifera*, is found in use for the same nefarious purpose in the delta of the Niger, for we find Mary Kingsley (1899, 488) stating that the fishing girls of Twon Town, at the mouth of the Bass river, are accustomed to resort to blind creeks 'where the currentless water permits them to use poison made from the pericarp of the fruit of this palm, pounded into a pulp. A supply of this is taken to the fishing-ground, mixed with water and baled out into the water of the creek. In a little over three hours you might see them paddling back, each tiny canoe (two or three girls in each) with from fifty to a hundred small grey mullet, sometimes with more and occasionally with a few small river soles.'

In Abyssinia, *Millettia ferruginea* has been recorded as a fish-poison. (Moloney, 1883, 31–2.)

In Asia, records of fish-poisons are incomplete and discontinuous. Omitting Palestine for the moment, we find that Habshush (1941) states that large fish (barbels) are caught in the River Kharid, north-east of San'a in the Yemen, after being thrown into a state of coma by the stupefying action of the black seeds of a wild shrub called *dhafar*; under this name several species of *Tephrosia* are known in Southern Arabia.

The Armenians of the head-waters of the Euphrates are another people addicted to this practice, and it is likely that they, too, use the crushed seeds of *Tephrosia* for the purpose, for Southgate (1841, I, 192) says that these hillmen 'knead into dough the powder of the *black* kernels of a poisonous plant and then throw bits of it into the water which the fish devour and soon rise to the surface dead'. He adds in a footnote that *Nux vomica* is used for a like purpose in Persia.

It is, however, in India that fish-stupefying is most extensively practised. No district is free from this abuse, and the variety of the substances used is astonishing. In Day's *Report on the Fresh-water Fish and Fisheries of India and Burma* (1873, lxxxviii and elsewhere), the Collector of South Canara is quoted as listing among these, such diverse ingredients as Croton-oil seeds, soap-nuts, *Cocculus indicus*, chillies and even fowls' dung.

Usually the poisonous mush is thrown into pools when the rivers are at their lowest, for then the fishes are massed together in such pools as remain. 'A regular time is fixed, and the villagers unite to dam the stream, collect poisons and gather the fish'—a most destructive and uneconomic form of fishing for, apart from those fishes which are of usable size, an immense quantity of fry is destroyed.

The use of tobacco leaves and the milk-bush (an *Euphorbia*) has been reported from the Bombay Presidency, together with numerous other plants not properly identified.

Stirring up of the muddy bottom is another of the practices employed at times; this causes partial suffocation, enabling the fishes affected to be caught with ease.

When on fishery duty in Palestine and Fiji, I was so fortunate as to learn many details concerning fish-poisoning as practised there as this was a subject which came directly under my notice when investigating fishery problems in these localities on behalf of the respective governments. In Fiji, I had unusually good opportunity to study the method used, for the principal Fijian authority in the island of Ovalau, Ratu Edward Thakombau, was so extremely kind as to arrange a communal fish-drive and the poisoning of a reef lagoon in order that I might become fully conversant with all details. Below I give all the relevant particulars obtained in these two localities:

PALESTINE. Everywhere in this country I found a knowledge of fish-poisons widely disseminated. Prior to the War of 1914–18, poison-fishing in ponds, lakes and slow-running streams was a common practice whenever conditions were favourable. To-day, this illicit method of fishing is greatly reduced; dynamite and other explosives have been found to be more lethal and effective, with the added advantage that their use is not restricted to quiet waters: a stick of gelignite or a Mills' bomb, relic of a war-time *cache*, is equally effective for its purpose whether thrown into placid enclosed waters or into the open sea. This substitute, frowned on by the authorities with just cause, is extremely difficult to suppress when explosives are obtainable easily during war-time and the years that follow. Even so late as 1934, when I was in Palestine, Arabs of the southern district were still unearthing unexploded bombs and shells, lost or hidden, some left by our own troops, but the greater part abandoned by the Turks during their retreat in 1917. The local Arabs had learned to extract the explosive very cleverly, but sometimes the results were tragic.

In the north of the country, little war material has been available, but the construction of Haifa harbour and the extensive quarrying operations in that neighbourhood for some years past have given plentiful opportunity to obtain illicit supplies.

Although the use of poison has been superseded to a large extent by dynamiting, it is still extensively practised, especially in the inland parts, as around Tiberias and Huleh, and in the various rivers when they run low and form quiet pools where fish tend to congregate; a condition necessary to the successful use of poison is that the water shall be still and without current.

The plants commonly employed by the Palestinian Arabs are three in number:

1. *Cyclamen latifolium.* In Arabic *rakaf* and *sabūnet er-r'ai* ('shepherd's soap'); less commonly it goes by the names of *zūkruk, zūknuk, zūkzuk, zūzu* and *zēmbak.*

2. *Styrax officinalis.* In Arabic the plant is called *abhar*, with *hauz* as the name of the seeds.

3. *Verbascum sinuatum* and other species of mulleins. In Arabic, *awar-war.*

Of these, the first two are those in most common use.

Cyclamen latifolium has a wide range in Palestine, growing most freely on the hills, but also creeping down the river valleys, as on the right bank of the Auja or Yarkon river near its mouth, and on the border of Lake Tiberias between Kennereth and the town of Tiberias.

Fishermen and others employ for their purpose the tuberous root, which usually has the form of a large and flattened potato. They pound it until it becomes of the consistency of soap and then throw it into the water. As it dissolves and spreads, fishes that come within the area of contamination become stupefied and float helpless on the surface; this poison has so powerful an influence that this method of fishing is extremely profitable, large quantities being netted out under favourable conditions.

The active principle is the alkaloid cyclamin which produces effects similar to those of the deadly arrow-poison *curare*, used by South-American Indians. Fishes are so susceptible to the baneful influence of cyclamin that dilution to the extent of one part to three thousand is sufficient to cause them to float to the surface in an inert condition; death results quickly in small fishes.

The people living at Athlit are credited with being particularly partial to this practice; they are, or were, accustomed to use this poison in the bay during periods of dead calm. Those of Haifa and Acre were also offenders in past years, using it both in the rivers and in the sea, but dynamite is now found to be more effective.

Styrax officinalis, which grows wild on the hills, is especially abundant in the region north of Lake Huleh, on the high ground between Metulla and Banias. The poisonous principle resides in the seeds; these are known under the name of *hauz* in the bazaars where they are generally obtainable at shops known to those who require supplies.

For the purpose of obtaining fish-poison from these seeds, they are first ground and afterwards boiled in water to which a small quantity of wheat flour has been added; to this they subsequently add some sheep's gall and a further small amount of flour, boiling the mixture until it becomes of the consistency of paste. This is afterwards dried; when required it is broken up and the crumbs are thrown upon the surface of any pool or quiet backwater where fishes are known to be abundant. As with *Cyclamen*, it is also used on occasion in the sea when conditions are exceptionally tranquil. Some fishermen affirm that the use of *Cyclamen* paste is most effective in brackish and in fresh water, whilst *hauz* is the better poison for use in the open sea.

Regarding the third vegetable poison, extracted from *Verbascum*, I learned nothing definite, but, according to Dr Rabinovitch, the plant when dried is thrown upon the surface of the water to be contaminated and then is beaten with sticks until its juices turn the water yellow. How this procedure can have the result stated is difficult to understand; I should judge that the beating is done *prior* to throwing into the water. Fishes which come within the area affected are stupefied, float up and are netted out as in the case of fishes stupefied with the other two poisons.

None of the three poisons named renders fishes unfit for human consumption, if they are properly gutted and washed before cooking. The vital objection to their employment is the wastefulness of the method; in most instances the great majority of the fishes affected are too small to be of any market value and are left to die on the banks or in the water.

Unslaked lime is also occasionally thrown into pools to kill or stupefy fishes, but few professional fishermen use either this or any of the poisoning methods; these are practised mainly by fellahin without any stake in the waters.

FIJI. Travelling to the other side of the world, I found poison-fishing a common usage in the lagoons of many islands of Oceania. In Fiji in particular is it prevalent; its popularity vies with that of the fish-drive. Whenever conditions are favourable and a decision is made by the elders of a village, everyone gets busy raiding the nearby forest for the material requisite. This consists preferably of the roots of two species of *nduva*, plants belonging to the genus *Derris*, which is otherwise valued as the basis of a potent insecticide.

One species of *Derris* which is indigenous is called *nduva nganga* or *nduva-ni-Viti* (=*Derris uliginosa* Benth.); the other (*Derris malaccensis* Prain) is reputed to have been introduced from New Guinea, as is recognized by Fijians, who term it *nduva-ni-niukini*. *Tephrosia pescatoria* (*nduva-kei*) and a species of *Pittosporum* (*nggoling-goli* and sometimes *nduva-kalou* in Fijian) are also reputed to be employed for a like purpose.

When the villagers return laden with their spoil, they set to work to pound the roots and make the crushed mass into small bundles of convenient size to hold in the hand. Everybody works with a will, with much talk and jollity, anticipatory of the fun to come and the feast to follow.

The conditions of fishing differ entirely from those that prevail in continental lands. Instead of being restricted almost entirely to inland waters, in Fiji poison-fishing takes place in the lagoons bounded on the seaward side by the encircling coral reef. Here, when calm weather prevails, the water, sheltered from surf and swell by the reef, is still as a millpond at low tide, the time chosen for poisoning operations. An hour or so before dead low water the villagers load all their available dugout canoes with bundles of the crushed *nduva* roots. The crews paddle out to the area selected, followed by a crowd of their friends wading quietly, for now a ban of absolute silence is enforced lest the fishes be alarmed. All are armed with fish-spears, single-pointed. Reaching the chosen place the canoes are distributed over the area to be fished, an area characterized by cavernous rock masses such as dead coral-heads, ideal hiding-places for rock-haunting fishes. In hushed silence all await the signal to begin. When at last this is given the crew of every canoe dive simultaneously to the bottom, each man with a bundle or mass of pounded *nduva* in one hand or the bundle may be impaled on the point of a stick or spear, according to the nature of the rock cavities. The advantage of the spear or stick is that by its use the bundle may be pushed farther into the hole if it penetrate deeply into the rock. Each man may place in this way several handfuls. When this operation is complete, the men wait in a surrounding circle while the poison does its work. Within a few minutes the effect is seen. Some of the larger fishes, more resistant than others, dart out from their holes in the endeavour to escape the toxic influence of the drug—their fate is to be speared as they flee. Those that receive a sufficient dose become stupefied and float to the surface, more or less inert, to be gathered in by the hands or by the spear (Pl. xxvii, figs. A and B).

The factors of tide, weather and local physical conditions are all carefully considered before the fishing area, date, and hour are selected. Should there be any wind, the *nduva* is placed preferably in holes on the windward side of each rocky mass. The run of any current has also to be considered; the ideal conditions are a perfectly smooth sea with the operations timed to coincide with the slack water period at low tide.

Under the conditions in which poison-fishing is conducted in Fiji, the evil consequences entailed by this practice elsewhere are eliminated in great measure. The fishes caught sheltering in rocky cavities are, in the main, adult and of good size; small shoaling fish and fry are seldom involved. Hence if carried out according to the recognized Fijian usage, no serious objection need be taken; indeed, under the conditions implied in the agreement made with the Fijian chiefs, when they voluntarily ceded the islands to the British Crown, the continuation of the right of Fijians of indigenous race to practise this fishing method cannot well be withheld; people of other origin have no such claim to this privilege.[1]

Elsewhere in Oceania and Indonesia we find the tuba-plant (under which name several species of *Derris* are included) to furnish most of the raw material of the poison commonly used for stupefying fishes. The method in Borneo is more elaborate and destructive than usual. Having chosen a suitable stream, the natives erect a palisading across its mouth, with a bagnet fitted at an opening about the centre. The pounded tuba-root is then scattered broadcast over the surface; after a short interval to give the poison time to work, all the people, men, women and children, rush in to catch whatever they can by spearing, by plunge-basket or by hand, as the fishes begin to rise to the surface. Most of the larger fishes, having greater resistance to the poison, endeavour to escape and are caught in the bag-net fitted at the centre of the palisaded barrier.

In the Marquesas Islands fish-poisoning was formerly done both by men and women. The root of the *kohuhu*, 'a kind of broom' (evidently *Tephrosia*) was the agent commonly used. 'It was rubbed on the rocks enclosing pools filled with sea-water in which fish had been stranded at low tide, or it was carried down among rock crevices along the shore by divers.' (Handy, 1923, 178.) Evidently the procedure was identical with that employed in Fiji; Handy reports this from information received from some of the old men, and this accounts for whatever obscurity there is in the description.

The fruit of the *hutu* tree (*Barringtonia speciosa*) was also used for the same purpose. According to Jardin (1862, 38–9) the fresh fruit was broken open with a stone and rubbed on the rocks. Fishes were sometimes poisoned in deep water, men diving with the crushed *hutu* in their hands, and releasing it under water. All poison-fishing was done on the coast, for the fishes in the freshwater streams were too small or too few to make this form of fishing worth the trouble.

Few of the alkaloids present in these poisonous plants have been separated or fully studied. Of these few, mention has already been made of cyclamin. Tephrosine is another and even more peculiar poison and this has been proved to be a poison to which fishes are specifically and peculiarly susceptible, whereas mammals and marine invertebrates are immune unless the dosage is of concentrated strength. Its chemical formula is $C_{31}H_{26}O_{10}$.

---

[1] Since writing the above I have received from Sir Harry Luke, then Governor of Fiji, a copy of the Fisheries Ordnance recently enacted by the Fijian Legislature; in this it is gratifying to find that provision is made for the establishment of a committee to make inquiry into the nature and extent of the customary fishing rights of each village community prior to British rule, with instruction to codify these and to define the boundaries of each village area.

By this measure the good faith of the British Government is vindicated in the eyes of the Fijian people and the possibility of discontent eliminated for the future.

Various ceremonial observances attend the opening phases of some of these peculiar fishing operations, but the people are extremely reticent on this subject and our information is meagre. From the scraps available we find that the Cameroon negroes when beginning a communal fish-poisoning take great care to ensure that the first handful of *Tephrosia* mush shall be thrown by a virgin youth or by a man who has abstained for 2 or 3 days at least from sexual intercourse (Monod, *l.c.*). This has its parallel in India, where many fishing operations are subject to the latter restriction.

In Mexico, where fish-poisoning has been practised from time immemorial, 'when the Tarahumares are preparing to poison the waters of a river...they take the precaution of first making offerings to the Master of the Fish by way of payment for the fish of which they are about to bereave him. The offerings consist of axes, hats, blankets, girdles, pouches and especially knives and strings of beads, which are hung to a cross or a horizontal bar set up in the middle of the river;...next morning the owners of the various articles remove them.' (Lumholtz, 1903, 1, 403.)

POISON-WHALING. Any account of poison-fishing would be incomplete without reference to the use of poison for the killing and capture of whales, a method formerly prevalent among several maritime peoples living on the extreme northern coasts and islands of the Pacific Ocean. Technical objection may be taken to the inclusion here of means designed specifically for use in the whaling industry, seeing that whales are mammals and not fishes. The fact that their habitat and many of their ways of life are similar to those of fishes must be my excuse for introducing this ingenious phase of primitive man's resourcefulness in devising means to supplement his otherwise puny equipment for the capture of these leviathans of the sea.

The people who first made use of the idea appears to have been the Ainus, the folk who occupied the whole of Japan with an extension into the Kamchatka Peninsula before the irruption into their territory of intruders from the mainland of China and from the northern islands of Indonesia.

Within historical times poison-whaling extended from Yezo or Hokkaido, northernmost island of Japan, through the Kurile chain of islands as far as Kamchatka where it was once in current use along both the eastern and western coasts. Northward of this region it seems never to have been adopted by the circumpolar peoples. It passed neither to the Koryaks, nor to the Chukchi nor to the Asiatic Eskimos. Instead, with the intermittent flow of migrant bands of Mongoloid Asiatics to North America via the Aleutian chain of islands, it became known to and practised by the Aleuts of the islands and by the Koniags of Koniak Island and the adjacent Alaska Peninsula. On this side of the Pacific also it appears that poison-whaling failed to pass northward into Eskimoland; the reasons suggested are (1) evidence which points to a marked reduction in toxicity of poisonous plants when they grow in high latitudes, and (2) the fact that knowledge of how to prepare the material in a fully toxic form was kept a close guild secret by the possessors of the technique. That the knowledge passed to America via the Aleutians, points to this route—Kuriles–Kamchatka–Aleutians—having been a most important highway from Kamchatka. To a maritime people coming from lands to the southward this course afforded a more suitable route than did the short crossing at Bering Strait, which lay through a harsh and forbidding countryside, bare of any of the amenities familiar to migrants coming from a country favoured with a milder climate.

Wherever poison-whaling was practised, the people watched eagerly for any sign of the approach of a whale. When the watchers—'huers' as they would be called in Cornwall—gave warning of a whale in the offing, the quiet of the village dissolved into noisy activity as the men, shouting excitedly, raced to man their kayaks (*baidarkas* as the Russians name them). In the Aleutian Islands these craft are of the two-man type, the two man-holes arranged tandemwise; the man in front, the lance-thrower, the one aft, the paddler when his mate is otherwise engaged. In Kodiak Island the one-man kayak is favoured.

Steller (1774, 98, 103) tells us many details of the way the Kurile Islanders caught whales in the eighteenth century. Around the southern end of Kamchadal, the people put to sea in baidars,[1] searching the places to which the whales usually resorted:

If any are found [he says] they are shot with poisoned arrows [lances]; when the poison takes effect, the whale goes into a terrific flurry and sounds. Usually the Kurilians did not follow up the attack, preferring to look for another whale and to attack again with their poisoned weapons. All that they dared hope for was that out of several whales lanced and killed, one would be carried by current or tide to a neighbouring island and there cast on shore. The lance heads being of smoothed slate barbed on each side, it was easy for the owner to scratch his private mark upon the surface; custom ruled that any dead whale cast ashore belonged to the man whose mark was on the lance head embedded in the blubber or flesh—his to give away in portions and thereby to earn honour among his people.

The reason why they did not follow up the first whale lanced was that their kayak had insufficient man-power to enable them to tow it ashore should it die at a distance from their home village. The Eskimos, who used unpoisoned harpoons but who employed umiaks, manned by ten or twelve paddlers, were well-fitted to tow their captured whale; in an illustration given by Eggede in 1763, we see three well-manned umiaks engaged in towing a dead whale, the umiaks arranged in line ahead.

---

[1] Said by Heizer (1943, 421) to connote in this instance boats with a dugout base and built-up side planking; usually *baidar* is to-day the equivalent of the Eskimo *umiak*, a boat of open framing covered with skin.

Steller adds that 'when the Kuriles obtain a whale, no one begins to cut it up till all are assembled. First shamanizing takes place, each one puts on his best clothes and carries home his portion of the flesh or blubber. After this, one yurt entertains the other. Before and after the entertainment they give a dance and otherwise delight themselves in all sorts of ways.'

Although poison-whaling originated in Asia, the details of this practice are more fully known and better authenticated for the Aleutian-Koniak Island region than for its use in Asia. Heizer (*l.c.*) has collated all the descriptions on record, written mostly in German and Russian, and from these we are able to build up a fairly complete picture of this strange fishing method.

In all instances the American procedure was either identical with that employed in the Kurile-Kamchatka area or else so closely related to it as to be classed as of the same origin. Where differences occurred, we may presume with safety that they would be found to be equally characteristic of the original Asiatic practice, did we know as many details thereof as we happen to know of the American.

Kodiak whalers were accustomed to leave shore early in the morning in their two-man kayaks and to paddle to a place where whales—usually the humpback (*Megaptera kuzira*)—were expected to be encountered. When one was located, the kayak was paddled as silently as possible till within throwing distance. If the men succeeded in approaching unobserved, the forward man poised his lance and with the help of a spear-thrower, hurled it with all his strength into the whale; if possible, he planted it beneath or just behind the fore flipper or, alternatively, close to the dorsal fin if it happened to be a humpback. The lance, about 3 ells in length, say about 10 or 11 feet, was tipped with a stone point fitting loosely in the head of the shaft so as to become readily detached after entering the whale's body. If the poisoned lance-head penetrated well into the flesh, the poison quickly diffused and the whale usually died within 2 or 3 days; the quantity of the poison absorbed was never sufficiently concentrated to bring about death quickly.

Several writers (Markoff, 1856 and Von Kittlitz, 1858, quoted by Heizer, *l.c.* 430) have attributed the animal's death to inflammation caused by the irritation of the barbed lance-head embedded in the flesh; this is incorrect, for the true cause lay in the poisoning of the barbed head with smears of an aconite mixture. As already noted, this preparation and its application was carefully guarded as a close and valuable secret among the whaling families, who constituted the wealthy *élite* of the whaling centres. To maintain the secret of the essential ingredient, these people added a substance to the poison, which though actually quite innocuous, was, in common belief, considered to be peculiarly dangerous if handled; this ingredient was fat rendered down from dead bodies, preferably those of successful whalers, who by reason of the wealth so obtained, held high social position. This explanation of the tremendous effectiveness of the poisoned lance-heads sufficed to still the curiosity of those who were not members of the closed inner circle of the whaling fraternity—a bluff which seems to have been fully successful.

The stone points, smeared with this devil's mixture of human fat and deadly aconite poison were formed either out of smoothed pieces of slate of dagger-shape armed with a barb on each side, as was the preference of the Koniag whalers of Kodiak Island and of the neighbouring Alaskan Peninsula or else they were chipped out of fragments of glassy obsidian, or of fine-grained gritty trachyte.

The origin of poison-whaling in the Kurile-Kamchatka-Aleutian area was due undoubtedly to direct transfer of the custom of using poisoned arrows and lances in the chase once widespread throughout Eastern Asia, from the Naga Hills of Assam (Hutton, 1929, 58), through China to Japan where the Ainu hunted and killed the bear with arrows poisoned with aconite.

The aconite poison is prepared from the roots, according to Sauer (1802, 181). These roots after being dried are pounded or grated; water is then poured upon the powder and the mixture kept in a warm place till fermentation takes place; when this stage is reached, it is considered ready for use and it may then be smeared upon the points of arrows or lance points. With weapons thus anointed sea-lions as well as whales were hunted.

Modern usage. During the nineteenth century several attempts were made to modify and improve this aboriginal method of poison-whaling in such wise as to enable it to be adapted to modern commercial whaling. The first to enter the field was the Scottish firm of Messrs W. and G. Young, of Leith; they commissioned R. Christison in 1831 to devise a method and to prescribe the dosage of poison to be used. This he did and he also designed a form of harpoon head with hinged barbs which would spread open and thereby smash a glass container filled with prussic acid which was to be attached to the shaft opposite these movable barbs. Unfortunately, the vessels equipped with this weapon were crushed in the ice-pack and lost on their first voyage before the method could be tested. Success, however, attended a second expedition; one whale was hit by the poison-carrying harpoon fired from a harpoon-gun and surfaced dead soon after. The awesome result so unnerved the crew that they are said to have refused to use the dreadful weapon again. It appears that some doubt attached to this statement which may have been put abroad in order to deter competition by rival firms. This doubt is strengthened when we learn that a total of twenty-four whales were caught in the course of the vessel's voyage, an unusually high record and one which no other whaler, using normal methods, ever reached in voyages made about this period. The news of the successful use of a poisoned harpoon eventually became known and this led to a second attempt on the part of other Scottish whalers about the year 1838 or 1839 (Heizer, *l.c.*, 445). But again we hear of the crew refusing to flense those whales that were shot with the poisoned weapon.

Another vessel which attempted to use this new method of whaling was the American vessel *Susan Swan*; equipped with the necessary apparatus she sailed out of Nantucket in 1833 but the voyage was once again a failure so far as the new weapon was concerned, for the crew refused to handle the blubber of whales killed by means of the deadly prussic acid.

The idea of using poison in the whaling industry lay dormant for many years and it was not till 1861 that some Scottish whalers made another effort to revive it by varying the procedure; instead of a poisoned harpoon they proposed to use a rifle firing a shell filled with half an ounce of prussic acid. By means of a small powder charge fired by a 10-second fuse the shell was timed to explode after lodgement in the whale's body. The first trial of the new method proved successful (12 May 1862) but for some unexplained reason it did not lead to the establishment of a fishery based upon this technique.

It was left to a French scientist, M. L. Thiercelin, to carry out whale poisoning experiments on scientific lines and to publish the results in detail (1866).

He began by experiments upon horses, dogs and rabbits to ascertain the most effective poison to employ and the minimal dose necessary to kill a mammal of the great size attained by whales. The poison selected eventually was soluble strychnine salts mixed with one-twentieth part of curare. A dosage of 0·005 g. of this mixture per kilogram of the animal's weight if it weighed more than 10 kg., was found to cause death within from 10 to 40 minutes. From these results, Thiercelin estimated that a cartridge containing 30 g. of the mixture would be sufficient to kill a whale of 60,000 kg. weight, and that two cartridges would suffice to kill the largest whale to be found in the Arctic. To verify his conclusions he shipped on a whaling cruise. Ten whales were shot with bomb-lances carrying poison-cartridges of this toxicity. All died within periods corresponding with Thiercelin's calculations, death supervening within a period of time varying from 4 or 5 minutes to 18 minutes, the average being 10 to 11 minutes.

Of the ten poisoned whales, six were tried out without any accident resulting from the handling of the poisoned carcasses. Even those sailors with open wounds on their hands suffered no ill effects.

Notwithstanding the success which crowned this cruise in 1863 and the proved absence of danger to those who flensed the blubber, this method of killing whales has never been exploited commercially. What the original reason may have been we do not know, but in later years there is no doubt that the extensive use of whale fat and oil in the manufacture of margarine and the consumption of whale meat in time of stress or of war, would be adequate reasons to discredit the method and cause it to be abandoned. Advance in the technique of shooting whales with an improved form of harpoon-gun and the use of explosive shells have rendered the employment of poison unnecessary; these later measures have the additional advantage of removing any danger of the crew refusing work because of fear lest by some accident they might absorb some appreciable quantity of the dreaded poison while handling the blubber.

XIX

SEEKING PEARLS IN CEYLON AND INDIAN WATERS

THE pearl fisheries of South India and Ceylon are confined almost entirely to the Gulf of Mannar. The Indian pearl banks front the coast in a long chain of detached beds stretching from Manapad to Kilakarai, with the most prolific beds off the port of Tuticorin. Those on the Ceylon side are more compact in their distribution; the principal beds lie from 15 to 20 miles from land, stretching athwart the mouth of the shallow bay north of the island of Karativu and of Kudiramalai ('Horse-hill') Point, the Hippurus of the *Periplus of the Erythraean Sea*, written about the middle of the first century A.D. Less productive beds stretch southward, parallel with the coast from Karativu to Chilaw.

The average depth where the beds lie is 8 fathoms, but beds as shallow as 5 fathoms have occasionally yielded good results, and a few beds occur between 8 and 10 fathoms; these last seldom bring their harvest to a fishable age. Because of the relatively shallow depth, fishing has been carried on from the earliest historic period by naked or 'skin' divers.

The Sinhalese Chronicles mention pearls among the gifts and dowries passed between the Royal House of Ceylon and that of the Pandyan kings of South India in the closing centuries of the last millennium B.C. After the occupation of Alexandria by the Romans, pearls became particularly fashionable among Roman ladies according to Pliny,[1] who records that in his time the vogue had spread even to the poorer classes—'People are in the habit of saying that a pearl worn by a woman in public is as good as a lictor walking before her.'

With the arrival of the Portuguese in Ceylon early in the sixteenth century, that power acquired by conquest the sovereign rights in the fishery on the eastern side of the Gulf; those on the western side were obtained peacefully when the oppressed fisher-class on the Pandyan coast appealed for protection against the exactions of their overlord, the Naik of Madura. Thereafter the records of the pearl fisheries were carefully maintained, for they yielded a substantial revenue to the power in control.

From these records we learn that an outstanding characteristic of past fisheries was their erratic occurrence. A short series of productive fisheries usually alternated with a longer series of blank years, when the banks were either bare of pearl-oysters or were covered with oysters too young to be worth fishing. Another notable feature was that a good fishery on one

[1] *Nat. Hist.* ix, 54–8.

side of the Gulf seldom if ever coincided with one on the opposite side, a fact which leads to the inference that when conditions are favourable for a generous spat-fall on one side of the Gulf, the contrary is the case on the other side: the controlling factors are many, but it is certain that the most important are the character of the weather and the direction and strength of the currents at the time when spawning takes place.

Pearl-fishing exercises a compelling fascination upon all who come within reach of its spell; its story, staged in the Gulf of Mannar, has been told time and again from the days of Marco Polo and the medieval Arab travellers, down to our own time, when visiting globe-trotters splash the scene with picturesque purple patches.

All the boats used by the divers in their operations are open, undecked craft, hailing mainly from the small ports on the Indian side of the Gulf of Mannar and of Palk Strait; the remainder are contributed by the fishermen of the Jaffna coast villages in the extreme north of Ceylon. No Sinhalese craft participate, neither are any Sinhalese to be seen among the motley crowd of divers who flock to the fishery from Indian and Arabian fishing ports and from the Tamil provinces of Ceylon.

The lure of the pearling gamble suffices to attract an adequate contingent of volunteer divers and boat-owners. Some weeks before the date fixed for the commencement of operations, the Government concerned (Madras or Ceylon) broadcasts an advertisement throughout the Indian and Arab worlds proclaiming the prospective fishery; divers are invited to attend and boat-owners to bring small sailing craft. The sole conditions are obedience to the regulations and remuneration on the share system—one-third of the catch to the divers, two-thirds to the Government.

The vessels participating in a fishery vary greatly both in numbers and in types from time to time. The Ceylon fishery enjoys a superior reputation for rich yield over the Indian, and thereby attracts craft of all kinds from nearly all the fishing centres in the Indian districts of Tinnevelly and Ramnad; some, too, from Tanjore and a fair number from the northern province of Ceylon. The less productive Indian fisheries rely to a greater extent upon local craft; because their pearl beds lie closer inshore, many canoe craft unfit for work in Ceylon waters are enabled to participate. Off the Tinnevelly coast, the craft employed comprise large cargo lighters from Tuticorin, the dugout fishing canoes in use from Tuticorin to Manapad, outrigger canoes from Kilakarai and transom-sterned boats from Pamban; in the rare instances when a pearl fishery takes place in Palk Bay, the local balance-board canoes furnish the bulk of the small fleet employed; outrigger canoes from Kilakarai, Pamban dhonis and a few Tuticorin lighters constitute the remainder.

A few days before the date proclaimed for the start of a pearl fishery, the divers and their boats begin to arrive in the camp. The men have their own section allotted to them, where they run up rude shanties; each diver and each boat have to be registered with the beachmaster, who allots a distinctive number to each boat to be displayed prominently on hull and sail (Pl. xxix A). If a larger number of boats arrive than can be handled conveniently on the fishing-ground, two 'fleets' are formed, the red and the white; these fish on alternate days; if the beds prove prolific, the divers are so eager to fish that though only half the total number of boats are allowed out, each boat carries wellnigh a double crew—the native is resourceful and, if he is barred in one way, he exercises great ingenuity to keep within the letter of the law and nevertheless have his own nefarious way!

The great day at last arrives; notice has been given that fishing will begin soon after sunrise on this date; the preceding night saw the fleet set sail for the fishing-ground which lies generally about 20 miles off the coast in an average depth of about 8 fathoms. The Inspector of the Pearl Banks has already marked the limits of the day's fishing area with bamboo buoys carrying red flags, and has anchored his Indian-built inspection barque at the centre. With daybreak the whole fleet lie at anchor around the ship, the divers awaiting the gunfire signal to begin work.

As yet it is but a few minutes past six o'clock; the night chill will not be dissipated for another half-hour; till then some 9000 men—divers, line-tenders, guards and boatmen—who crowd the pearling craft will lie like shrouded corpses, covered even to their faces with whatever wraps they possess.

When at last the sun rises over the ragged silhouette of forest jungle that covers the greater part of the mainland of Ceylon in the region off which the pearl fishery is carried on, the sheeted figures begin to arise, stretching and yawning noisily after the manner of the East. From the boats manned by Tamils from South India a babble of voices rises; all have something to say (of no consequence whatever) and all say it simultaneously at the full pitch of voices that cannot be deemed musical by any stretch of courtesy. These men are Roman Catholics, descendants of converts more or less forcibly made by that most militant missionary, St Francis Xavier, nearly 400 years ago. The Muhammadans are quiet by comparison; just on our port quarter is a Jaffna dhoni, full of Arabs from Koweit, a small but independent state at the head of the Persian Gulf. At the stern they have fitted up a sand-filled firebox; on three stones arranged around a small fire of short sticks, a brass coffee-pot is set, a handsome, brightly polished vessel with an immense curved spout, reminiscent of the great bill of the toucan. As soon as the coffee boils, it is passed round in tiny cups; the aroma reaches me across the water as I lean on the rail watching—why cannot our Indian cook make a brew so strong and good, I wonder? It seems so delightfully simple; you put a handful of finely ground coffee into the pot with a generous allowance of sugar, add water sparingly and boil directly on the fire. One of these Arab coffee-pots I was able to secure; the inside is crusted thickly with a black deposit and for months it was a delight to lift the lid and take a long whiff of the lingering aroma.

Seven o'clock approaches. The voices take on an altered tone and from the nearer boats come appeals to make the signal to begin fishing. It still lacks some minutes of the hour, but the sea is placid, the sky cloudless and the air already balmy; in answer to a nod, the tindal breaks out a flag at the fore and I let off a couple of rounds from a rifle, for the authorities do not approve of the custom of arming the Inspection Vessel with cannon as in the turbulent days of Portuguese and Dutch domination when piracy and enemy action had to be guarded against.

Hardly has the sound of the shots died away before a great clamour rises from the crowded boats of the fishing fleet. The crews are galvanized into intense activity as they get busy hauling up their anchors—usually massive blocks of coral stone, holed at the centres—and row off in search of a rich patch of oysters. Usually, before they start work in earnest, the divers make a few trial dives; when satisfied, they anchor and the diving gear is got ready. This consists of two ropes for each pair of divers, who dive alternately. On the end of one rope is a heavy sinker to carry the diver rapidly to the bottom; the other serves as a life-line to haul him up when ready to ascend to the surface—a bag is attached to the lower end (Pl. xxix). The conservative Indian (Tamil) uses a granite sinker, weighing about 56 lb., the Arab prefers a leaden weight, the shape of a plummet, as being less clumsy to handle.

When all is ready the divers jump overboard; each seizes his pair of ropes; the sinker of the diving rope he adjusts so that his feet rest upon it; the net on the life-line he slings round his neck. The coils of both are held loosely by the diver's tender, ready to throw into the water when the diver pulls the slip-knot that releases the sinker rope. The weight carries the diver very quickly to the bottom, descending feet first. The moment he reaches bottom he steps off the sinker and releases his grip on the rope which is hauled up at once by the tender, ready for another descent. As soon as free, the diver starts to swim over the bed looking for oysters. Any seen, he pulls off the rock by a twist of the wrist, depositing it in the coir-bag slung round his neck, if an Indian, or in a light net-bag around his waist, if an Arab. The catch varies greatly; from none to fifty or sixty or even more on specially prolific ground.

All has to be done in an amazingly short time; no diver whom I ever saw at work in this fishery remained below water for more than 90 seconds if he had to collect oysters. Only the best of the Arabs stay underwater for more than 85 seconds when working; Indians are far behind; the ordinary Tamil, whether Hindu or Christian, scarcely ever remains under water for more than 50 seconds, but if he be a Muhammadan he is usually able to stay about 10 seconds longer—his physique and stamina are generally superior to those possessed by men of other religions.

No special preparations are made by divers before commencing work other than abstention from food from the preceding evening. The Arab carries a horn clip on a string around his neck, and this clip he adjusts upon his nose before descending (Text-fig. 44). The Indian closes his nostrils with the fingers of one hand and stubbornly declines to follow the example of the Arabs in spite of the obvious advantage it confers of allowing the use of both hands in place of one only.

Soon after the work of the morning has begun, the Inspector calls up one of the inspection launches and sets off on a very necessary tour of the fleet, to ensure that fitting respect is being paid to the fishing limits of the day's operations and to do what is humanly possible to check malpractices.

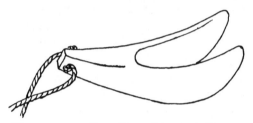

Text-fig. 44. Nose-clip used by Arab divers.

Passing a boat manned by Arabs, we note the unduly large proportion of faces pitted by smallpox. Many are fine featured with clear-cut profiles that bespeak the purity of their ancestry; a few are unmistakably negroid, the offspring of slaves, and others are half-breeds, Arab out of Negro. They come mostly from Bahrein and Koweit. At previous fisheries Arab divers gave the authorities much trouble, but my own experience of their conduct has been uniformly good. They require to be treated justly and firmly; they have contempt for anything that savours of weakness or indecision but will take reasonable punishment if it be shown that this is justifiable. They are essentially reasoning people and they appreciate and listen carefully to a friendly explanation of any regulations put into force. The men from Koweit at the time I refer to, were particularly quiet; their chief was then the famous Sheik Mubarrak, an Arab of Biblical character. My old friend Abdul Karim, a patriarchal diver who concealed his greying beard with the aid of flaming henna, once said to me:

'Yes, the Sheik, he rules justly; the foot of the runaway is cut off; the slanderer loses his tongue, and the prying one sees no more.'

Mubarrak was austere at home, but rumour (whose tongue certainly should be cut out) used to hint that the occasional visits paid to his pleasure-loving friend, the Sheik of Mohammerah, were periods of relaxation, when host and honoured guest looked upon the wine when it was red and perchance, occasionally, upon the rounded limbs of dainty dancing girls from Damascus and Aleppo.

Poor old Abdul Karim! He fell upon evil days in the end, when his strength began to fail. One day he came to me in great distress to beg a loan to pay his fare back to distant Koweit; when he got it, he insisted on giving me his ancient and rather dirty-looking rosary. The gift did not seem of any intrinsic value, but some years later, when the beads were washed and cleaned, I learned my mistake; the beads were fine examples of the rare and valuable Persian amber.

At midday, when the sea breeze generally begins to blow, the cease-fishing signal is made; the boats weigh anchor and head for the fishery camp. On landing, their catches are carried into a huge palisaded enclosure, the *kottu*, where division is made on the basis of one-third share to the divers, the remainder being that apportioned to the Government according to immemorial custom. As soon as this division is complete, the number of oysters in the Government share is ascertained by counting or, of recent years, by measurement in tubs of known capacity; the total number is sold by auction the same evening in units of a thousand oysters.

The divers are free to dispose of their share in whatever way they please: some sell to the smaller merchants; some hawk them about the camp, selling in twos and threes to the poorer people who are as eager to gamble as their wealthy brethren, while others try their luck by opening the shells themselves, especially if they know that the bed fished has proved to be rich in pearl-bearing oysters.

The majority of the more productive pearl banks lie far off shore, so the return run takes from 3 to 4 hours' sailing according to the strength of the wind even when favourable; indeed, if the breeze is light or if the midday calm is overlong continued, the fleet may not straggle to their moorings until evening.

With nothing to do during the run home, the itch for illicit gain becomes overpowering; after all, think the men, out of our labours only one-third of our catch is allowed to us. Let us see what good fortune Allah may grant if we fill in time by opening some of the oysters. With knives surreptitiously carried, they set to work cutting open the most likely looking shells—those thick at the hinge or heavily wormed and of an aged appearance. The work is roughly and hastily done; just a quick and dextrous twist of the knife and a rapid run over the flesh with the fingers, feeling anxiously for that big pearl of which the men dream of finding—the pearl that will ensure them affluence for the rest of their days. As the search goes on, the opened shells are thrown overboard, welcome dainties for the many species of rock fishes living on the banks.

To minimize illicit operations various expedients have been tried from time to time, but as soon as a novel one is introduced, the wits of the divers are keen to devise some form of evasion. For long it was customary to put a one-man guard aboard each boat; paid a coolie's wage, a small contribution from each of the divers aboard sufficed to blind his eyes to the practice; as one official sagely remarked, the employment of one of these guards on a boat, merely added one more to the number of thieves aboard!

The abuse at last became so flagrant that during the long series of successful fisheries which began in 1903, the Inspector pitted his wits against those of the divers, to devise effective safeguards. The best result was found to be the issue of three empty sacks to each diver every day the fleet sailed out, with the instruction that he should divide his catch equally between these sacks. When fishing ceased each day, carefully selected European checkers boarded the boats in turn, numbering and affixing seals to all the bags. This procedure was fully successful for the first season, but during the following one, it was found that the divers had thought out a clever counter-measure; they unstitched part of one of the seams in selected bags and in this way were able to abstract oysters without breaking the seals, afterwards resewing the seams with sufficient neatness to pass hurried observation!

Sunday brings agreeable relief to the staff afloat. By common consent, alike of the Muhammadans as of the Christians, no diving takes place then, so the week-end is usually spent ashore. Welcome as this is as a break in the week's monotony, 24 hours suffice to make one hanker for clean, fresh sea air, uncontaminated by the pungent odour given out by heaps of decaying oysters.

Tastes differ, however, even in this and there was a notable exception in the case of the late Sir William Twynam, a youthful civil servant of eighty, who chose to remain in Ceylon after a late retirement from Government service, and who was ever ready, even then, to resume office in time of emergency. I must explain that on the morning after each day's sale of the Government's share of the day's catch, the buyers pay the cost of their purchases into the local treasury, and then hire coolies to carry the oysters away to be piled in mat-covered heaps within privately owned palisaded enclosures. The odour from these heaps attracts myriads of flies, which lay untold millions of eggs on the oysters. The maggots that emerge eat out the flesh of the oysters within 7 to 10 days according to their numbers; the more flies, the quicker is the process. At the end of this period nothing remains except the shells, some sand and dirt, and whatever pearls there may be. To separate these, the shells are rinsed in water and thrown aside, the pearls being afterwards picked out of the residue when the rinsing water is decanted. During the 'rotting' process, the stench given out by the heaps is overpowering and most nauseating to those unaccustomed to it, but old Sir William was fond of taking a preprandial walk among the oyster enclosures; he stoutly maintained that the odour was wholesome and actually stimulating to the appetite, as good an aperitif as could be had anywhere! He had other curious predilections. His daughter had a large coconut estate in the sandy north of the island and Sir William declared that he found the best way to keep fit was to take a daily 6-mile tramp through the plantation, the softer the sand the better the exercise!

I am inclined to think he was right about the appetizing quality of the odour of decaying oysters; I attained after a while a certain tolerance myself, and, provided one can endure the experience without being sick, the desire for some form of liquid refreshment, if not for a meal, becomes overpowering. But no one whom I ever knew had the hardihood to say that he could enjoy the company of the pearl-camp flies. There are two outstanding species of these tormentors, one much like our own ordinary house-fly, mild and companionable compared with the other, a bluebottle with ferocious red eyes. The persistence of Bruce's spider sinks into insignificance beside that of the latter. This troublesome insect, presuming it would seem upon its birth within the shell of a pearl-oyster, considers itself the equal of the highest in the land (if they be visiting the camp) and insists on feeding with them and upon the same morsels. Indeed, it is quite willing to accompany the morsel down the diner's throat if forcible objection be not taken. Gauze-covers endeavour to protect the dishes on the table, but alas! these have to be raised occasionally and the buzzing hordes know neither fear nor shame. They are bibulous too, with a devouring thirst for whisky and soda. They love to swim in beer. There is no bravery like theirs, they die by hundreds and by thousands, yet ever are reinforcements coming up. As for the mosquitoes, well, they are reasonable creatures compared with old 'red-eyes'. They do respect the sanctity of a mosquito net, if it is kept in a state of repair, and they are sufficiently humane to rest from their search for blood during many hours of each day.

XX

THE WOMEN DIVERS OF JAPAN

SOME years ago when on a visit to Japan to learn what I could of the methods of fishing employed there and particularly those used in the culture of pearl-oysters, I had the pleasure of meeting a very courteous gentleman, the late Dr K. Kishinouye, the head of the Bureau of Fisheries and a scientist of world-wide reputation. In many ways he was unlike the ordinary Japanese type; although distinctly Mongoloid in features, he had a beard of sufficient strength to suggest a touch of another race; probably some blood of the old Ainus, earliest inhabitants of Japan, flowed in his veins. In disposition he was frank and free, with an appreciation of humour that made him a genial companion; apart from a quite reasonable indisposition to divulge trade secrets, he gave freely of his knowledge. Among the hundred and one things which I learned from him before going out on my own to observe at first hand, was that the motto of the diving community in Japan is *Place aux dames*; in most coast villages it is the women who do the diving. Usually husband and wife work in partnership, the wife diving while the husband tends the lifeline and rows the boat; if there is a grown-up daughter she too takes a share in the diving.

Such a topsy-turvy procedure tickled my curiosity and so it was that a few days later I found myself sitting cross-legged on a hard cushion on the matted floor of the best room in a little native inn in the town of Toba in the province of Shima, waiting for the rain to cease and the wind to abate that I might visit the fishing-grounds out in the bay. I doubt if anything is more irksome than to sit trying to do nothing day after day, cooped up by bad weather in a Japanese inn. The language difficulty precludes any but the scantiest conversation; sitting on the floor spells discomfort and occasional cramp; even an outlook on the dismal rain-soaked landscape is denied, for oiled paper takes the place of glass in the sliding panels that are the Japanese substitute for windows. The frailness of the house itself, a wooden frame filled in with these oiled paper panels, quivering under the gusty assaults of a howling, whistling wind, adds to the general discomfort. Nor did the nasal singing of doleful hymns in Japanese by a Christianized family on the other side of the paper partition wall of the room contribute to my happiness although the hymns were set to English tunes.

The only relief and a very welcome one is the periodical visits of the little waitress; in she comes with an obeisance that brings her forehead bumping gently on the floor, and asks with a delightful shyness and a dimpling smile whether his honourable self is ready to partake of the honourable tea. He certainly is, but he would have preferred it to be stronger and a little hotter than the lukewarm infusion which is poured into a cup wholly inadequate in capacity.

However, everything comes to him who waits; at the end of 3 days the weather cleared and my boatman announced that he was ready to take me to see the women divers working off the islands out in the bay. After a stiff pull we reached Sugashima; owing to the day being a village festival no serious work was being done and it was with difficulty that a diving crew were engaged. These consisted of three stoutly-built ladies of courtly manner as befitted their nationality and, therefore, unlike the traditional fishwives of our own country. But in face and figure they would have had no chance in a beauty competition.

While they were getting ready their equipment, a number of other diving women, mostly younger and more comely, were preparing to set out to the inshore shallows to collect seaweed of the kind from which vegetable isinglass (agar-agar) is made. They were gathered round a big fire on the beach to get some reserve warmth into their bodies on the same principle as is followed by Japanese youngsters who have a dip from time to time in the family hot bath on cold wintry days. But the bashful damsels espied me in time, focusing my camera—off they ran shrieking with delight at my discomfiture, and so, instead of the close-up I had intended, all I got was the distant view I had taken before my approach was discovered.

At last my three mermaids were ready; the equipment consisted of a pair of diving spectacles and a net-bag tied by a cord round the waist for each, and a single heavy stone sinker about 40 lb. in weight. Tending them was an elderly man, husband of one of the divers.

The spectacles consisted of a pair of goggles fitting close to the orbits and provided with an air-bulb at each side behind the ear to equalize the air pressure and so exclude the sea-water from the eyes (Pl. xxx, fig. B). The use of these spectacles is an immense help to the diver. Adopted or evolved about the beginning of this century they quickly became popular, for they enable the diver to see more clearly and thereby to work at greater depths than formerly—so much so that in some villages a mutual arrangement exists whereby their use is prohibited except outside the village limits lest the prosperity of the home-grounds should be impaired by overfishing.

When a depth of 7 fathoms was reached, the boatman anchored his craft by throwing overboard one of the heavy diving-stones. The three diving women divested themselves of all their clothing save a cloth bound tightly round the head and a short white cloth wrapped round the loins and thighs. The net-bag, roomy and of large mesh, made of twisted rice-straw, the mouth distended by a stiff circular ring, was now tied on in front, the mouth horizontal; into this is placed whatever catch is made during each dive (Pl. xxxi, figs. A and B). Various ways of reaching the bottom are employed, varying with the depth of water. When it is very shallow, 2 to 3 fathoms, the mermaid, who in this case brings up the catch in her hands, executes an acrobatic turn—she is already in the water—up-ending herself suddenly and so quickly that all the camera can usually record are a pair of feet and a big splash. In a moderate depth, 4 to 7 fathoms, as it was on the occasion now being described, the diver reached the bottom by swarming head foremost down the anchor rope. In greater depths, 8 to 12 fathoms, a heavy stone attached at the end of a long rope is slung over the side of the boat, the line held in position on the gunwale by the attendant's foot after passing between his big toe and the next one. When the diver is ready, she gives the tender a signal, turns over in the water, seizes the sinker rope close to the stone, and is carried swiftly to the bottom, head first, by the descent of the stone released by the tender simultaneously with her initial somersault. Just before reaching the bottom, she relinquishes her grasp of the rope and swims away over the bottom intent on her search. When a diver goes down in this way, it is usual to have a second line, a life-line, attached to her waist; when her breath is nearly exhausted, she signals her wish to rise by a jerk on the line, which is then hauled in rapidly by the tender. Once up, she rests for a few minutes against the side of the boat, throwing her arms over the gunwale. Not till the diver is up does the tender haul up the sinker stone. In this way the stone serves a double purpose; it carries the diver to the bottom and at the same time anchors the boat. In shape the stone is squat and wide based, not an elongated cone as that used in the Ceylon pearl fishery. From what I could learn this method of using a stone to carry the diver quickly to the bottom is of comparatively modern adoption; one woman by referring to the age of her son, about 22 years old, fixed its introduction at about 20 years previous, her son being then a baby. It was adopted or evolved to obviate the fatigue occasioned by having both to swim to the bottom and to swim up, hampered in the latter case by the weight of the catch. By its introduction the divers are enabled to work longer on the bottom and to work profitably at greater depths than is possible without such help.

But to return to my diving lady whom I have left overlong in the water. On her reappearance at the surface, the tender in the boat extends a long bamboo pole towards her whenever she rises some distance away; she grasps the end and is hauled by it through the water to the side of the boat—her strength must be conserved to the utmost or the number of her dives will be reduced, to the detriment of the family exchequer.

On the way back, we passed through the fishing-ground of another village whose divers were not on holiday. All were out fishing or rather diving for *awabi*, the Japanese name for the lovely ear-shell (*Haliotis*). The sea was alive with small skiffs and bobbing heads, everybody happy as the catches were reported to be good. This *awabi* is an enormous relative of the common limpet, encased in an iridescent oval shell, 4 to 6 inches long, sparkling with vivid iridescent blues and greens when the rough outer coating has been removed. A smaller species of ear-shell, the ormer or *oreille-de-mer*, common in the Channel Islands and on the rocky Brittany coast, is there esteemed the most delicious of that miscellaneous collection of minor sea-products that the Italians so felicitously call *Frutti del mare*. Some of the Japanese ormers attain a great size and may weigh anything up to 2 lb. With the rapid increase of population during recent years, coast fishing became so intensified that the *awabi* and the pearl-oyster were threatened with extinction. To remedy this, various regulations are in force; in some villages a local arrangement forbids the use of diving spectacles on the fishing-grounds within the village area, while permitting them on the common ground outside.

Pearl-fishing in the land-locked bays and fiords of Japan is an industry that has existed from time immemorial; in recent years, thanks to the discovery of methods to induce the pearl-oyster to manufacture to order a kind of pearl marketed under the name of 'culture-pearls', a great extension of the industry has taken place. Diving for pearl-oysters on the open or common grounds is still prosecuted, but many of the smaller and younger ones are sold to the people who run 'culture-farms', situated in specially sheltered areas or inlets over which they have exclusive fishing rights. The young oysters are laid down on a bottom which is as carefully tended and weeded as any land garden till they are old enough to have the operation performed upon them that will induce them, willy-nilly, to form a culture-pearl of whatever size the operator considers most suitable, or most in demand by the feminine fashion of the moment, that is unless they choose to die in the meantime or are able to dislodge the intruding body by a combined effort of will power and muscularity. As with human surgery, although the operation is invariably a success, the patient not infrequently succumbs or fails to carry out the result expected.

By Dr Kishinouye, I was introduced to Mr T. Nishikawa, a biologist engaged upon the then unsolved problem of producing spherical culture-pearls, and the son-in-law of Mr K. Mikimoto, the world-famed marketer of culture-pearls. By his good offices I was able to visit the Mikimoto pearl-farm on the Bay of Agu, and there to learn a great deal about the methods of cultivating the oysters and of the treatment employed to induce them to form the button-pearls which are those sold originally under the name of 'culture-pearls'.

The centre of the organization is located on the small island of Tadoka. A little harbour and landing place have been built on the south side and everything there bespeaks order, good organization and prosperity.

Immediately opposite the landing place is the family house, a long, low wooden building, two stories in height, fronted by a wide veranda. To the left is a building occupied by the jewellers' department; here work the skilled mechanics who cut off and otherwise manipulate the pearl blisters or buttons attached on the inner side of the pearl-oyster shell by artificial stimulus. On the other flank of the main building is a small dwelling house, a guest house for Japanese visitors, while to the right again is the biologist's laboratory, where I was accommodated. Farther along, still on the sea front as are all the buildings, are the storehouses and workshops for the surgical treatment of the oysters.

The Bay of Agu, where this establishment is located, is a rock-bound inlet of considerable area, land-locked and abounding in side-branches sheltered so effectually that work can be carried on the whole year round. The bottom is rocky and stony, ideal ground for pearl-oyster cultivation but only parts of this bay are under the Mikimoto control, for in Japan every fishing village has prescriptive proprietary rights over a defined area of the sea adjacent to the village; here no outsider may fish without permission from the village concerned. In the present instance Mikimoto pays the villagers agreed compensation for the temporary abandonment of their privileges, for a specified term of years.

Outside of these leased areas, the villagers may fish for pearl-oysters under certain regulations; the chief of these forbids the removal of oysters under a size of 2 inches, except for cultural purposes, while another enforces a close season from 1 August to the end of October.

Mostly the small-sized oysters are bought by Mr Mikimoto to increase his stock in the oyster farm. The large ones are searched for pearls and the flesh used as food, for pearl-oysters when cooked form a dainty dish, as I know well by experience for without this addition to the cuisine, I should have fared badly when anchored for weeks at a time on the Ceylon Pearly Banks, a hundred miles from any source of European market supply.

A large staff of divers has to be employed at the Mikimoto farm; young oysters brought in from the open grounds have to be relaid, older ones have to be fished up and selected for treatment and these again have afterwards to be relaid once more; those judged to have lain long enough to have coated the introduced nuclei with a sufficiently thick layer of nacre have to be collected; in addition the beds have to be kept clean and free from those vermin of the sea, the starfish and the octopus. Starfish are picked up individually—they make good manure for the land, but the octopus has to be trapped. The usual traps are narrow-necked earthenware jars attached at short intervals along a line laid on the bottom and left there for some hours. Dark cavities have great fascination for the octopus and many seek shelter in the jars, to be captured and destroyed when the line of jars is hauled up. Seaweeds have also to be rigorously cleared out.

The water over much of the farm area is shallow and while this is an advantage from the cultural standpoint as the abundance of food material there favours rapid growth, there are times when this shallowness is a danger through the influx from the sea of poisonous water called from its colour the 'Red Current'. When it comes, the stock of oysters runs the risk of being poisoned or asphyxiated, so all hands have to turn to and move as many as possible from the shallow-water areas where the danger is greatest. As the current usually disappears quickly, the oysters are kept ashore for some hours; if the peril persists, the only alternative is to relay them in the deepest water available.

In the busy season as many as 600 divers are employed, an index to the extent of this industry and incidentally to the wealth of the Mikimoto family; *more Japonico* the whole of the management and skilled work is a family concern. At the time of my visit, the entire management was in the hands of six brothers, whilst every one of the sixty inhabitants of the Mikimoto island was related by blood or by marriage to the head of the clan!

Diving does not begin till the sun has risen and warmed the air. On the day I was there, four boats laden with divers, all women, left shore at 8.30 a.m. Three boats carried eight divers each, the fourth twelve. Arrived at the appointed place, where the depth of water was from 3 to 4 fathoms, the women slipped overboard, each equipped with a pair of the latest form of water-spectacles, and a wooden tub in which to place her catch on coming to the surface. A line from her waist connected with the tub, to prevent it floating away out of reach. Three to five pearl-oysters was the average catch at each dive.

On several occasions I tried to obtain a photograph of a crowd of these women divers when at work in the water, but either they were in an unusually modest mood or, more probably, were possessed by playful humour, and saw their way to tease the stranger; they splashed about and jabbered freely until they judged I was on the point of pressing the button, when, with a parting joyous shout they made a simultaneous dive; all I could record were a lot of empty tubs and about the same number of splashes. In the end I did manage to get a close-up of one diver alongside her bucket but it was at the expense of the Japanese equivalent of baksheesh (Pl. xxx, fig. B).

As the depth over this ground is mostly from 3 to 5 fathoms, no special apparatus is needed to carry the diver to the bottom. When rested sufficiently she turns a somersault in the water and swims downwards head first. Some 7 seconds suffice to reach bottom, where she stays about 40 seconds, quartering the ground in search of oysters; 5 seconds more bring her to the surface, with the catch in her hands, which is then deposited in the tub. When a number of the Agu women divers are at work, a shrill whistling sound fills the air; every time a diver breathes she rounds her mouth and protrudes the upper lip, and it is the violent expulsion of her breath through this small orifice that produces the whistling noise.

In winter the water is too cold for diving. In April the women begin the diving season by working three spells a day, each of about 10 minutes' duration, the water temperature registering about 10° C. In summer, while still adhering to the three spells per day, each is lengthened to from 1 to 1½ hours. Between the spells of work and also before beginning work the women warm themselves at a fire.

Like any *enfant terrible* I was persistent to ascertain the reason why it is customary for women to take the place of men as divers in some districts in Japan. Three explanations were offered. The first and most reasonable is that the superior plumpness of women over men in Japan, enables them to withstand the numbing effect of prolonged immersion longer and with less discomfort than is possible with men. Truly the Japanese woman is remarkably plump considering the smallness of her bones; by comparison the Japanese man of the working classes is thin and scraggy, muscular and lithe though he really is.

Another reason given is that in the districts where women monopolize the diving, the menfolk were so frequently away from home for prolonged periods in pursuit of the tunny and the bonito that the women, with little to do and nothing much to eat unless they caught it themselves, began to fish for shellfish and took to diving when the riches of the littoral were exhausted.

The third and last reason is given in a legend current in Shima. According to this the men did all the diving until one unhappy season when a large number of vicious sharks made their appearance. Although they were not man-eaters, they effectually scared the divers from pursuing their calling, for the sharks contracted the habit of emasculating them. This would never do; the men refused to go diving and all fishing for shellfish ceased. It was the stormy season when no offshore fishing was possible. Food grew scarce; the spectre of famine stalked grim and threatening through the villages. All were in despair till one bright intellect conceived a solution. 'Teach the women to dive', he said, 'and send them out fishing. The sharks will take them for eunuchs and will not molest them.' Hope returned; the advice was acted upon and the result was entirely satisfactory. Lest the sharks should return, the women of Shima Province continue to deputize for their husbands and fathers and brothers.

On a subsequent occasion I had an opportunity to visit an experimental pearl-culture station on the little island of Aoshima set in the northern section of Nanao Bay, a beautiful miniature inland sea, well sheltered and ideal for pearl-oyster culture. The station was run by the local authorities, and the officer in charge was an old pupil of Professor Kishinouye, in whose company I visited the place. It was the Professor's first tour in this district and he was just as eager as myself to see everything of note. With him were a number of other former students, now the fishery experts of various prefectures and private fishery establishments—a happy party.

We circled the island to see what progress the experiments had made. The water being shallow and pellucid, everything on the bottom showed up clearly when viewed through a water-glass, a conical cylinder with glass inserted at the broader end. Mostly it consisted of rounded stones, varying in size from gravel to boulders. Pearl oysters were abundant and healthy. With the water less than 2 fathoms in depth, divers are not needed, their place being taken by a pair of tongs worked at the end of a long bamboo pole. From the oysters brought up and the descriptions of my friends I learned exactly how the culture-pearl is induced. Having caught the oyster, the first procedure is to induce it to open its mouth. A judicious exposure to warm air soon overcomes this reluctance. The operator is alert and no sooner do the valves gape than he thrusts in a wedge to gag them apart. The oyster passes to the next operator who with a specially formed spatula carefully raises the delicate 'mantle' that lines one of the valves and pushes in as far as he can a small rounded nucleus with the aid of a pair of forceps cupped at the tips. This nucleus was originally made from a fragment of mother-of-pearl; an alternative procedure is to use a small spherule of glass. The operation over, the oyster is laid with other companions in a tray divided into compartments, one for each oyster. This is placed in the sea and kept under observation for a few days to ascertain which of the oysters retains the nuclei within their shells. Those that do not, have to be relaid for a time before a second course of treatment is tried, while those that do retain the nuclei are laid on the culture grounds, thirty to a *tsubo*, equal to four square yards. Here they lie for a period varying from 2 to 3 years. By the end of that time the nuclei are covered with a coating of nacre, which also cements them to the inner surface of the shell, forming what are known as 'blister' or button-pearls. Those oysters which, when opened, show satisfactory 'blisters' at Mikimoto's establishment are passed to special workers who cut off the blisters from the shell beneath. After this, the process as described to me by Mr Mikimoto's son-in-law is to extract the nucleus, usually a glass spherule, from the blister; the cavity thus formed is cleaned out and a mother-of-pearl spherule of appropriate size is cemented into it. Finally the base is cut off and a closing disk of pearl-shell fitted over the cut surface, converting the button into a sphere. The original glass nucleus is readily dislodged as the pearl-oyster forms a brown membraneous layer over it soon after its introduction and before the pearl-oyster regains its nacre secreting power, which is temporarily impaired locally for some time after the shock sustained during the operation of introducing the nucleus under the mantle.

Pink culture-pearls are made by replacing the nucleus with a red coral one. The demand for these cultured buttons is now less than the supply, for pearls of this description are useful only for rings and other settings for which half-pearls are suitable, as the base of each is then hidden by the setting.

Of recent years spherical culture-pearls have been produced in considerable quantity. These are excellent imitations of the natural gem, but can never have the lasting value of the real thing, for the lustrous coating of nacre is thin and is subject to damage from fracture if subjected to a blow. Real pearls on the contrary receive no injury if struck; indeed the Ceylon gem dealers often guarantee the genuine nature of the pearl they offer by inviting a dubious customer to lay it on the ground and stamp on it with any force he pleases. Resistance to such rough treatment is possible, because the true pearl is homogeneous through and through, whereas in the spherical culture-pearl the real pearl substance consists of a mere skin of nacre divided from the foreign nucleus by a membrane which forms a plane of weakness between the two.

The Japanese pearl-oyster resembles very closely in size and shape that of Ceylon and South India, if indeed it is not merely a variety of the same species. Years ago I succeeded in inducing the formation of free spherical pearls in the Ceylon pearl-oyster by a different method from that followed in Japan, and one which if the experiment had been carried on longer, would have given a pearl vastly superior to that produced in Japanese pearl-culture farms.

Plans to form a pearl-culture farm on an island off the Indian coast were actually drawn up and the island purchased for the purpose of the scheme by the Madras Government. Lord Pentland, then Governor of Madras, was a keen believer in the proposal, and backed it up vigorously. Unfortunately the Great War of 1914–18 broke out before work was commenced, and postponement became necessary. With the end of the war, financial stringency and the coming of the Montague-Chelmsford reforms made the Government reluctant to ask the Legislative Council to vote money for an excursion into unknown fields, and so a scheme that might have proved exceedingly profitable to the country was abandoned without trial.

XXI

FRUITS OF THE SEA

Our likes and dislikes in respect of what we eat are largely a matter of early acquired prejudice. Like the caste people of India, we almost invariably limit our appetite to the things our fathers ate; the foods we were given as children. And these prejudices lie heavy upon us. Let frogs' legs be ever so tender and desirable, if we be not introduced to this delicacy while young, how many of us are able to relish a dish of this sort in later years? Frenchmen love the Apple Snail when cooked properly and the poorer among them are happy even with the slimy Garden Snail, but how many of us are able to face the thought of such fare without shuddering?

Insular prejudices deprive us of much gastronomic enjoyment, for there are many tasty products of Nature, particularly of the sea, which we scorn, but which in many other parts of the world are valued as toothsome delicacies.

Go to the Mediterranean or to China and Japan and there you will find squid, cuttlefish and octopus laid out on the market slabs, commanding good prices, the result of popularity in the homes of the people. And with them are a dozen minor dainties gathered from off the bed of the sea—*Fruits de mer* and *Frutti del mare* as the French and Italians appropriately name them.

On the quayside or in the fish market of any coast town in Italy or the south of France, the variety of these unfamiliar fruits of the sea is amazing. Most conspicuous are piles of purple and of dark-green sea-urchins, covered with long, sharp-pointed spines that certainly give them a forbidding aspect, viewed as prospective items of a meal. (In Malta they are carried round the town on Friday mornings in sacks by hawkers who peddle them from door to door.) How, indeed, can they be eaten? Well, if you will ask the old lady in voluminous skirts who presides at the stall, she will look at you with just a suspicion of contempt. 'Its only a mad Englishman,' she probably says to herself, 'what can you expect him to know?' And then, humouring such silly ignorance she will deftly knock off the lower half of the spiny ball and turn the upper half over to show five masses of orange-coloured egg-masses radiating star-like from the centre. 'V'la, Monsieur, c'est bon, ça.' (Pl. xxxii, fig. A.)

Other heaps are still less familiar; they consist of gristle-like elongated bags, indefinite in colour, and about $2\frac{1}{2}$ inches long, known to zoologists as simple ascidians and to our fishermen as sea-squirts, degenerate things whose larvae show aristocratic relationship to the fishes by beginning life as tadpole-like creatures armed with a long tail for swimming; as they grow older they lose the tail and settle down on rock or stone after the fashion of an oyster, with the 'works' protected like the mechanism of a watch by a stout, protective case. After slicing off one side of the gristly envelope you eat the contents oyster-fashion, 'off the shell'.

Piles of many kinds of shellfish are present; some few among them we know and appreciate—oysters and mussels—but there are others with which we have a nodding acquaintance as seaside shells but which we never think worth eating. Of these are the large family of clams, big and little, the long, scabbard-shaped razor-shells, and the date-like rock-borer (*Lithodomus*).

Appreciated most of all are the octopus, the squid and the cuttlefish. On the market slab, lying in slimy, slithering masses, the octopus is far from attractive in appearance, but all three kinds are delicious when properly cooked if not old and tough. The family to which they belong, the Cephalopods, is widespread throughout all seas, yet, strangely enough, those of temperate latitudes grow to much larger sizes than those of the tropics—a characteristic common also to numerous other groups of marine life. (Pl. xxxiii, fig. A and Text-fig. 34.)

Everywhere except in the British Isles and in India, where the people are as fastidious as ourselves, the cephalopods are valued as good food. Quite close home, in the Channel Islands and on the Brittany coast, the octopus in particular is held in great favour; a catch of big octopus hung out to dry, pegged to a clothes' line, is a common object in the gardens of a fishing village. (Pl. xxxiii, fig. B.)

Limpets and their kindred are also to be seen in the Jersey markets in great piles and their collection is one of several allied minor industries. At the times of the greater spring tides, when the sea at low water lays bare many square miles of weed-covered rocks, scores of men are to be seen searching for the ear-shell or 'ormer' (*Haliotis tuberculata*), a flattened ear-shaped shell about 3 inches in length and a giant cousin of the limpet; it is a delicacy vastly esteemed by all classes. The Chinese in particular are inordinately fond of it and the shores of the Pacific are ransacked to supply their needs. Great quantities are canned on the Californian coast for the Chinese market under the name of *abalone*, and elsewhere the thick fleshy 'foot' that serves as a sucker to anchor this mollusc to the rock is sun-dried to the consistency of horn for the same destination. (Pl. xxxiv, fig. A.)

Then there is *bouillabaisse*, the fish-soup familiar to every traveller passing through Marseilles. As served in the restaurants there, it is an emasculated form of the real thing. Actually it is a fisherman's soup or broth, compounded of all the oddments found in the nets—things which our fishermen throw overboard as worthless rubbish, even if their families are on short commons at home! All sorts of little crabs and fishes, bullheads, little loach and the like, of no market value, are the principal ingredients, plus anything else that may be available. Everything goes into the pot just as it comes to hand, a veritable *olla podrida*, and yet no other fish-stew or soup can compare with it, when hunger is the relish.

But the so-called Latin races do not limit themselves to crabs and molluscs. Barnacles both stalked and sessile are eaten whenever procurable of sufficient size. In Spain the naked *Conchoderma*, a near relative of the ship-barnacle, is esteemed a great delicacy in southern coast towns. It figures even in the cuisine of Madrid, where it appears on the table in the roasted form as a hors-d'œuvre; the stalks only are eaten, after the tough investing skin is peeled off.

Madeira adds another unusual sea-dainty to our expanding list, for in that happy isle a large acorn-barnacle, called *craca*, an overgrown relative of the tiny species that covers our rocks near high-water mark and makes them a terror to the barefooted, is in esteem as a particularly dainty morsel. Care has to be taken that the base of the tulip-shaped 'shell' is not broken, otherwise the luscious body juices will escape; for this reason a piece of the mother-rock remains adherent to the lower side, so shell and stone have both to go into the pot to be boiled, the usual method of cooking the acorn-shell. A special instrument, a *craqueira*, has been devised to break them from the rock. It has the shape of a small pickaxe or mattock, but with the end of each arm broad and chisel-shaped.

But to find the fruits of the sea most fully utilized we must go to Japan. Life for the poorer classes there is very hard, the standard of life incredibly low as judged by the British yardstick. Fortunately this seemingly unhappy lot is not realized by the people themselves, for their wants are few and simple. Given good weather, the coast folk fare well according to their own standard, for they have no prejudices in regard to what they may eat out of the sea. All that comes is grist to their mill. So varied is this class of food that the only satisfactory way to enumerate the kinds is to follow a zoological classification, beginning with the lower forms of life and thence ascending.

So far as I know there is no kind of sponge eaten, but of the jellyfishes one large species, *Rhizostoma*, is extensively utilized. It has a thick, stout mushroom-shaped umbrella or disk and four stout bifid arms pendant around the mouth, suggestive of a multiple stalk. Swarms enter the bays when the wind is in a certain direction; women and children paddle out to the harvest and scoop up the jellyfishes in hundreds. Taken ashore they are preserved with salt and alum or else by tanning with an infusion of oak leaves! Those preserved by the latter method are the more esteemed. Morgan's famished buccaneers on their march to Panama managed to stay their hunger by eating the boiled leather of their boots, so, presumably, tanned jellyfishes are also digestible!

Another strange food resource in Japan is the sea-anemone. Several species are large and fleshy and furnish a very nutritious dish when boiled.

The roes of sea-urchins are as greatly esteemed as in France and Italy. Sea-cucumbers, the trepang and bêche-de-mer of commerce, are also valued highly. A spinous-looking species, common in many places on the Japanese coasts, is extensively cured and dried; it is very much in evidence in the dried-fish shops. But not only do the Japanese eat the body-wall as do the Chinese, they also eat the roe when present and even the intestine when emptied of sand. Should any reader wish to try bêche-de-mer soup it can be had in London's Chinatown. The following is the recipe of a Chinese chef:

Clean, wash and mince finely; soak in cold water for 5 hours; boil for 1 hour; add salt, pepper, butter, and some beef or chicken stock. Serve hot or iced.

Here it may be appropriate to mention the other great Chinese marine delicacy—shark's fins. The trade in these ranks next in volume to bêche-de-mer and in value probably surpasses it. This article is also used in soups, the fin-rays being boiled till they soften and gelatinize.

The long-stalked brachiopod *Lingula* is eaten both in Fiji, Japan and the Philippine Islands where it occurs in abundance in muddy bottoms. This curious animal, although not a mollusc, exactly simulates in its shelled body the outward form of a bivalve shellfish; it has an unbroken pedigree from ancestors of *precisely* the same form that lived in all but the oldest of our fossiliferous rocks, untold millions of years ago. When alive, one end of a long stalk, comparable to that of a ship-barnacle, passes through a hole in one valve close to the hinge and serves to secure the animal to a stone deep buried in the mud in which it elects to dwell. (Pl. xxxiv, fig. B.) Nothing shows above ground except perhaps a few bristles edging the mouth of the shell, which project from a slit-shaped aperture on the surface of the mud when uncovered by the tide. The animals are dug out at low water and their stalks are eaten exactly like those of the ship-barnacle in Spain.

It is doubtful whether any kind of shellfish is considered inedible in Japan. Chitons, limpets, ear-shells, clams, mussels, oysters, scallops and all kinds of univalves, from winkles to the giant triton, are eaten. The adductor muscle of *Pinna*, the leg-of-mutton shell, is a delicacy eaten both raw and cooked, and that of a large scallop (*Pecten*) is dried extensively for export to China. The fishery for the ear-shell (*Haliotis*) is of great commercial value; these molluscs are obtained by diving and it is curious that in certain districts it is the women of the village who are the divers, their husbands and brothers managing the boats and tending the life-lines while their womenfolk are below, as described in Chapter xx.

Pearl-oysters are eaten in Kyushu during the winter, for then they are in prime condition and the water so clear that the fishers can discern them on the bottom and so can fish them out by means of a long-handled pair of tongs.

In the Dutch Indies and in South China the adductor muscle of the window-pane oyster (*Placuna*), so called because the half-grown shells are used instead of glass in old style Chinese houses, is also sometimes used as food. It is very thin but as the shells form immense beds on many brackish mudflats, the poor people who search these oysters for the minute pearls they produce, easily obtain enough to give welcome relish to their dry and insipid meals of boiled rice.

Octopus, cuttlefish and ascidians are as highly valued as in France.

In the South Sea Islands the choicest marine delicacy is furnished from an unusual quarter. On the occurrence of one particular phase of the moon toward the close of the year, incredible numbers of a sea-worm, known as *palolo* in Samoa and Tonga and as *mbololo* in Fiji, rise to the surface of the sea from the submerged coral reefs which encircle these islands. This swarming is limited to two particular days, one usually in October, the other in November. The natives know from experience exactly when to expect them. The moon's phases are closely watched. If the moon is full about mid-October, the main swarm of *palolo* is sure to come during the last quarter of this moon. Otherwise it will be deferred for a month. When the signs are recognized, every available canoe is manned and paddled out to the reef shortly after midnight; here they eagerly await the coming of the worms. If their calculation is correct, as it generally is, the swarm begins to appear on the surface about 2 hours before sunrise. Work is carried on with feverish haste. All are armed with hand-nets of some sort or other. Almost anything will serve, so dense are the writhing, wriggling masses of worms. Every canoe and receptacle must be filled before sunrise, for the moment the flaming rays of the sun strike the water, the worms, which are mere delicate-walled tubes filled with eggs or with sperm, burst and shed their contents into the water. Within a few minutes the swarms have vanished like smoke before the wind; no sign remains except a thin whitish scum floating on the surface.

Feasting and revelry continue among the islanders until the whole of their enormous catch has been consumed. With the usual improvidence of these people all has to be eaten up in the shortest possible time. In a week or, at the outside, 10 days, every morsel of the cooked food has disappeared.

In some of the atoll islands in the Low or Dangerous Archipelago, away in the centre of the Pacific, one of the principal food supplies of the island folk consists of extensive beds of that giant clam, the holy-water shell (*Tridacna*), so often seen in Catholic churches, fulfilling the duty from which it takes its common name. As indicating how important is this clam to the islanders, the lagoon within the encircling reef in some instances is dotted with tiny islets rising a foot or two above the sea-level; each is composed of a solid mass of millions of the discarded shells.

From these notes it is clear that our coast people in Great Britain do not make anything like the use they might and ought of the minor products of our shores and seas. And the irony of the situation is that prejudice against the use of much of this good and wholesome food is most strongly held among the classes which stand most in need of cheap and nutritious supplies. The use of the dog-fish, now sold extensively under the euphemistic names of 'flake', 'rock salmon' and 'huss', became fairly general solely because of the scarcity of other supplies during the late war. Previous to that, dogfishes found their way chiefly to the dissecting tables of the medical schools and that was indeed but a limited market; the rest were thrown away or used as manure. Many other and more tasty sea foods, in company with caviare, are viewed askance by the majority of our people; even the large spider-crab (*Maia squinado*), sweeter and juicier than the common or 'edible-crab' so called, is thrown away as valueless by our south-coast fishermen, who hold that it is unwholesome! Equally heedless are the mass of our people of such excellent food as the roe of the sea-urchin and the flesh of the squid and the cuttlefish; clams are generally ignored although the larger make excellent chowder, loved of Americans.

Among molluscan dainties only the lordly oyster, the toothsome scallop and the plebeian cockle, mussel, whelk and periwinkle find considerable appreciation in Britain and these only within fairly clear-cut strata of the population.

With regard to shellfish found in estuaries, and apart from oysters dredged up in tidal waters, there are few of any edible importance. One exception requires mention. It concerns the fine clam, *Batissa violacea*, which bulks largely in the dietary of many people in Fiji. Every market-day many basketsful of this shellfish are conspicuous objects offered for sale in Suva, brought into town by countryfolk eager to make a little money wherewith to buy some item of foreign luxury, such for example as the tin of salmon which they esteem far more highly than any fish caught in their home waters. These *Batissa* shells, covered with a black skin, the periostracum, are notable for the beautiful violet colour of the interior surface of the shell, whence the specific name of *violacea*. (Pl. xxxv.)

BIBLIOGRAPHY

ALDABA, V. C. (1931). Fishing Methods in Laguna de Bay. *Philippine Journal of Science*, vol. XLV, pp. 1–28. Manila.
ALDABA, V. C. (1931 a). The Dalag Fishery of Laguna de Bay. *Philippine Journal of Science*, vol. XLV, pp. 41–57. Manila.
ALDABA, V. C. (1932). Fishing Methods in Manila Bay. *Philippine Journal of Science*, vol. XLVII, pp. 405–23. Manila.
BALFOUR, H. (1913). *Kite-fishing. Essays and Studies presented to W. Ridgeway on his 60th birthday*. Cambridge.
BALFOUR, H. (1915). *Note on a new kind of Fish-hook from Goodenough, New Guinea. Man*, art. 5.
BANFIELD, E. J. (1908). *The Confessions of a Beachcomber*. London.
BERTRAM, MRS C. K. R., BORLEY, H. J. H. & TREWAVAS, MISS E. (1942). *Report on the Fish and Fisheries of Lake Nyasa*. London.
BLACKWOOD, MISS B. (1935). *Both sides of Buka Passage*. Oxford.
BOULENGER, E. G. (1925). *Queer Fish and other inhabitants of the Rivers and Oceans*. London.
BURNETT, F. (1911). *Through Polynesia and Papua*. London.
BURROWS, G. (1898). *The Land of the Pigmies*. London.
CLAVIGERO, F. S. (1788). *History of Mexico* (English trans.). London.
CHRISTISON, R. (1860). On the capture of Whales by means of poison. *Edinburgh New Philos. Journ.* (n.s.), vol. II, pp. 72–80.
DAVIS, F. M. (1923). An account of the Fishing Gear of England and Wales. *Fishery Investig.* (2nd ser.), vol. V, no. 4. London.
DAY, FRANCIS (1873). *Report on the Sea Fish and Fisheries of India and Burma*. Calcutta.
DEANE, W. (1910). *Fijian Fishing and its Superstitions*. Suva.
DONNELLY, I. A. (1936). Strange Craft of China's Inland Waters. *Mariner's Mirror*, vol. XXII, pp. 410–21.
EDGE-PARTINGTON, J. (1890–8). *Ethnolog. Album of the Pacific Islands*. Series 1–3. Manchester.
EDGE-PARTINGTON, T. W. (1912). Kite Fishing by the Salt-water Natives of Mala or Malaita Island, British Solomon Islands. *Man*, vol. XII, p. 9.
EGGEDE, H. (1763). *Description et histoire naturelle du Groenland*. Copenhagen and Geneva.
ELDRIDGE, S. (1876). On the Arrow Poison in use among the Ainos of Yeso. *Trans. Asiatic Soc. of Japan*, vol. IV, pp. 78–86.
ELLIS, W. (1829). *Polynesian Researches*. London.
FENG, D. R. & KILBORN, L. G. (1937). Nosu and Miao poisons. *Journ. West China Border Res. Soc.* vol. IX, pp. 130–4.
FINSCH, O. (1888). *Samoafahrten*. Leipzig.
FRASER, T. R. (1916). The poisoned arrows of the Abors and Mishmis of North-east India. *Trans. Roy. Soc. Edinburgh*, vol. L, pp. 897–930.
FRENCH, D. D. (1916). Fishing at Santa Catalina Island. *Calif. Fish and Game*, vol. II, pp. 15–16. San Francisco.
GOMES, E. H. (1907). *The Sea Dyaks of Borneo*. Westminster.
GRAHAM, M. (1929). *The Victoria Nyanza and its Tributaries*. London.
GRAY, J. H. (1878). *China: a history of the laws, manners and customs of the people*. 2 vols. London.

GRUVEL, A. (1928). *La Pêche dans la Préhistoire, dans l'Antiquité et chez les Peuples primitifs.* Paris.
GUDGER, E. W. (1926). Fishing with the Cormorant: I. In China. *American Naturalist,* vol. LX, pp. 5–41.
GUDGER, E. W. (1927). Fishing with the Otter. *American Naturalist,* vol. LXI, pp. 198–225.
GUDGER, E. W. (1929). Fishing with the Cormorant in Japan. *The Scientific Monthly,* vol. XXIX, pp. 5–38.
GUDGER, E. W. (1930). Poisonous Fishes and Fish Poisonings. *Amer. Journ. of Tropical Medicine,* vol. X, pp. 43–55.
GUDGER, E. W. (1937). Fooling the Fishes. *Sci. Monthly* (April), pp. 295–306.
GUDGER, E. W. (1942). Swordfishing with the Harpoon in New England Waters. *Sci. Monthly,* vol. LIV, pp. 418–30 and 499–512.
HABSHUSH, H. (1941). *Travels in Yemen; an account of J. Halévy's Journey to Najran in the year 1870.* Jerusalem.
HADFIELD, EMMA (1920). *Among the natives of the Loyalty Group.* London.
HAMILTON, F. (1824). An account of a genus including the *Herba toxicaria* of the Himalaya mountains or the plant with which the natives poison their arrows. *Edinburgh Journ. Sci.* vol. II, pp. 249–51.
HANDY, E. S. C. (1923). The Native Culture in the Marquesas. *B. P. Bishop Mus. Bulletin,* No. 9. Honolulu.
HEIZER, R. F. (1943). Aconite poison whaling in Asia and America. *Anthrop. Papers of the Bureau of American Ethnology,* No. 24 of Bull. 133. Smithsonian Instn., Washington.
HENRY, T. A. (1924). *The Plant Alkaloids.* Philadelphia.
HOLMWOOD, F. (1883). *Zanzibar: Official Catalogue of the Internat. Fisheries Exhibition,* London, 1883 (4th ed.), pp. 380–2.
HORNELL, J. (1924). The Fishing Methods of the Ganges. *Mem. Asiatic Soc. of Bengal,* vol. VIII, pp. 201–37. Calcutta.
HORNELL, J. (1928). The indigenous fishing methods of Sierra Leone. *Sierra Leone Studies,* no. 13, pp. 10–21.
HORNELL, J. (1931). *The Fishing Industry in Malta.* Valetta.
HORNELL, J. (1934). Indonesian Influence on East African Culture. *Journ. Royal Anthropological Institute,* vol. LXIV, pp. 305–32.
HORNELL, J. (1941). Fishing Poisons. *Man,* art. 87, pp. 126–8.
HORNELL, J. (1946). *Water Transport.* Cambridge.
HOSE, C. (1929). *Field-book of a Jungle-wallah.* London.
HOSIE, ALEX. (1897). *Three Years in Western China* (2nd ed.). London.
HUTTON, J. H. (1929). Diaries of two tours in the Unadministered Area east of the Naga Hills. *Mem. Asiat. Soc. of Bengal,* vol. XI, pp. 1–72. Calcutta.
JARDIN, E. (1862). *Essai sur l'histoire naturelle de l'archipel des Marquises.* Paris and Cherbourg.
KILLIP, E. P. (1930). The Use of Fish Poison in S. America. *Annual Report, Smithsonian Institution for 1930,* pp. 401–8.
KINGSLEY, MISS MARY (1899). *West African Studies.* London.
KISHINOUYE, K. (1911). Prehistoric Fishing in Japan. *Journ. College Agric., Imp. University, Tokyo,* vol. II, no. 7.
LEITH, T. & LINDBLOM, K. C. (1933). Two kinds of Fishing Implements. *Riksmuseets Etnograf. Avdelning, Smarre Meddel.,* no. 11, pp. 3–48. Stockholm.
LEO AFRICANUS (1896). *The History and Description of Africa.* 3 vols. London: Hakluyt Soc.
LING ROTH, H. (1896). *The Natives of Sarawak and Br. N. Borneo.* London.
LITTLE, ARCHIBALD (1898). *Through the Yang-tse Gorges.* London.
LITTLE, H. W. (1884). *Madagascar; its history and people.* Edinburgh and London.
LUMHOLTZ, C. (1903). *Unknown Mexico.* London.

Moir, Gordon (1909) Some methods of fishing in China. *Badminton Mag.* vol. XXIX, pp. 279–81.
Moloney, C. A. (1883). West African Fisheries. *Internat. Fisheries Exhibition, Papers of the Conference.* London.
Monod, Th. (1928). *L'industrie des Pêches au Cameroun.* Paris.
Montilla, José (1931). The Ipon Fisheries of Northern Luzon. *Philipp. Journ. of Sci.* vol. XLV, pp. 61–75. Manila.
Nordhoff, C. (1930). Notes on the Off-shore Fishing of the Society Islands. *Journ. Polynes. Soc.* vol. XXXIX, nos. 2 and 3. Wellington, N.Z.
Oppian. *Halieutica.* Diaper and Jones' version, 1772.
Parona, C. (1919). Il Tonno e la sua Pesca. *R. Com. Talassografico Italiano, Mem.* 68. Venice.
Percival, W. S. (1889). *The Land of the Dragon.* London.
Regan, C. Tate & Trewavas, E. Deep-sea Anglers. *The Scientific Results of the 'Dana' Exped. round the World, 1928–30.* Copenhagen.
Reynolds, A. J. (1932). *By Desert Ways to Indian Snows.* London.
Sauer, M. (1802). *An account of a Geographical and Astronomical Expedition to the northern parts of Russia...by Commodore J. Billing, 1785–94.* London.
Southgate, H. (1840). *Narrative of a tour through Armenia, Kurdistan, Persia and Mesopotamia.* London.
Steller, G. W. (1774). *Beschreib. v. dem Lande Kamtschatka.* Frankfort u. Leipsic.
Stokes, J. F. G. (1921). Fish-poisoning in the Hawaiian Islands. *Occas. papers, B. P. Bishop Mus.* VII, 10, pp. 219–33. Honolulu.
Talavera, F. (1932). The Fisheries of Lake Sampaloc...Luzon. *Philipp. Journ. of Sci.* vol. XLVIII, pp. 411–27.
Talavera, F. & Montalban, H. R. (1932). Fishing appliances of Panay, Negros and Cebu. *Philipp. Journ. of Sci.* vol. XLVIII, pp. 429–83.
Thiercelin, M. L. (1866). Action des sels solubles de strichnine, associés au curare, sur les gros cétacés. *C.R. Séances Acad. Sci.* vol. LXIII, pp. 924–7. Paris.
Thiersant, P. Dabry (1872). *La Pisciculture et la Pêche en Chine.* Paris.
Torii, R. (1919). Les Ainou des Iles Kouriles. *Journ. Coll. Sci., Tokyo Imp. Univ.* vol. XLII, pp. 1–337. Tokyo.
Waterton, C. (1836). *Wanderings in S. America* (3rd ed.). London.
Weber, Max (1902). *H.M. 'Siboga' Expedition, 1899–1900.* Leiden.
Whitehead, S. S. (1931). Fishing Methods for the Bluefin Tuna (*Thunnus thynnus*). *Bureau of Fisheries Bull.* 48, pp. 1–13. Sacramento, U.S.A.
Wilkinson, Sir J. G. (1837–41). *The Manners and the Customs of the Ancient Egyptians.* London.
Williams, J. (1837). *A narrative of Missionary Enterprises in the South Sea Islands.* London.
Worthington, E. B. (1929). *A report on the Fishing Survey of Lakes Albert and Kioga.* London.
Worthington, E. B. (1932). *A report on the Fisheries of Uganda....* London.

PLATE I

A. How the swordfish is lured within reach, Laccadive Islands; a demonstration

B. Harpooners watching for swordfish, Strait of Messina

PLATE II

A. Shooting fish with a cross-bow, Malabar

B A Chinese illustration of cormorant-fishing

PLATE III

A. Adjusting a cormorant's harness

B. The head cormorant wearing its harness

PLATE IV

A. Night fishing with cormorants, Gifu, Japan

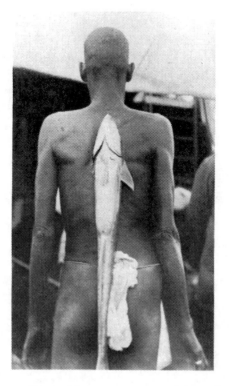

B. An experiment with a remora, at a pearl fishery in Ceylon

PLATE V

A. A negro woman making a *bimbé* net, Sierra Leone

B. Fishing with a *bimbé*-net, Sherbro, Sierra Leone

PLATE VI

A. A Kru fisherman landing with a catch of tarpon

B. A Sierra Leone fisherman using four fishing-lines

PLATE VII

A. The Chinese lever dip-net in use in South India, at Beypore, Malabar

B. Bonito-fishing in Japan: a lookout boat

PLATE VIII

A Solomon islander freeing a garfish's beak from the threads
of the spider's web lure used in kite-fishing

PLATE IX

A. Collecting bait for the bonito fishery, Maldive Islands

B. The Maldivian bonito fishery: the crew engaged in fishing

PLATE X

A. A store-basket for live bait, Minicoy Island

B. A store-basket for bonito live bait as used by the Japanese

PLATE XI

A Samoan bonito-boat showing how two men ply three rods

PLATE XII

A. Doing tots on his thigh; a Gujarat fisherman calculates his earnings

B. Shooting an anchored bag-net off Velan, Kathiawar, India

PLATE XIII

A. Stringing 'Bombay-ducks' to dry at Velan, Kathiawar

B. The fishermen's shrine to Madhvar Devi at Diu, Kathiawar, India

PLATE XIV

A. Drying the threefold portion of a veranda-net, Mauritius

B. Egyptian mullet-fishers: their veranda-net is rolled up at the stern of each boat

PLATE XV

The *changodam* method of catching mullet in Cochin backwaters

PLATE XVI

A. Two of the Italian fishing-boats which trawl in pairs off Port Said

B. Ancient Egyptians using a primitive trawl
(*From a model in the Metropolitan Museum of Art, New York.*)

PLATE XVII

A. A large catamaran used in the flying-fish fishery, Coromandel coast of India

B. The same catamaran under sail

PLATE XVIII

A. A prawn trap, Chilka Lake, Ganjam, India. These traps are set in long rows across the current

B. Quadrangular fish and prawn traps, Kolair Lake, India

PLATE XIX

A. Hand-traps used in Malabar. Left, a sieving device; centre, a plunge-basket and right, a fishing scoop

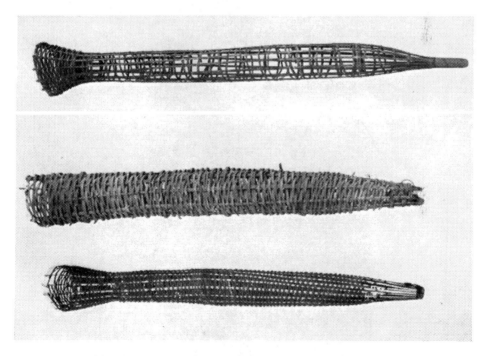

B. Tubular traps of split cane used in Fiji. At bottom is an eel trap; above are two wider woven fish-traps

PLATE XX

B. A large fish-trap (*nassa*), Malta

A. Fish-traps (*nasse*) on the quay, Palermo, Sicily

PLATE XXI

B. A small type of *nassa* (fish-trap) usually hung from a buoyed rope, Malta

A. A hooded fisherwoman and her fish-trap, Aramia river, Papua

A. A stellate five-way fish-trap, Kilakarai, South India

B. Heart-shaped fish-traps, Madeira

PLATE XXIII

A. A two-way fish-trap (*uwea*), Mbau, Fiji (1939)

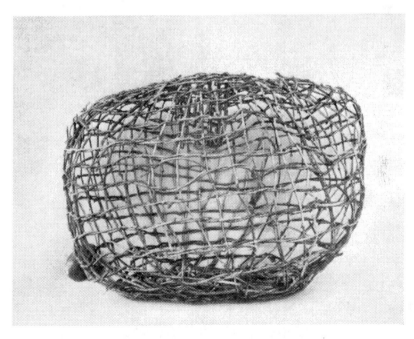

B. A one-way fish-trap (*susu*) with entrance on top, Mbau, Fiji (1939)

A. Eel-trap of *uwea* type, Fiji (1939)

B. A shark-fisher of Aua Island, Melanesia

A. Walled enclosures used to trap fishes on the Darling River, Australia

B. A screen-barrier, trapped at the centre, in a Cochin backwater, South India

PLATE XXVI

A. Outer view of a cordate terminal fish-trap used at Comacchio, Italy

B. View of the same from within

PLATE XXVII

A. A poisoning fish-drive at Ovalau Island, Fiji: hauling in the net

B. The end of the fish-drive; hauling the net aboard, Ovalau, Fiji

PLATE XXVIII

A fish-drive for a shoal of hilsa at the Lower Anicut, Kaveri River, South India

A. Divers at work on the pearl banks, Ceylon

B. Divers from Tuticorin at work on the South Indian pearl banks

PLATE XXX

A. Muhammadan divers with their catches of chank shells in net-bags. Rameswaram, South India (1914)

B. A Japanese woman diver on the pearl bank, the Bay of Agu, Japan
(Note the goggles)

A. Three Japanese women divers and their male attendant

B. The same family group at work, Toba, Japan

PLATE XXXII

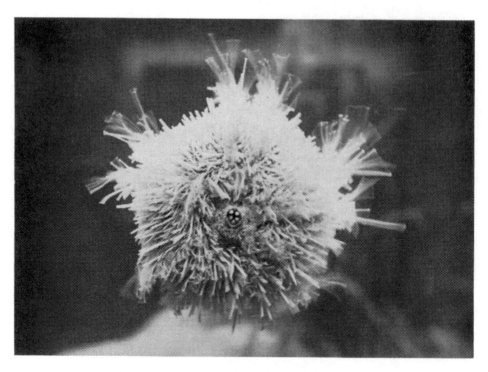

A. Life appearance of an edible sea-urchin (*Echinus esculentus*); many tube feet are shown fully extended

B. Shells of *Pteroceras* (five-fingered chank) used as octopus-traps, South India

A. The common octopus; attitude when resting

B. A large catch of octopus drying outside a village in Mauritius

PLATE XXXIV

A. The 'ormer' (*Haliotis tuberculata*) of the Channel Islands. Above, the inner surface of an empty shell; below, the under surface of the animal and (right) the outer surface of the shell. Jersey

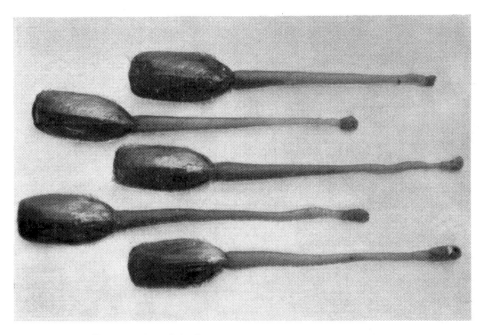

B. A number of the Brachiopod *Lingula* dug out of sand, Fiji

Baskets of the Fijian river-clam, *Batissa violacea*, on sale in Suva market, Fiji (1939)

PLATE XXXVI

Strings of crabs on sale on the roadside in Fiji (1939). Most of them are swimming crabs

INDEX

Africa: methods of negro fishing, 46–61; mullet-fishing on Congo, 104–5, 107; spear and harpoon in Central Africa, 11
Albacore, 79–80, 83–4
Aleutian Islands, poison-whaling, 177–9
Alligators, 91–3
Andaman Islands, bow and arrow, 12
Angler-fish, 38–40
Arabia, shark-fishing, 45
Archer-fish, 40
Australia, turtle, 36–7

Bait, 23–5, 26–7; for bonito-fishing, 66–7, 72; for tunny-fishing, 81
Barnacles, 201
Barracuda, 45 n., 47
Bengal: bait, varieties of, 23–5; bush-fishing, 123–6; crocodiles, 91–2; fish-traps, 52, 136–44; mullet, 101, 103; otter-fishing, 34; rod and line fishing, 22–3
Bismarck Archipelago, shark-fishing, 43–4
Blow-gun (*thumbithan*), 16–21
Blow-pipe fish, 40
Bombay-duck, 94–8
Bonito: in Japan, 70–4; in Maldive Islands, 65–9; in Polynesia, 74–8; *and see* 'Skipjack'
Borneo, blow-gun, 16
Bouillabaisse, 200–1
Bow and arrow, 4, 12; *and see* Cross-bow; Fishing-bow
Brazil: bow and arrow, 12; fish-traps, 148; spear, 11
British Guiana, alligators, 91
Bush-fishing, 123–9

California, tuna-fishing, 80
Ceylon: pearl-fishing, 182–9; squid-fishing, 134–5
Channel Islands, 21, 130, 193, 200
China: bush-fishing, 127; cormorant-fishing, 30–1; fish-traps, 146; food from the sea, 202–3; mullet, 104, 106–7; otter-fishing, 33
Clam, 203–4
Cochin, 12, 16
Cochin State Museum, 18
Columbus, 35, 36
Cook Islands, octopus-fishing, 130–1
Cormorant as fisher, 29–33
Crab, blue-clawed, 115
Crocodiles, 87–93
Cross-bow, 12–16
Cuttlefish, 133–4

Dog-fish, 204
Dummy fish, in Laccadive Islands, 6–8

Dutch East Indies: fishing-weirs, 156–7; window-pane oyster, 203

Eels: farmed at Comacchio, Italy, 162–7; trapped in Fiji, 152; *and see* Sand-eels
Egypt: crocodile baiting, 90; frescoes of fishing scenes, 2; seine-netting, 116; *and see* Port Said
Etroplus surantensis. *See* Pearl-spot
Eunicid worm, 26–7

Fiji: fish-traps, 149–53; poison-fishing, 171, 173–5; pounds, 153–5; prawn-traps, 146
Fish-drive, 29
Fish-fences: in Fiji, 155–6; in French Cameroons, 56–7; in Lake Victoria, 53; in Sudan, 55
Fish-poisons: *Balanites*, 129, 169–70; *Cyclamen*, 168, 172–3; *Derris*, 173, 175; *Tephrosia*, 168–70, 175–6
Fishing-boats: Bombay-duck boats, 94–5; Ceylon pearl-fishers, 183; Indian catamarans, 119–21; Maldivian bonito-boats, 66–8; negro dugouts, 59–61; Port Said feluccas, 114–15; Samoan bonito-canoes, 75; *tira*-canoes, 78–80
Fishing-bow, 12
Fishing-rafts, 101–3
Fly-fishing, 27
Flying-fish, 118–22
France: cuttlefish, 134; fish-sickle, 21; octopus, 130
Fruits de mer, 199–204

Gaff, 25
Gannet as fisher, 29
Garfish, 62–3
Greeks: fishing-spears, 3; and sucker-fish, 36

Hand-line, 26
Harpoon, 2–11
Henry the Navigator, Prince, 61
Herodotus (quoted), 90
Hilsa, 88, 108–13

India: angler-fish, 39; Bombay-duck, 94–8; crocodiles, 87–9, 91–2; deities of fishing castes, 87–8, 98; fish-drives, 29; flying-fish, 118–22; hilsa, 108–13; marine traps, 147–8; mullet, 102–3; murrel-traps, 144–5; octopus-traps, 132–3; otter-fishing, 33–4; pearl-fishing, 182–9, 198; plunge-basket, 52; poison-fishing, 170–1; shark-fishing, 43–4, 45 n.; *and see* Bengal, South India
Indonesia: fish-poison, 169 n., 175; kite-fishing, 62–3
Italy: eel-farming, 162–7; fish-traps, 147; octopus-traps, 131–2

INDEX

Japan: bonito-fishing, 70–4; cormorant-fishing, 31–3, 107; food from the sea, 201–2; octopus traps, 131–2; pearl-fishing, 190–8; poison-whaling, 176, 179
Jellyfish as food, 201
John Dory, 40
Juti (compound harpoon), 5

Kishinouye, Professor, 31, 190, 193, 196
Kite-fishing, 62–4
Konch (compound spear), 4–5

Laccadive Islands: dummy fish, 6–8; spear and harpoon, 5–6
Landing-net, 25
Limpets, 200
Lingula, 202

Madagascar, crocodiles, 93
Malabar, 12, 16–19
Maldive Islands, bonito-fishing, 65–9
Malta: cuttlefish, 134; fish-traps, 147; octopus, 132; squid, 134
Marquesas Islands, fish-poison, 175
Mauritius, grey mullet, 100–1
Melanesia: fish-traps, 150; kite-fishing, 63–4; spear and harpoon, 8–9
Messina, Strait of, swordfish, 8
Mexico, fish-poison, 176
Moray (*Muraena*), 147
Mugilida. *See* Mullet, grey
Mullet, grey, 21, 99–107, 116; red, 115, 116
Murrel, 20, 138; as bait, 23; traps, 144–5

Negro: bush-fishing, 127–9; freshwater-fishing, 50–61; methods of sea-fishing, 46–50; poison-fishing, 169–70
Nets: cast-net, 60; dip-net, lever, 57–60, 159; Egyptian seine, 116; handkerchief net, 126; hilsa net, 108–13; purse-seine, 80; veranda net, 99–101
Newfoundland banks, 97

Octopus, 130–3, 147, 194, 199–200
Ophiocephalidae. *See* Murrel
Oppian, *Halieutica* (quoted), 168
Ormer (*oreille-de-mer*), 193
Otter-fishing, 33–5
Oysters. *See* Pearl-fishing

Palestine: grey mullet, 99–100; poison-fishing, 171–3
Pearl-fishing: in India and Ceylon, 182–9, 198; in Japan, 190–8
Pearl-spot, 21
Pearly nautilus, 149
Pediculati. See Angler-fish
Pelicans, fishing methods, 28–9
Periplus of the Erythraean Sea, 45, 182
Philippines: cross-bow, 15; fish-traps, 145; pounds, 153

Plunge-basket, 50–2
Port Said, 114–17
Pounds, 85–6, 145–6, 153–7

Rainbow trout, 27
Rat-lure, 130–1
Remora. *See* Sucker-fish
Retarders, 10, 43–4
Rod and line, 22–3, 25–6, 75–6; in tunny-fishing, 81–3
Romans: fishing-spears, 3; moray, 147; and pearls, 182

Salmon, 108
Samoa: bonito-fishing, 75–8; fish-traps, 149
Sand-eels, 21
Scare-lines, 53–4
Sea-anemone, 201
Sea-cucumbers, 202
Sea-squirts (ascidians), 199–200
Sea-urchins, 199, 202
Sea-worms, 203
Shad, 48–9; *and see* Hilsa
Shark, 41–5
Sickle, 21
'Skipjack' (Atlantic bonito), 80–1
Snare, baited spring, 137
South India, 12–21, 27, 98, 105–6, 126–7
Spear, forms used in fishing, 1–6, 8–9, 11, 47
Spider-crab, 204
Spider's web as lure, 63–4
Squid, 134–5, 199–200
Starfish, 194
Sucker-fish, 35–8
Sudan: bush-fishing, 127–9; fish-fences, 55
Superstitions: Egyptian, 117; Indian, 87–8, 98; Japanese, 196
Swordfish, 6–8

Tahiti, 29
Tarpon, 49
Thiercelin, M. L., 180
Thumbithan. See Blow-gun
Tonga: fish-fences, 156; shark-fishing, 41–2, 44
Torches: used with raft, 103, 104; with sickle, 21; with spear, 5, 8
Traps, marine: Indian, 147–8; Italian, 147; Oceanic, 148–51
Traps, riverine: box-traps, 143–4; cage-traps, 141–3; plunge-basket, 52–3, 137–9; prawn-traps, 146; scoop-traps, 139–41; tubular traps, 134–5; *and see* Pounds
Travancore, 12, 14, 16, 19–20
Tuna. *See* Tunny
Tunny: in Bay of Biscay, 83–4; in California, 80–3; in Japan, 85–6; in Mediterranean, 84–5, 153
Turtle, 9–10, 35–8

Walton, Izaak, 23, 25
Whales, poison-whaling, 176–81

Zanzibar, turtle, 37–8

Printed in the United States
By Bookmasters